AF065042

Valentina Marinescu,
Bianca Mitu,
Silvia Branea (eds.)

Critical Reflections on Audience and Narrativity

New Connections, New Perspectives

Valentina Marinescu,
Bianca Mitu,
Silvia Branea (eds.)

CRITICAL REFLECTIONS ON AUDIENCE AND NARRATIVITY

New Connections, New Perspectives

ibidem-Verlag

Bibliografische Information der Deutschen Nationalbibliothek
Die Deutsche Nationalbibliothek verzeichnet diese Publikation in der Deutschen Nationalbibliografie; detaillierte bibliografische Daten sind im Internet über http://dnb.d-nb.de abrufbar.

Bibliographic information published by the Deutsche Nationalbibliothek
Die Deutsche Nationalbibliothek lists this publication in the Deutsche Nationalbibliografie; detailed bibliographic data are available in the Internet at http://dnb.d-nb.de.

Cover picture: © Petra Bork / pixelio.de

∞

Gedruckt auf alterungsbeständigem, säurefreien Papier
Printed on acid-free paper

ISBN-13 Paperback edition: 978-3-8382-0609-7

ISBN-13 Hardcover edition: 978-3-8382-0680-6

© *ibidem*-Verlag
Stuttgart 2014

Alle Rechte vorbehalten

Das Werk einschließlich aller seiner Teile ist urheberrechtlich geschützt. Jede Verwertung außerhalb der engen Grenzen des Urheberrechtsgesetzes ist ohne Zustimmung des Verlages unzulässig und strafbar. Dies gilt insbesondere für Vervielfältigungen, Übersetzungen, Mikroverfilmungen und elektronische Speicherformen sowie die Einspeicherung und Verarbeitung in elektronischen Systemen.

All rights reserved. No part of this publication may be reproduced, stored in or introduced into a retrieval system, or transmitted, in any form, or by any means (electronic, mechanical, photocopying, recording or otherwise) without the prior written permission of the publisher. Any person who does any unauthorized act in relation to this publication may be liable to criminal prosecution and civil claims for damages.

Printed in Germany

Contents

Does the cultural capital compensate for the cultural discount?
Why do German students prefer US-American TV series? — 7
Daniela Schluetz, Beate Schneider

Awake, or the multiplication of the realities Contemporary Television Series:
Narrative Structures and Audience Perception — 27
Mathieu Pierre

"Three hundred channels and nothing's on":
Metaleptic Genre-Mixing in *Supernatural* — 35
Michael Fuchs

Appreciating Nietzsche in Episodic Drama:
The Highbrow Intertextuality and Middlebrow Reception of *Criminal Minds* — 49
Michael Wayne

The Seed of an Idea and its Cognitive Field:
Minding the Gap of Alternate Reality in Flash Forward and Fringe — 63
Inbar Kaminsky

Breaking Narrative: Narrative Complexity in Contemporary Television — 77
Oliver Kroener

The Walking Dead and the Truly Monstrous... on Television — 89
Atene Mendelyte

Television Cosmo-Mythologies: The Return to Mythological Narratives
in Television Fiction, from *The Prisoner* to *Lost* — 103
Raquel Crisóstomo Gálvez, Enric Ros Zofío

Breaking Bad, a Character-Based Formula — 117
Rodrigo Mesonero

Representing Occupations in Media and Audience Perceptions of TV Series — 133
Valentina Marinescu

Homeland: War on Terror Revisited — 141
Marc Perelló-Sobrepere

Understanding Health in Grey's Anatomy Television Series — 155
Bianca Mitu

Fiction Television in Brazil: New Perspectives — 165
Lilian Fontes Moreira

TV Series *Bolji život* (1987–1991): View from the Future — 179
Natasa Simeunovic Bajic

The *X-Factor* of Singing Competitions TV Series — 195
Maria Dicieanu

TV Drama as a Narrative form: Scenes from a Gendered and
a Sacralized Cultural Sphere in Turkish Society 213
Nuran E. Işık

The hero's journey 227
*María Teresa Nicolás Gavilán, Lourdes López Gutiérrez,
Carmen Silvia Sánchez Arana, Tania Alejandra Benítez Sánchez*

About the contributors 237

Does the cultural capital compensate for the cultural discount? Why do German students prefer US-American TV series?

Daniela Schluetz, Beate Schneider

Many European countries but also other countries worldwide experience a predominance of US-American TV products. This is mainly due to the globalization effects rather than to the audience's choice because viewers usually prefer products that are culturally proximate (Straubhaar, 1991). German television ratings confirm this situation (Zubayr & Gerhard, 2011) with the exception of younger, well-educated viewers who seem to favor US-American fictional television content (Zubayr & Gerhard, 2010), particularly series (Gerhards & Klingler, 2009). In this paper, we examine cultural proximity from an audience point of view posing the following question: how do young highly educated viewers evaluate non-nationally produced TV series? Germany serves as a case study for the present study.

In the last 20 to 30 years, US-American content has become an important part of television programming in Europe and especially in Germany—both quantitatively and qualitatively speaking. Since the establishment of the commercial television sector in 1984, more and more television channels have distributed more and more content—much of which originates from the USA (Europäische Audiovisuelle Informationsstelle, 2010). All over Europe, the share of national fictional TV programs is on decline (Hallenberger, 2005). To a large extent, this is a reflection of economic globalization effects of television production and distribution as purchasing content is often less expensive than producing it. Thus, the predominance of US formats seems to depend on structural reasons rather than audience choice: "More than audience tastes, trade practices and costs better explain the content of schedules" (Waisbord, 2004, p. 369). Nevertheless, with almost a third of the total programming, Germany has the highest percentage of nationally produced fictional content in Europe (Hallenberger, 2005, p. 15). German productions are the domain of public television channels (ARD/ZDF) while commercial channels broadcast less German productions.

Indigenous productions, expensive as they might be, they deserve the price because viewers usually prefer "home grown" television products. This can be explained by the concept of 'cultural proximity' brought forward by Straubhaar (1991; 2002; see also de Sola Pool, 1977). Straubhaar argues that a discussion about globalization disregards the influence of audiences' national identities in selecting and interpreting cultural products (2002, p. 182). By several Latin American case studies, he shows that audiences tend to prefer national entertainment products to foreign ones, for instance Hollywood productions. Viewers actively look for cultural cues in TV productions and derive pleasure out of symbols and practices they can relate to. That is why national formats are appreciated more. Non-national genres are more popular if they are linked to a similar culture connected by, for instance, language, geography or history and values (La Pastina & Straubhaar, 2005). As Straubhaar puts it: "Since the 1990's it has almost become commonplace to say that audiences prefer culture-specific or national television programs that are as close to them as possible in language, ethnic appearance, dress, style, humor, historical reference, and shared topical knowledge." (2008, p. 15) Language, Straubhaar argues, is the most important factor, with some genres such as comedies relying more on it than the others. One may call it the smallest common denominator for cultural proximity (cf. Ksiazek & Webster, 2008). Language is not the only relevant factor, though. The US-American TV industry even adapts formats from the British market (see the example of 'The Office', Beeden & de Bruin, 2010) and in Germany, for instance, national programs are more popular although all foreign content is dubbed (Tinchev, 2010). The concept of cultural proximity, however, has been challenged by the widespread availability and global appeal of US-American fictional productions (cf. Kerr & Flynn, 2003).

A lack of cultural proximity leads to 'cultural discount' (Hoskins & Mirus, 1988). This concept argues that a "particular program rooted in one culture, and thus attractive in that environment, will have a diminished appeal elsewhere as viewers find it difficult to identify with the style, values, beliefs, institutions and behavioral patterns of the material in question. Included in the cultural discount are reductions in appreciation due to dubbing or subtitling. [...] As a result of the diminished appeal, fewer viewers will watch a foreign program than a domestic program of the same type and quality." (Hoskins & Mirus, 1988, p. 500) Thus, US-American series should be less appealing to foreign audiences than their own. There seems to be empirical support for this argument in Germany (cf. Zubayr & Gerhard, 2011): The top 15 in television ratings 2009 comprised only German fictional films. In 2008, only one US-American production entered the top ten ('Ice Age 2'; Zubayr & Gerhard, 2010, p 116). The same was true for television series (Zubayr & Gerhard, 2010, p. 117). The rule, however, does not seem to apply to all audience groups. Younger viewers preferred US-American series like 'The Simpsons' (Gerhards & Klingler, 2009, p. 674). Table 1 shows ratings and market shares of younger, highly educated viewers in Germany. Their 2009 top ten in television ratings included only two German productions: 'Stromberg', which is the German version of 'The Office', and 'Doctor's Diary' (a comedy/drama series, comparable to 'Scrubs'; original title in English) (cf. Table 1).

Why is it that young, well-educated Germans prefer foreign, particularly US-American TV content regardless of cultural discount? We want to propose two possible explanations for this preference which might apply to other, non-US-American nations as well. The first one is related to the texts in question. Hoskins and Mirus (1988) argue that US program exports have a rather low cultural discount due to high production values and undemanding content. Therefore, they lend themselves to worldwide distribution. Olson (1999) adds the concept of 'narrative transparency' of US-American television texts that open them to 'different readings' (Hall, 1992; cf. Fiske's notion of 'polysemy', 1987). Varying audiences can thereby relate to the text and identify with the personae based on their individual interpretation and sense making of the text: "Transparency is the capability of certain texts to seem familiar regardless of their origin, to seem a part of one's own culture, even though they have been crafted elsewhere." (Olson, 1999, p. 18) The consequence of transparency in a television program is its appeal to a larger and more diverse audience—as is the case with many US-American TV series.

Table 1: Top ten TV series on German TV 2009

Top 10	Channel	Origin	Adults 18–28 years with higher education (2.73 Mio., N = 456)		Adults 14–49 years (35.56 Mio., N = 5289)	
			Rating in Mio.	Market Share in %	Rating in Mio.	Market Share in %
Grey's Anatomy	ProSieben	USA	0.23	40.9	1.54	14.4
Two and a Half Men	ProSieben	USA	0.22	33.4	1.79	13.5
Desperate Housewives	ProSieben	USA	0.19	31.2	1.77	15.0
Private Practice	ProSieben	USA	0.19	31.6	1.28	11.3
Stromberg	ProSieben	Germany	0.18	37.1	1.36	13.3
House MD	RTL	USA	0.18	28.0	3.07	24.2
Doctor's Diary	RTL	Germany	0.18	30.5	1.89	17.1
Lipstick Jungle	ProSieben	USA	0.14	24.5	1.30	10.3
Fringe	ProSieben	USA	0.13	23.0	1.93	16.5
Monk	RTL	USA	0.13	25.8	2.11	22.0

Note: All shows, Mo–Sa., 5–11 p.m., SAT.1, ProSieben, kabel eins, RTL, VOX, RTL II, ARD, ZDF
Source: AGF/GfK-Television-Research

The second explanation for the worldwide popularity of US-American television content refers to viewer characteristics. Central to the understanding of cultural proximity is Pierre Bourdieu's (1984) concept of cultural capital. As opposed to economic and social capital, cultural capital refers to education and knowledge. It creates a "familiarity based in language, education, or travel that enables someone to understand a language- or culture-based [...] program from elsewhere" (Straubhaar, 2008, p. 17). Cultural capital fosters the understanding and enjoyment of foreign media content because it bridges gaps between culturally positioned audiences and television products drawing on other cultural symbol systems. Consequently, cultural capital has a bearing on cultural proximity and, indirectly, on media selection: "Cultural capital focuses on the sources of knowledge that permit people to make choices among media and other sources of information and culture." (Straubhaar, 2007, p. 202–3) The more cultural capital somebody has at his or her disposal, the more prone he or she is to choose non-national media content. Thus, higher educated viewers are more likely to derive pleasure from foreign TV content than less well-educated ones.

Moreover, cultural proximity is a dynamic concept based on identifications with national offerings (Straubhaar, 2008, p. 16; cf. Iwabuchi, 2002). Social changes influence the perception of cultural proximity in cultural artifacts by historically and socially positioned groups. Younger people's liking of US-American television would then be a cohort effect rather than a consequence of a certain age. Having been raised with a lot of exposure to US-American lifestyle, culture or values (be it fictional sources like media exposure or factual ones like exchange programs, for instance), younger people might feel closer to the USA than members of an earlier cohort (i.e., elder generations). A closer proximity to US-American culture might be due to more knowledge about the USA, a more positive image of the USA as a country or a higher proficiency of the English language (cf. Elasmar, 2003; Schlütz, 2012). A distinct national identity[1], on the other hand, should have a detrimental effect in this process. National identity is formed culturally and suggests a sense of unity and belonging based on a shared territory (Beeden & de Bruin, 2010, p. 5; cf. Straubhaar, 2002). Communication practices, thus, influence national identity: "The mass media, and television in particular, are powerful nation-building tools, which serve as a main communication space for defining what our country is and what it is like." (Castelló, 2009, p. 315) On the other hand, it is plausible that national identity has a bearing on cultural activities, the reading of cultural texts and—at the end of the day—on media choice. A pronounced national identity should therefore lead to less selection of foreign media content.

In this paper, we regard cultural proximity from an audience point of view: How do viewers with a certain amount of cultural capital perceive cultural proximity and how important is this perception for their evaluation of (entertaining) media content? We focus on a special audience fragment: highly educated, younger people (in Germany). This choice is based on the assumption that education is connected to the accumulation of cultural capital. Cultural capital, we argue, helps to overcome effects of cultural discount. We chose a cohort of young viewers because they seem to have developed

---

[1] "A nation can [...] be defined as a name human population an historic territory, common myths and historical memories, a mass, public culture, a common economy and common legal rights and duties for all members." (Smith, 1991, p. 14)

specific viewing habits and tastes. At least in Germany, they do not seem to prefer national TV products in general. We therefore surveyed such young, highly educated viewers regarding the genre of TV series to examine the following research questions:

> RQ1: To what degree do German students prefer US-American TV series?
> RQ2: What do they appreciate in US-American TV series?
> RQ3: How do factors of cultural capital and national identity influence this preference?

Method

In May 2010, we conducted an online survey with German students to address our research questions (Couper & Miller, 2008). Both nationality and the fact that the respondents were enrolled in a university program were secured by corresponding screening questions. The questionnaire was distributed using a snowball system and filled in completely by 3404 respondents. The questionnaire comprised 37 questions addressing uses and preferences of US-American TV series, nation images, aspects of national identity and further aspects irrelevant to this discussion. The average completion time was 21 minutes.

Measures

Viewing volume: The average time spent watching TV series per week was measured by the question: "Approximately how much time do you spend watching television series? Please estimate the time devoted to watching television series during an average week." Answers were given in a closed format with response options ranging from "7 hours or more per week" (code 5) to "I hardly ever watch television" (code 0) with two-hour-steps in between ($M = 3.6$, $SD = 1.2$).

Evaluation: The liking of US-American series was measured by two questions. The first one was open ended ("Which is your favorite television series?"). In the second one, the respondents were presented with a list of 15 shows (cf. Table 2) in a randomized order to rate on a scale from (1) "don't like it at all" to (5) "like it very much". To capture their evaluation criteria, we asked the respondents to rate a number of items on a scale from (1) "does not apply at all" to (5) "applies completely". The statements were customized to include aspects regarding both form and content of TV programs (cf. Table 3).

Language proficiency: As a proxy for linguistic proficiency relevant to media use, we determined the preference of the original (i.e., not dubbed) version of a program with the statement: "I like to watch American TV series in the original version." The item was rated on a Likert-type scale from (1) "does not apply at all" to (5) "applies completely" ($M = 3.8$, $SD = 1.4$).

Affinity to the USA: The respondents were asked to indicate on a 7-point semantic differential (Osgood, Suci, & Tannenbaum, 1978) whether the USA was familiar (code 7) to them or alien (1) and whether it was likable (7) or unlikable (1) ($M_{familiar} = 3.85$, $SD = 1.4$; $M_{likable} = 4.2$, $SD = 1.4$).

National identity was encompassed with the question "How proud are you to be German?" taken from the World Values Survey[2]. The answers were "very proud" (code 3), "quite proud" (2), "not very proud" (1) and "not at all proud" (0) ($M = 1.9$, $SD = 0.8$).

Sample structure

From the 3404 participants in our study, 56 percent were female. On average, the participants were 24 years old ($M = 23.8$, $SD = 3.6$). Most of the students who filled in the questionnaire were TV afficionados: 32 percent devoted seven or more hours to watching television series during an average week, only four percent watched one hour or less. This suggests that our sample tilts towards heavier users of television series.

Not all of the series chosen as favorites by our respondents are accessible on German television permanently or at all, for that matter. Accordingly, many students in the sample did not watch them on regular German television channels. Instead, 27 percent reported that they watched series on DVD or Blu-Ray and 51 percent of the respondents claimed to follow their favorite series over the Internet using both legal and illegal channels to download or stream them (multiple responses possible). One of the reasons of non-linear use seemed to be that most viewers (64 %) preferred the original versions (OV) of the shows to dubbed ones (OVs are not accessible on German free TV).

---

[2] Source: http://www.worldvaluessurvey.org/

Results

The surveyed German students distinctively preferred US-American productions (RQ1): The ten most frequently named shows in the open ended question were (in this order) 'Scrubs', 'How I Met Your Mother', 'Grey's Anatomy', 'Two and a Half Men', 'Lost', 'House MD', 'The Simpsons', 'Gilmore Girls', 'CSI/CIS', and 'Desperate Housewives' (N = 4012). Not one German series made it in the participants' top 40. The closed ended question revealed the same pattern. Table 2 illustrates that all of the presented US-American shows were liked almost equally by the respondents: On a 5-point Likert-type scale (5 denoting the highest evaluation), thirteen out of fifteen series were rated 4 or higher with an overall mean of 4.3 (SD = 0.5). The best liked show was 'How I Met Your Mother', followed by 'Lost' and 'Scrubs'. 'Lost', 'Californication' and 'The Simpsons' were more popular with men, while female students preferred 'Grey's Anatomy' and 'Desperate Housewives'. There were three comedy shows within the first five positions. This finding strikes us as particularly interesting, since humor is said to be highly susceptible to cultural discount because it lacks cultural proximity (Straubhaar, 2008; cf. Beeden & de Bruin, 2010).

What is it that German students like about an US-American TV series? (RQ2) We asked the participants to evaluate US-American TV series in general by assessing several items in terms of applicability to their own opinion (cf. Table 3). Subsequently, all items were submitted to a Principal Component Analysis (PCA) with Varimax rotation. Five factors with eigenvalue > 1 were extracted accounting for 49 percent of the variance.[3] Responses to all items per factor were then averaged for each participant to yield a single score. Higher index scores indicated higher importance of the dimension in question.

---

[3] The item "A television series is good if it touches me emotionally" is not a part of the solution because it has no clear-cut classification.

Table 2: Evaluation of US-American TV series by German students

Title	Main Genre*	All participants N**	All participants M	All participants SD	Females M	Females SD	Males M	Males SD	p <
How I Met Your Mother	C	1709	4.5	0.741	4.5	0.77	4.5	0.714	n.s.
Lost	F	1007	4.4	0.913	4.3	0.987	4.5	0.844	.000
Scrubs	C	2278	4.4	0.768	4.4	0.797	4.5	0.731	.010
Californication	D	800	4.4	0.821	4.2	0.888	4.5	0.773	.000
Two and a Half Men	C	2024	4.4	0.828	4.3	0.859	4.4	0.785	.000
Grey's Anatomy	D	1495	4.3	0.880	4.4	0.811	3.9	0.950	.000
House MD	D	1840	4.3	0.806	4.3	0.800	4.3	0.812	n.s.
The Mentalist	F	719	4.3	0.823	4.2	0.845	4.3	0.794	n.s.
Navy CIS	Cr	1050	4.2	0.883	4.2	0.907	4.3	0.846	n.s.
The Simpsons	C	2346	4.2	0.855	4.1	0.905	4.3	0.787	.000
Fringe	F	746	4.2	0.887	4.1	0.918	4.2	0.861	.050
Desperate Housewives	D	1384	4.1	0.957	4.2	0.913	3.8	1.008	.000
Monk	Cr	1035	4.0	0.859	4.1	0.832	4.0	0.882	.01
CSI	Cr	1023	3.7	0.915	3.8	0.914	3.6	0.896	.000
Heroes	F	839	3.7	1.016	3.9	0.994	3.6	1.018	.001

Question: *"Now we are interested in how you appraise the television series you actually watch. (1) means "don't like it at all" and (5) means "like it very much"."You can use the numbers in between to grade your opinion."*

*C: Comedy, Cr: Crime, D: Drama, F: Fantasy
**Number of respondents who watch this show at least occasionally
Note: Randomized item order in questionnaire

Table 3: Evaluation criteria (Factor Analysis)

		Factor Loadings				
	Item Mean	Cultural Ties	Serial Structure	Production Values	Characters	Morality
I think it's important that a television series is close to reality.	2.79	0.729				
A television series should present solutions for personal problems.	2.14	0.668				
I like a television series presenting a lifestyle I can identify with.	3.02	0.661				
I like television series that deal with current social issues.	2.75	0.589				
I like to find out what's up to date through watching a television series.	2.08	0.465				0.446
I prefer television series where each episode has an ending and the story doesn't continue in the next episode. (reversed)	2.41		-0.771			
I prefer stories that continue from episode to episode. That way, it remains exciting.	2.98		0.732			
What's especially good about a television series is when the story never ends.	3.69		0.606			
I like distinctive camera work.	3.17			0.721		
It's important that a television series is very well produced.	2.42			0.593		0.411
I think the music of a television series is very important.	3.6			0.485		
The more different threads of action there are, the better the television series gets.	3.23			0.464		

Item	Item Mean	Cultural Ties	Serial Structure	Production Values	Characters	Morality
The delightful part of a television series is that one always returns to the same people and scenery.	3.51				0.592	
I like to identify with the behavior patterns of the characters.	3.43	0.516			0.539	
The cast of a series is extremely important to me.	3.73			0.417	0.448	
I like to see a few bizarre characters in a television series.	4.08				0.446	-0.443
It is important to me that I can clearly distinguish the "good" and "bad" characters of a television series.	2.08					0.731
It bothers me when the main characters in a television series act against my beliefs.	2.57				0.403	0.425
Eigenvalue		3.4	2.2	1.4	1.2	1.1
Variance explained (%)		17.9	11.7	7.3	6.5	6.0
Factor Mean (overall loading items/factor)		2.5	3.4	3.1	3.7	2.3

Note: Scale: from (1) "does not apply at all" to (5) "applies completely"; Extraction Method: PCA; Rotation Method: Varimax (13 Iterations); N = 3404; total variance = 49,3 %

We found three more important clusters of criteria (i.e., with an overall mean above 3.0)—characters, serial structure and production values—and two less important ones (with an overall mean below 3.0)—cultural ties and morality:

Characters (M = 3.7, SD = 0.6): Most important for a good TV series is—as far as the respondents were concerned—a good cast: recurrent personae lending themselves to identification, real people (maybe a little bit bizarre) who can easily be made friends with.

Serial structure (M = 3.4, SD = 0.9): Beyond that, what makes a series[4] worth seeing is the ongoing narrative, the potentially never-ending story.

---

[4] To be precise, one has to distinguish serial from an episodic series (cf. Cantor &

Production values *(M* = 3.1, *SD* = 0.7): Distinctive camera work, a high-quality production, music and a complex narrative structure are important for a well-liked program.

Cultural ties *(M* = 2.5, *SD* = 0.7): The respondents found it slightly less important that the show relates to (their) reality, that it presents a lifestyle they can identify with or that it deals with current social issues and the "dernier cri", respectively.

Morality *(M* = 2.3, *SD* = 0.9): The surveyed German students found it less appealing to watch series with clear-cut characters who act according to the respondents' beliefs.

Regarding this factor solution, the notion of 'cultural proximity' does not seem to be the most important criterion for evaluating US-American TV series within our sample. If it were, the factor 'cultural ties' should be rated much higher by the respondents. 'Morality' should be a relevant dimension as well because values and beliefs are deeply rooted in a nation's culture. The respondents, however, appreciate the personae—American folks—they observe on the screen; people they apparently can relate to and identify with although they are from a different cultural background. Apparently, US-American texts offer enough narrative transparency (Olson, 1999) to facilitate this reaction.

To find out to what extent these evaluative criteria explain the amount of TV series consumption in our sample (RQ3), we conducted a stepwise regression analysis with frequency of use as dependent variable. Evaluation dimensions, affinity to the USA, language proficiency, national pride as well as gender and age served as regressors.

Pingree, 1983; Creeber, 2004).

Table 4: Factors influencing frequency of use (Stepwise Regression Analysis)

Independent Variables	Coefficients		
	B	SE B	Beta
(Constant)	1.665	0.247	
Serial Structure (Index)	0.303	0.028	0.213
Gender (1 = male)	0.244	0.047	0.098
Language Proficiency	0.074	0.017	0.085
Affinity to the USA: Familiarity	0.062	0.016	0.073
Cultural Ties (Index)	-0.131	0.033	-0.078
Characters (Index)	0.128	0.04	0.065
Production Values (Index)	-0.083	0.036	-0.046
National Identity	0.065	0.028	0.044
Age	0.013	0.006	0.038

Note: Dependent variable: Average time spent watching television series per week (quasi-metric); R^2 adj. = .09; method stepwise; criteria pin (.05) pout (.10); excluded variables: Morality (Index); Affinity to the USA: Likability

The analysis revealed several variables that significantly influenced the exposure to TV series. Together they explained 9 percent of the variance of the dependent variable. The most important aspect is the show's seriality: The more the respondents appreciated the ongoing narrative, the more time they devoted to watching series. The second most important factor was gender: Male respondents reported consistently more exposure to US-American TV series than women. Language proficiency (enabling the respondents to follow the series in the original version) influenced frequency of use positively as well as familiarity with the USA. Consistent with our assumption was the fact that the factor 'cultural ties' was negatively associated with viewing frequency. Respondents who valued a show relating to their reality were less prone to watch a lot of US series. The same was true for production values. The preference of high-quality production leads to less series consumption. This result seems to contradict Hoskin and Mirus' (1988) argument that high production values diminish cultural discount. Interestingly, the B value of national identity was positive. This suggests that respondents with a more pronounced German national identity watched more foreign series instead of less as we had assumed.

Discussion

In this paper, we posed the question whether cultural capital can compensate for effects of cultural discount. In this context, we discussed the concept of 'cultural proximity' (Straubhaar, 1991) with regard to TV viewing habits of German students. We chose this specific group because of their higher education that allowed them to accumulate cultural capital. Cultural capital, we argued, can help to overcome detrimental effects of cultural discount in cultural artifacts. The study was conducted in Germany, one of the European countries with a lot of US-American television content. As object of investigation we chose US-American TV series as they are very popular with young Germans. They are, in fact, much more popular than German TV series although the notion of 'cultural proximity' would suggest otherwise. To address our questions, we conducted an online survey with 3404 German students. We found that the respondents distinctively preferred US-American TV series to German ones. The answers to both open-ended and closed-ended questions showed that US-American programs were the respondents' favorites. We suspect that this preference depends at least partly on their better education. Language proficiency, for instance, seems to play an important role in this process. Many German students are more or less fluent in English due to their education, foreign exchange programs and—not least—the viewing of English TV shows in the original version. This "multicultural fluency" (Ksiazek & Webster, 2008, p. 500) seems to be an important factor in diminishing effects of cultural discount.

Additionally, we found that German students seemingly did not suffer from a feeling of cultural discount when watching US-American television series—even though many of them watched the shows in American English, commonly on the Internet. A certain amount of cultural capital is a precondition for this kind of cultural practice. Another indicator for the lack of feeling cultural discount was the Germans' preference for Hollywood comedies. Humor is usually thought to be deeply rooted in culture and therefore especially prone to effects of cultural discount. This was not the case with our sample. Apparently, there were other criteria for evaluating US-American fiction. For our respondents, likable characters were the most important criterion, while the opportunity to connect the scene and plot with their own experiences and values seemed less important. These results suggest that the narrative transparency of US-American series makes them more accessible for foreign viewers.

The amount of exposure to TV series was mainly influenced by the serial character of the narrative.[5] Viewers who preferred continuous serials to episodic series tended to watch more of them than other viewers. This is comprehensible as you "get hooked" much easier by the story of these formats. Another important factor influencing frequency of use was language proficiency. Respondents who preferred original versions to dubbed ones watched more series. This might be due to the fact that they have generally a broader range of shows to choose from. Another reason might be that they possess more cultural capital and that their multicultural fluency enables them to appreciate foreign media content more. The latter argument is supported by another factor: affinity to the USA. The more familiar somebody in our sample was with the USA, the more time he or she devoted to watching TV series. The importance of recognizing cultural cues within a program, on the other hand, reduced viewing hours of foreign TV content (at least in our sample). Finally, a distinct (German) national identity leads to slightly more demand of US-American series. This result struck us as particularly interesting because it was unexpected. When scrutinizing the patriots' image of both Germany and the USA, it appears that they like both countries better than German non-patriots (Schlütz, Schneider, & Stipp, 2011). The feeling that Germany is "good" apparently does not coincide with the feeling of the USA being "less good". On the contrary: The USA seems to be some kind of idol, an aspired culture one wants to be close to. This suggests another explanation why so many German students embrace US media content—the people, places and issues in those programs are interpreted as proximal because the students feel close to the USA and its culture.

Thus, our study supports the assumption that cultural capital can compensate for cultural discount to a certain extent. German students prefer US-American series (among other reasons) because their education and knowledge about the country and the language allows them to appreciate US-American TV content as well. The narrative transparency that these programs offer adds to this effect.

Due to our sample, we cannot prove that this is especially the case with young, highly educated Germans but the notion would be plausible. This

---

[5] The rather small amount of explained variance indicates that there are other relevant factors we did not capture.

generation has been raised in a globalized world where the effects of 'deterritorialization' (Beck & Beck-Gernsheim, 2007; cf. Glanzner, Schlütz, & Schneider, 2012) are experienced, i.e., the disconnection of culture from social and geographical territories. Thereby, the process of national identification is influenced in manifold ways. It is less linked to territories and more to mediated experiences. As Hollywood television is part of these experiences, it might influence the process of identity forming and change the way we perceive national identity as a concept—not only in Germany but anywhere in Europe.

Limitations

Despite the cohesive findings of our study, we have to address some limitations. First, the findings are limited by the homogeneity of the sample both in terms of nationality and socio-demography (mainly education and age). As we were still in an exploratory state of research, this was consciously decided to work out the effects more clearly. In the future, however, we wish to include respondents from different national backgrounds and social strata to be able to compare subsamples and analyze the influence of these criteria. Another limitation of the study is its cross-sectional design that cannot account for causal relationships. In future research, we would like to use an appropriate approach, preferably a panel, to address developments and changes over time. The question whether the affinity to non-national TV products is a cohort rather than an age effect strikes us as particularly interesting when analyzing long-term effects.

Conclusion

Our study showed that young, highly educated people prefer foreign TV content to national productions. Elasmar and Hunter (2003) argue that repeated exposure to foreign media content influences attitudes and values with regard to the production country. In this process, values can be complemented or altered. Elasmar (2003) models this relationship of the 'Susceptibility to Imported Media' (SIM) and labels the process 'Media-Accelerated Culture Diffusion', i.e., the process of cultural hybridization on an individual level (cf. Schlütz, 2012). Effects are enhanced when viewers appreciate the country of origin of the media content, share similar values and are exposed to the content frequently. Cultural capital is a prerequisite for the selection and appreciation of foreign media content. At the same time, it is enhanced by watching this specific content. Thus, cultural capital facilitates the approximation to foreign values by compensating for cultural discount in foreign media products. This process can be modelled as a self-reinforcing process of cultural deterritorialization (Glanzner, Schlütz & Schneider, 2012). Thus, the prolonged exposure to (and enjoyment of) US-American series might have manifold consequences (in terms of attitudes, (cultural) values, cultural capital, felt proximity etc.) in the long run.

Tomlinson reminds us that "globalization fundamentally transforms the relationship between the places we inhabit and our cultural practices, experiences and identities" (1999, p. 106). If this is true it should have consequences on the development of cultures: Is there a globalization of tastes? Maybe there are socializing effects of American television on international audiences as Tan, Tan, and Gibson (2003) propose or Quick (2009) shows for 'Grey's Anatomy'. This would argue for a cohort effect that should become more pronounced in the future. Maybe learning effects can explain the rising interest in US-American commodities: The repeated and long-lasting consumption of entertaining Hollywood products might a) change the expectations of television content and b) foster change in the perception of cultural proximity (cf. Moyer-Gusé & Nabi; 2010, Shrum, 2004 for effects of narrative persuasion). Both effects might lead to an altered perception and evaluation of these products in the long run. Because of their routinized use and their potential endlessness, series (and particularly serials) might play a special role in this process (cf. Castelló, 2009, p. 307; Tamborini, Weber, Eden, Bowman, & Grizzard, 2010).

In their in-depth study on cosmopolitan communications, Norris and Inglehart (2009) showed that individual news media use encourages more cosmopolitan, more modern orientations—while simultaneously strengthening feelings of nationalism. According to the authors, national identity is not "a zero-sum game, but it seems more accurate to understand modern identities as multiple and overlapping" (Norris & Inglehart, 2009, p. 304). We observed something similar in our sample.

References

Beck, U., & Beck-Gernsheim, E. (2007). Generation Global. In U. Beck (Ed.), *Generation Global: Ein Crashkurs* [Generation global: A crash course] (pp. 236–265). Frankfurt am Main: Suhrkamp.

Beeden, A., & de Bruin, J. (2010). The Office: Articulation of national identity in television format adaption. *Television and New Media, 11*(1), 3–19.

Bourdieu, P. (1984). *Distinction: A social critique of the judgment of taste*. Harvard: Harvard University Press.

Cantor, M. G., & Pingree, S. (1983). *The soap opera*. Beverly Hills, CA: Sage.

Castelló, E. (2009). The nation as a political stage: A theoretical approach to television fiction and national identities. *International Communication Gazette, 71*(4), 303–320.

Couper, M. P., & Miller, P. V. (2008). Web survey methods: Introduction. *Public Opinion Quarterly, 72*, 831–385.

Creeber, G. (2004). *Serial television: Big drama on the small screen*. London: BFI.

de Sola Pool, I. (1977). When cultures clash: The changing flow of television. *Journal of Communication, 27*(2), 139–150.

Elasmar, M. G. (2003). An alternative paradigm for conceptualizing and labeling the process of influence of imported television programs. In M. G. Elasmar (Ed.), *The impact of international television: A paradigm shift* (pp. 158–179). Mahwah, NJ: Lawrence Erlbaum Associates.

Elasmar, M. G., & Hunter, J. E. (2003). A meta-analysis of crossborder effect studies. In M. G. Elasmar (Ed.), *The impact of international television: A paradigm shift* (pp. 133–155). Mahwah, NJ: Lawrence Erlbaum Associates.

Europäische Audiovisuelle Informationsstelle [European Audiovisual Observatory] (2010). *Jahrbuch 2010: Film, Fernsehen und Video in Europa. Band 1: Fernsehen in 36 europäischen Staaten* [Yearbook 2010: Movies, TV and video in Europe. Volume 1: TV in 36 European states]. Straßburg: Europäische Audiovisuelle Informationsstelle.

Fiske, J. (1987). *Television culture*. London: Routledge.

Gerhards, M., & Klingler, W. (2009). Das Programmjahr 2008: Sparten- und Formattrends im deutschen Fernsehen [The program in 2008: Format trends in German television]. *Media Perspektiven, n.v.*(12), 662–678.

Glanzner, B., Schlütz, D. M., & Schneider, B. M. (2012, May). *The self-reinforcing process of cultural deterritorialization: Intercultural capital, transnational media representations and cultural vicinity—An empirical study*. Paper presented at the Annual Meeting of the International Communication Association, Phoenix, AZ. Retrieved 2013-06-25 from: http://citation.allacademic.com/meta/p553415_index.html

Hall, S. (1992). Encoding/decoding. In S. Hall, D. Hobson, A. Lowe, & P. Willis (Eds.), *Culture, media, language* (pp. 128–138). London: Routledge.

Hallenberger, G. (2005). Eurofiction 2003. Deutlicher Angebotsrückgang [Eurofiction 2003: Considerable decline in supply]. *Media Perspektiven, n.v.*(1), 14–22.

Hoskins, C., & Mirus, C. (1988). Reasons for the US dominance of the international trade in television programmes. *Media, Culture and Society, 10,* 499-515.

Iwabuchi, K. (2002). *Recentering globalization: Popular culture and Japanese transnationalism.* Durham, NC: Duke University Press.

Kerr, A., & Flynn, R. (2003). Revisiting globalisation through the movie and digital games industries. *Convergence, 9*(1), 91–113.

Ksiazek, T. B., & Webster, J. G. (2008). Cultural proximity and audience behavior: The role of language in patterns of polarization and multicultural fluency. *Journal of Broadcasting & Electronic Media, 52*(3), 485–503.

La Pastina, A. C., & Straubhaar, J. (2005). Multiple proximities between television genres and audiences: The schism between telenovelas' global distribution and national consumption. *Gazette: The international Journal for Communication Studies, 67*(3), 271–288.

Moyer-Gusé, E., & Nabi, R. L. (2010). Explaining the effects of narrative in an entertainment television program: Overcoming resistance to persuasion. *Human Communication Research, 36,* 26–52.

Norris, P., & Inglehart, R. (2009). *Cosmopolitan communications: Cultural diversity in a globalized world.* Cambridge; MA: Cambridge University Press.

Olson, S. R. (1999). *Hollywood Planet: Global media and the competitive advantage of narrative transparency.* Mahwah, NJ: Lawrence Erlbaum Associates.

Osgood, Ch. E., Suci, G. J., & Tannenbaum, P. H. (1978). *The measurement of meaning* (4th ed.). Urbana, IL: Board of Trustees of the University of Illinois.

Quick, B. L. (2009). The effects of viewing Grey's Anatomy on perceptions of doctors and patient satisfaction. *Journal of Broadcasting & Electronic Media, 53*(1), 38–55.

Shrum, L. J. (2004). *The psychology of entertainment media: Blurring the lines between entertainment and persuasion.* Mahwah, NJ: Lawrence Erlbaum Associates.

Schlütz, D. (2012). Der Prozess grenzüberschreitender Medienwirkungen: Das Susceptibility to Imported Media (SIM)-Modell am Beispiel US-amerikanischer Fernsehserien [Modelling cross-border media effects: The ‚Susceptibility to Imported Media' (SIM) model and US-American TV series]. In H. Wessler, & S. Averbeck-Lietz (Eds.), Grenzüberschreitende Medienkommunikation (pp. 183–202) [Transborder media communication]. Baden-Baden: Nomos.

Schlütz, D. M., Schneider, B., & Stipp, H. (2011, May). *Cultural proximity from an audience point of view: Why German students prefer U.S.-American TV series.* Paper presented at the Annual Meeting of the International Communication Association, Boston, MA. Retrieved 2013-06-26 from http://citation.allacademic.com/meta/p489059_index.html

Smith, A. D. (1991). *National identity.* London: Penguin Group.

Straubhaar, J. D. (1991). Beyond media imperialism: Asymmetrical interdependence and cultural proximity. *Critical Studies in Mass Communication, 8,* 39–59.

Straubhaar, J. D. (2002). (Re)asserting national television and national identity against the global, regional and national levels of worlds television. In J. M. Chan, & B. T. McIntyre (Eds.), *In search of boundaries: Communication, nation states and cultural identities* (pp. 181–206). Westport, CT: Ablex Publishing.

Straubhaar, J. D. (2007). *World television: From global to local.* London: Sage.

Straubhaar, J. D. (2008). Rethinking cultural proximity: Multiple television flows for multi-layered cultural identities. *Paper presented at the Annual Meeting of the International Communication Association, TBA, Montreal, Quebec, Canada.* Retrieved 2012-06-14 from http://www.allacademic.com/meta/p232732_index.html

Tamborini, R., Weber, R., Eden, A., Bowman, N. D., & Grizzard, M. (2010). Repeated exposure to daytime soap opera and shifts in moral judgment toward social convention. *Journal of Broadcasting & Electronic Media, 54*, 621–640.

Tan, A. S., Tan, G., & Gibson, T. (2003). Socialization effects of American television on international audiences. In M. G. Elasmar (Ed.), *The impact of international television. A paradigm shift* (pp. 29–38). Mahwah, NJ: Lawrence Erlbaum Associates.

Tinchev, V. (2010). Dexter's German reception: Why are German networks so obsessed (and troubled) with US shows? In D. L. Howard (Ed.), *DEXTER: Investigating cutting edge television* (pp. 157–171). London: I.B. Tauris.

Tomlinson, J. (1999). *Globalization and culture.* Cambridge, MA: Polity Press.

Waisbord, S. (2004). McTV: Understanding the global popularity of television formats. *Television and New Media, 5*(4), 359–383.

Zubayr, C., & Gerhard, H. (2010). *Tendenzen im Zuschauerverhalten: Fernsehgewohnheiten und Fernsehreichweiten im Jahr 2009* [Tendencies in viewing behaviour: TV habits and TV coverage in 2009]. *Media Perspektiven, n.v.*(3), 106–118.

Zubayr, C., & Gerhard, H. (2011). *Tendenzen im Zuschauerverhalten: Fernsehgewohnheiten und Fernsehreichweiten im Jahr 2010* [Tendencies in viewing behaviour: TV habits and TV coverage in 2010]. *Media Perspektiven, n.v.*(3), 126–138.

Awake, or the multiplication of the realities
Contemporary Television Series:
Narrative Structures and Audience Perception

Mathieu Pierre

Historians of the television are agreed to say that series are reaching for now several years. Its topics are deeper, its directions much more thoughtful and they have more than ever a critical look on the world, society and the Human being. It possesses this intrisic capacity to imitate reality by bringing it the necessary modifications to have its own speech. So, the fictional universe of *Desperate Housewives* (ABC, 2004–2012) can only exist if we accept that the world is governed by many secrets, the *Glee* (Fox TV, 2009) one by music, or simply by the existence of aliens in *The X-Files* (Fox TV, 1993–2002) or a supernatural island in *Lost* (ABC, 2004–10). We adhere to all these proposals because we are capable of measuring them thanks to our own perceptions of the reality. Nevertheless, the success of the fantastic or science-fiction series demonstrates, although we are conscious of their conflicting relationship with reality, we are capable and voluntary to envisage what doesn't exist. These shows wouldn't have the will to give a false image of reality in which our perceptions would be convened to offer a legitimacyto their "fictional reality".

It was already demonstrated that this one is a medium allowing these series to give a metaphoric speech on the world. Nevertheless, it is a question which does not seem to have been evisaged in general: the relationship that maintain the fictional universes of the series with the reality and the world. Indeed, a lot of programs wonder about our relationship to this one through the multiplication of ensuing realities, as Russian dolls, some of the others, developing the idea of a split of the reality represented sometimes by a principle of illusion. In this type of programs, neither the spectator, nor the characters know how to disentangle the truth of the forgery. Several series ventured to concern this look on the world. It's the case of several episodes of *Buffy the Vampire Slayer* (The WB, 1997–2003) when in one of them (Normal Again, 6x17), the sciptwriters go as far as denying and dismantling the fictional network set up since six seasons. Strangely, the same year, its spin-off *Angel* (The WB, 1999–2004), also ventures on it and puts us in front of an episode (Awakening, 4x10) where for the needs of the action, an illusion of the reality is created.

Recently, *Awake* (NBC, 2011–12) explores this idea according to which there would be several jointly linked realites which it can be hard to identify and legitimize according to our relationship in the sensitive, in our perceptions and our relation with the ouside world. These series ask the question of our capacity to determine what is real and what is not, claiming one idea: and if what I consider as reality is only an error of interpretation? The world I perceive is it the real world? Can we rely on our perceptions?

We want, through this reflection, to study these few leads (without claiming to be able to answar it totally) to show the look carrying about the television series, due to its status different from other medium that are the cinema or the literature, on the world and the reality.

To perceive the worlds

The synopsis of *Awake* seems relatively simple at first sight. Further to a road accidend which he had with his wife and his son, officer Michael Britten finds himself in a particular situation. Every time he wakes up, he seems to change of reality. In one, Hannah is alive and Rex didn't survive the accident. In the other, it's the opposite. The scenario would be simple if it stopped there and if these two stories were linked only by the disruptive element that is the car accident. Nevertheless, the real problem of the show is the fact that Michael is aware of the existence of these two worlds. He lives these two lives at the same time and can distinguish them only thanks to an rubber band of different color that he wears constantly at his wrist[1]. Naturally, further to this tragic incident, he has to conult a therapist, which is different in each reality[2]. Revealing them this trange phenomenon, his doc-

---

[1] Following the example of this rubber band which guide Michael in its recognition of the wolrds, the direction also helps the spectator in this way. In the screen, it is symbolized by the different tint of the image. So, the realtity in which Rex died is governed by bright and hotter colors whereas the second is colder. It may be necessary to see another level of reading there in which it would be possible to organize into a hierarchy these worlds according to an emotional logic : one of them would be more difficult to bear than the other one.

[2] It's interesting here to note the importance granted to these psychotherapy scenes. During the conversations, the camera realises a travelling around the characters and

tors remain a little stunned and pesisit in demonstrating him that the other wolrd is only a dream, an illusion. Nevertheless, Michael guesses this is quite different, particularly when both universes seem to answer one to the other and when new disjunctions appear. The departure idea of the show crystallizes numerous philosophic reflections on the reality and our means to dread with it. It's interesting here to go further to highlight the speech *Awake* holds on this point.

As every human being, officer Michae Britten uses his senses and his perception to seize the world which surrounds him. It's necessary, to envisage correctly this question, to distinguish percpetion and sensation. The latter is a sensitive representation of things by means of one of our senses. The perception would work as a syntheses of thses senses increased by our consciousness, to show how we "live" in the world. If we take the pilot of *Awake* as base of our reflection, we can say that Michael has no sensation defect: further to the accident its five senses seem intact. What would be failling with him, according to his therapists, is his capacity to perceive. If we take the empiricist point of view on perception, we are facing a problem. Indeed, the thesis defended by the Englis philosopher John Locke in the XVIIth century proposes the idea that the perception is the sum of the informations received by our senses in an emprical way. We interpret it intellectually only secondly. Michael, having no problem at this level, there should be no disjunction of reality. On the other hand, for Descartes, the senses teach us nothing, the perception would be the result of an act of thought because it's this is the one who produces the sens of what we see, hear or smell. Michael sees two different worlds but this is the spirit which says to him that they are both real, joining the allegory of the "wax piece": he is in front of two worlds having differences, but he can't decide which one is false because his understanding indicates him unquestionably that they are both valid because ensuing from the same reality.

---

always give the feeling that a cut is going to take place when it crosses behind one of them. Indeed, at this moment, the screen becomes black and the spectator expects that the interlocutor of Michael has changed. Yet, it's not the case. The realities, and at the same time the diagnoses of the doctors, don't become confused: the direction push them there but the convictions of Michael resist to it.

> Or quelle est cette cire, qui ne peut être conçue que par l'entendement ou l'esprit ? Certes c'est la même que je vois, que je touche, que j'imagine, et la même que je connaissais dès le commencement. Mais ce qui est à remarquer, sa perception, ou bien l'action par laquelle on l'aperçoit, n'est point une vision, ni un attouchement, ni une imagination, et ne l'a jamais été, quoiqu'il le semblât ainsi auparavant, mais seulement une inspection de l'esprit, laquelle peut être imparfaite et confuse, comme elle était auparavant, ou bien claire et distincte, comme elle est à présent, selon que mon attention se porte plus ou moins aux choses qui sont en elle, et dont elle est composée [...]. Nous disons que nous voyons la même cire si on nous la présente, et non pas que nous jugeons que c'est la même, de ce qu'elle a même couleur et même figure ; d'où je voudrais presque conclure, que l'on connaît la cire par la vision des yeux, et non par la seule inspection de l'esprit [...] (Decartes, 2010: 45–48).

We can ask ourselves from there the question of the legitimacy of the worlds which Michael perceives. For *Gestalt Theorie*, what we perceive is a shape. That is to say we perceive global structures. So, we don't perceive first of all leaves, then the tree, it's the tree in its entirety that is perceived at first. From there, we can distinguish leaves and the other parts. The perception is not from then a set of sensations. On the contrary, any perception is first the perception of a set. It is from then impossible for the character to emit any supposition on the prevalence or not of a world or the other one: the whole world seems coherent, nevertheless it's at the level of the parts that differences appear. These remain corresponding to the reason and thus don't prove only to prefer a reality to an other one. Michael realizes it and needs his rubber band of color to find a way there, the supposed tests to prove him that he's nots in a dream being decisive neither in a world, nor in the other one. Moreover, there are events appearing as failing in this process and which could allow to bring the idea that one of these worlds (and why not both) is created by the character. Indeed, repeatedly, elements relative to criminal investigations led by Michael echo in both worlds. So, in the second episode, a famous professor in a reality finds himself homeless in the other one. We undestand it can involve only of a failure of the system of Michael's perception because the life of the professor has no link with his and there is no reason that the car accident inaugurating the series also affected him. All the more, the homeless version of this character was never a professor. If the accident is the trigger of the split of reality, none disjunction can have take place before. In such case, we would leave Michael's point of view to suppose the idea that thousands of realities exist according to the persons and that they are quite imbricated the one in the others. It's a question which won't be treated here.

Of disorders of the perception

To return to the subject which interests us, we supposed that the perception gave us access to the only real world. Nevertheless, we saw that the reflection proposed by *Awake* damaged this idea. From then, how our perception could deceive us? How can the worlds perceived by Michael not be real while he feels them as such? The answer is maybe, as saying by his therapists, in a disorder of the perception provoked by the accident. But of what order would be these disorders? A structural deficiency such as would be an illusion of the reality or a false perception as an hallucination?

The term of "reality " implies that there is something who is not of it. There would be in *Awake* a real world and a world of the appearances in which everything is false. This one would be inevitably a less corresponding copy of the first one. Nevertheless, in our case, it is impossible to say which one is. It's there the heart of our reflection. For Descartes, you should not trust our senses, because they bring no certainty. It is necessary to question our sensory faculties because what deceives Michael is not its perception but maybe well its imagination and its trauma. His judgment became erroneous. What Michael sees, or has the impression to see, is very present. He really has the impression to have, in a world, his wife under eyes, and in the other his son. It is not exactly his senses which deceive him, but he didn't admit simply yet that one of these two options did not exist. It's much more an error of the reason than the illusion produced by its senses. These errors of interpretation which Michael appoints to every awakening without we can identify them are then understandable by a psychological mechanism basing on our desires: the believing. There would be from then good and bad perceptions. The first ones presuppose that to have clear and different ideas are not enough to establish the certainty. The phenomenological thesis supported by Merleau-Ponty asserts that it is necessary to trust in the world: "Percevoir c'est engager d'un seul coup tout un avenir d'expériences dans un présent qui ne le garantit jamais, à la rigueur c'est croire à un monde" (Merleau-Ponty, 1976: 343–344). Michael believes in what he sees, he adheres to it completely and announces it to his therapists. He's convinced that it's not about dreams and decides to live these two lives jointly because he finds his happiness there and because he totally relies on them.

Nevertheless, doctor Lee and Evans see in this disjunction of reality a bad perception. Michael would see there what he considers as the truth; supposing that he desires unconsciously that neither his wife, nor his son die in the accident, probably because of his sense of guilt bound to his too high alcohol level at the time of the drama. This illusion remains a different shape from believing which consists, this time, in falling there entirely because it is established on a very real desire. The illusion is inherent to any human consciousness because it is a projection of our desires, but in the case of Michael, it is at an almost pathological stage because these illusions come true. In this case, maybe it would then be more just to speak of hallucinations.

You should not understand the hallucination as being a bad perception but rather as being false. Michael believes what he sees, his understanding creates a mental representation of the world which becomes confused wrongly with its perceptions. Nevertheless they would be only mental images created and resulting from its unconscious. From there to say that it is about a dream, there is only a step because both feign the reality and correspond to an unconscious tension releasing itself such a valve of the spirit. Maybe Michael is plunged into the coma and his spirit would wander by imagining itself the consequences of the accident. Or then, his pathological state would be such as it would be incapable to doubt the reality of the worlds in which he lives because the hallucination leaves no space in the uncertainty. Michael does not hear the hypotheses of his therapists on his psychological state because, for him, the mental image is very real: he has not at all the impression to lie when he says to his wife he sees his son. The positive function of the illusion is not available any more. The believing he has in the world was replaced by the total certainty that he is the only one to know what is real, as implies it one of the conversations with doctor Lee in the second episode:

> Doctor Lee: Let me be clear, detective. Your condition is the result of a deeply fractured psyche. It is a problem. It is not a tool.
> Michael: Well, you can call it whatever you like, doctor. I seem to be doing alright with it.

In the light of these reflections, we understand how much the question of the reality is present within a series as *Awake*. However, it seems that the rough stop of the series at the end of one single season did not allow it to widen its reflection and to bring an answer of its own in this thorny problem. It is moreover rare that the series dealing with this notion dare to have a categorical position on the subject. For proof the episodes of *Buffy the vampire Slayer* and *Angel* quoted earlier: in the first one, the heroine chooses consciously to stay in her fantastic world because it is there that are the persons who are dearest to her. Nevertheless, the final plan of the episode returns on the other reality and shows us a catatonic Buffy sounded by her psychiatrist. This one declares that she is lost and condemns at the same moment the series to be the hallucination of a girl locked into a mental home. At the same moment, it cancels totally the legitimacy of the universe created in *Angel*. Spin-off of *Buffy the vampire Slayer*, if the first one is the frenzy of the slayer, the second cannot exist: Buffy cannot logically live and be the vector of the adventures of the vampire in Los Angeles. In the episode "Awakening" of *Angel*, a hallucination is provoked magically on Angel to make him taste the real happiness for him to lose again his soul. Once again, only the final plan, outside the hallucination, reveals the secret to the spectator, the vampire being always cornered there. This episode supposes that what makes justifiable the world is what we perceive due to our reason. Angel loses his soul while what he feels is only a created illusion of happiness. Demonstrating, somewhere, the existence of a world managed by the intellect. Received world, whatever it is, would be the real world because we would have other choices only to rely on it.

We did not evoke another way, more playful, that the series possess to think about the reality. It would nevertheless be interesting to see what these programs have to say to us on this subject. Much more rational, we can find series playing with the reality and its possible. In these, the spectator is aware straightaway of disjunction of reality because this one is artificial and does not question the principles pre-established by the fictional universe. To simplify, it is mainly about these episodes with parallel universes, the "what if" which are going to reinterpret everything or part of a universe to give it to see a new aspect. The examples are many there, some as *Sliders* (Fox TV, on 1995–2000) make their pitch of departure and reinterpret only the universe, the characters, the inter-dimensional travelers, still by being foreigners. Others, in the style of *Friends* (NBC, on 1994–2004) give to see what would have passed if a tiny change had intervened in the life of the protagonists. The series devoting to this plot game are numerous. On the other hand, in another case, quite recent *How I Met Your Mother* (CBS, 2005–) renews these questions by showing the various points of view which we can have of the same event, sometimes totally contradictory, as well as the idea according to which it is possible to reinterpret the reality as the memories return.

References

Descartes, R. (2010). *Méditations métaphysiques,* Paris : PUF.

Merleau-Ponty, M. (1976). *Phénoménologie de la perception.* Paris: Gallimard.

"Three hundred channels and nothing's on": Metaleptic Genre-Mixing in *Supernatural*

Michael Fuchs

Supernatural (WB 2005–2006; CW since 2006) has been described as "a testosterone-charged romp about two excessively good-looking brothers who, armed with phallic weaponry, roam the country in a '67 Chevy Impala hunting monsters from American folklore" (Tosenberger, 2008, par. 1.1). Indeed, on their journey across the United States, Sam and Dean Winchester have confronted the typical monsters of movieland that have run the gamut from vampires to *Christine*-esque haunted cars, faced the Riders of the Apocalypse, and even taken on Lucifer himself. In addition, they have found and lost their father, have tried to overcome their dead mother's specter, have repeatedly died, and have averted the apocalypse. At least, this brief outline roughly covers the show's first five seasons, which is when the episode under discussion, "Changing Channels," takes place.

Although one cannot claim that *Supernatural*'s individual episodes open in a conventionalized way, already the first few moments of "Changing Channels" feel different, for the episode begins with a view onto Sun 'n Sands motel, a motel that is surrounded by palm trees, and a bright blue sky in the background. If regular viewers are not at least a little surprised by these opening visuals, Dean's (or actor Jensen Ackles's?) voiceover, "*Supernatural* is filmed before a live studio audience," most certainly will have viewers puzzled. To top it off, the voiceover is followed by a scene reminiscent of a sitcom (which even features a laugh track) that pokes fun at Dean's food obsession while also underlining his tendency to get distracted from work when he encounters beautiful women. This scene segues into an extremely cheesy opening theme song accompanied by a montage that both pays tribute to and satirizes 1980s' sitcoms while also self-deprecatingly ridiculing *Supernatural*. All of these elements stand in stark contrast to both the typical opening sequence (which merely features a title screen that changes each season), visuals (as *Supernatural* is dominated by rather bleak landscapes and mostly employs nightly outside views onto motels), and—related to the visuals—the overall tone of the show.

The episode's title sequence—if one can term it as such, for it was only used in "Changing Channels"—is succeeded by a title card that introduces the setting: "Wellington, Ohio. Two days earlier." The black background overlaid by the white lettering indicating the setting is slowly replaced by what seem to be images of a hospital in Wellington. However, the attentive viewer will quickly notice a sign in the upper left-hand quarter of the frame which specifies that the hospital is, in fact, Seattle Mercy Hospital, i.e., a hospital in Washington State, not somewhere in Ohio. The narrative mystery surrounding the scene's setting is clarified rather quickly, for a zoom-out reveals Seattle Mercy Hospital to be the setting of *Dr. Sexy, M.D.*—a thinly veiled *Grey's Anatomy* (ABC, since 2005) parody that has Dean, who is sitting in a motel room in Wellington, glued to the tube. When Sam enters the room, *Dr. Sexy*'s magic spell over Dean appears to be broken, because after Sam has challenged Dean's masculinity ("When did you have menopause?"), the older brother stresses that he was merely channel-surfing while waiting for Sam.

This is when the episode finally, yet merely seemingly, comes to more clearly resemble a typical *Supernatural* episode. Disguised as FBI agents, Sam and Dean head over to the local police department in order to inquire about an apparent bear attack they believe to be of supernatural nature. Their suspicion is substantiated when the victim's wife tells them that she "could've sworn [she] saw the Incredible Hulk" rather than a bear. After finding several pieces of evidence, the Winchesters conclude that the creature they are looking for must be a trickster, possibly the one they had already encountered in the past (in the season two episode "Tall Tales" and the season three episode "Mystery Spot"). The brothers intercept a police call that leads them to an old paper mill on the outskirts of town, where they expect to find their foe.

When Sam and Dean go through the door, of course expecting that they will thus enter the paper mill, their passing through the door marks more than a simple "crossing of [a] basic topological border" (Lotman, 1977, p. 238) because they enter an alternate universe. Thus, "[t]he door not only signals the crossing from one physical space into another, but it also invokes the transport from one ontological... realm to another" (El-saesser & Hagener,

2010, p. 50). This second world is, however, not just any random additional timespace within *Supernatural*'s larger storyworld, for as the Winchesters pass through the door, they enter Seattle Mercy Hospital, effectively entering the storyworld of the (embedded) television show that Dean watched earlier in the episode. Entering Seattle Mercy Hospital, however, merely represents the starting point for the Winchesters' journey through TV land, as they subsequently move through the worlds of a sitcom, a Japanese game show, *Knight Rider* (NBC, 1982–1986), *CSI: Miami* (CBS, 2002–2012), and a genital herpes medication commercial.[1]

Stepping into TV Land: Metalepsis and Television

In narratology, this transgression of ontological boundaries is referred to as 'metalepsis'. Despite being rooted in Ancient rhetorics, 'metalepsis', as a representational phenomenon, has only been studied for a relatively short period of time. In his book *Narrative Discourse*, Gérard Genette describes the phenomenon as "any intrusion by the extradiegetic narrator or narratee into the diegetic universe... or the inverse" (1980, p. 234). Even though Genette's elaborations on metalepsis published between the mid-1970s and 1980s are still counted among the foundational texts in the study of the phenomenon, the increasing interest in metalepses in the early twenty-first century has led to several critiques of Genette's rather restrictive conceptualizations. For example, Genette disregarded transgressions between diegetic and extradiegetic worlds and extratextual reality—for instance, when a character directly addresses recipients—in his early publications on metalepsis. Additionally, his early focus on print fiction has opened up Genette's definitions to attacks from scholars working in the field of transmedial narratology. From such a transmedial vantage point, Werner Wolf has, for example, proposed a more inclusive definition of metalepsis as "paradoxical transgression of, or confusion between, (onto)logically distinct (sub)worlds" (2005, p. 91; original in italics). Another traditional notion concerning metalepses that has undergone re-consideration is related to the question of immersion. While conventionally thought to deconstruct texts and thus distance recipients, more recent studies have demonstrated that

---

[1] The metaleptic quality of the genital herpes medication spot is emphasized in "The Devil You Know" (2010), which, in part, is set at Niveus Pharmaceuticals' labs. At the labs, a Herpexia poster is prominently on display.

metalepses can, in fact, be employed to heighten immersion. Sonja Klimek has, for instance, shown that, especially in fantastic tales, metalepses can "celebrate the magical power of fantasy... and thus work towards... immersion" (2011, p. 37).

While these theoretical shifts have introduced new perspectives and allowed for an increased awareness of metalepses' varied functions to the theoretical discourses surrounding the phenomenon, television, especially live-action television, has been largely neglected in the field. Even though televisual metalepses have been broached in a handful of publications—most prominently in Erwin Feyersinger's piece on the metaleptic potentials of television crossovers (2011) and Jeff Thoss's chapter on the remote control as a kind of magic wand that allows viewers to enter televisual timespaces (2011)—the fact that these studies focus on television series from the 1990s onwards implies that metalepses in television are a side-effect of the proliferation of "metapop" (Dunne, 1992) in popular culture since the mid-1980s. Werner Wolf has termed this "remarkable change in the degree and quality of metareferentiality in a number (if not all) of (the) media and arts over the past few decades" (2011, p. 1) the 'metareferential turn'. Although Wolf employs various rhetorical tools in order to hedge some of his claims, one can discern that he believes this "'explosion' of metareferential phenomena" (Butler, 2009, p. 313) to be rooted "in more or less sophisticated highbrow literature" (Wolf, 2011, p. 9). Metaization, argues Wolf, has recently "become an almost hackneyed convention" that "has spread across... all levels in literature in addition to being found in most if not all popular media and genres" (2011, p. 9). In his abovementioned chapter, Thoss supports Wolf's thesis of a trickle-down effect from elite to mass culture by stressing that the 'metaleptic remote control' "appears as a genuine pop-cultural form of [metalepsis]," a "device that was formerly deemed to be rather avant-garde" (2011, p. 169).

One could argue that Thoss commits a fallacy not that dissimilar from the one made by several media scholars in the 1990s who were overzealous to claim that certain new TV programs (including *The Simpsons* [Fox, since 1989], *Beavis and Butt-Head* [MTV, 1993–1997 and 2011], and *The X-Files* [Fox, 1993–2002]) were indicative of television having (finally) become 'postmodernist', while ignoring that "[t]elevision has always been *textually messy*—that is, textural rather than transparent" (Caldwell, 1995, p. 23; italics in original). As John T. Caldwell continues:

> Any systematic look at the history of television soon shows that all of those formal and narrative traits once thought to be unique and defining properties of postmodernism... have also been defining properties of television from its inception... From a postmodernist point-of-view, 1940s and 1950s television had it all: self-reflexivity..., intertextuality..., direct address..., pastiche...; and social topicality... (1995, p. 23)

The Burns and Allen Show (CBS, 1950–1958) presents a perfect example of the 'textual messiness' outlined by Caldwell. *Burns and Allen* employed an elaborate "mise-en-abyme structure, an endless stage within a stage, a bottomless pit of representation" that caught audiences "in an endless quagmire of metarealities" (Spigel, 1992, p. 166). The season eight episode "Hypnotizing Gracie" wonderfully illustrates the show's narrative complexity: Following the opening scene, George (the titular 'Burns') is suddenly sitting in his study, watching the very scene the audience had seen only moments earlier on an intradiegetic screen. George thus occupies a borderland space between the fictional television show and the audience, similar to the Stage Manager in Thornton Wilder's *Our Town* (1938). The existence of these two distinct worlds within the show's storyworld is used for comic effect when George appears in the main world some minutes later (metaleptically transgressing ontological borders in the process) and tells a hypnotist that he "saw [him] on television." The hypnotist is confused, for he has "never been on television." However, George and the audience know better. This mutual understanding between George and the viewers concerning *Burns and Allen*'s textural quality is underscored by George's concluding wink at the audience.

Lynn Spigel has suggested that "viewers experienced a kind of layered realism" when watching *Burns and Allen*. Throughout its eight-year run, the program never "attempt[ed] to sustain the illusion that it [was] a real space at all" (1992, p. 167). Early sitcoms like *Burns and Allen* "brought to the forefront the theatrical nature of domestic life" (Spigel, 1992, p. 170). "Changing Channels" taps into this television tradition inspired by the *theatrum mundi*, for the episode stresses that Sam and Dean are expected to play their roles in a divine play that wants them to follow in the footsteps of

Michael and Lucifer and Cain and Abel, respectively, and enact the fraternal strife that defines their bloodlines and (life) stories. However, in the course of the fifth season, Sam and Dean actively resist this predestined existence by taking their lives into their own hands. In order to do so, they 'merely' need to re-write the word of the quite literal Author-God, which, in fact, allows them to avert the apocalypse at the end of the season.

This participatory and possibly subversive aspect proves crucial, for it underscores the recent re-consideration of immersion. While Klimek's above-mentioned notion of immersion originates in a (dated) literary studies perspective that assumes the creation of an alternative universe that (usually) appears to be unmediated, Frank Rose has proposed that immersion, today, means "to get involved in a story" (2011, p. 8). Contemporary audiences want "to carve out a role for themselves, to make [the story] their own" (Rose, 2011, p. 8).

But not only Sam and Dean become active agents on the battlefields of participatory culture; arguably, by merging various genres and appropriating other television texts, "Changing Channels" allows *Supernatural* per se to participate in contemporary remix culture.

(Re-)Mixing Television on Television

Sam and Dean's repeated transgressions of ontological borders separating (believed to be) distinct worlds are not merely random meta-lepses, because through their jumps from one televisual timespace to the next, *Supernatural* fuses genres. Indeed, a spatial metaphor may be employed here, too, for the characters transgress what were once believed to be fixed and clearly definable markers separating typically distinct genres. Of course, this notion of fixed and 'pure' genres has long been abandoned by scholars—and arguably much longer by the people working in the entertainment industry.

When tracing *Supernatural*'s generic genealogy, one will quickly realize that the show "was conceived as a hybrid of the horror and road movie genres" (Abbott, 2011, p. ix) from the get-go. Numerous allusions—to movies ranging from *Night of the Living Dead* (1968) to *The Shining* (1980)—and the employment of various conventions (settings, framings, scoring, etc.) highlight the program's roots in the horror tradition. The road movie genre, on the other hand, serves not only as a plot device (that is, to get the main characters from point A to point B), but is also used as a means for characterization (Dean and, to a lesser degree, Sam are free from certain societal constraints) and symbolism (their journey takes the brothers across the United States, turning their tale into an explicitly American story—filmed in Vancouver, British Columbia). Besides merging horror and road movie conventions, any regular *Supernatural* episode adds elements of mystery (several plots borrow from mystery programs and *The X-Files* is repeatedly explicitly referenced) and family melodrama (as so many American gothic tales had already done before *Supernatural*).

Yet, as indicated above, "Changing Channels" takes this genre fusion much further than the program-defining genre hybridity might suggest by sending its heroes on a journey through TV land, from a commercial to *Knight Rider*. On first glance, Sam and Dean's trip through seemingly unrelated shows and genres could easily be considered parodic in nature. In this context, Steve Neale and Frank Krutnik have pointed out that in contrast to genre hybrids, which combine generic conventions, parodies work by drawing upon such conventions in order to make us laugh... The result is not the combination of generic elements, but the subordination of the conventions of one genre to those of another. (1990, p. 19)

Even when ignoring the dated notion of genre purity implied in the quotation above, "Changing Channels" provides a more complex example than outlined by Neale and Krutnik, for the episode is not 'just' a parody of numerous past and present television programs that subordinates these shows' conventions to those established by *Supernatural*. Rather, several of the Winchesters' stops in the course of the episode prove to be highly meaningful in the larger context of the series and help *Supernatural* contextualize some of its running themes, such as gender, class, and fandom.

When Did You Have Menopause? Gendering the Winchesters

The first of these stops finds Sam and Dean in Seattle Mercy Hospital and contributes to *Supernatural*'s constant questioning of traditional (if not stereotypical) gender roles while also poking fun at *Supernatural* itself. *Supernatural*'s complex depiction of gender is too broad a topic to satisfyingly tackle within the confines of this chapter,[2] but let me here just mention that,

---
[2] See Calvert (2011), Palmer (2011), and Wright (2008) for some publications on gender in *Supernatural*.

generally, Dean, tellingly the older brother, is the strong, manly type, who loves porn, pie, and burgers, whereas Sam represents the more emotional, feminine man with a penchant for books and a healthy diet. With this in mind, Dean's (girlish?) obsession with a medical drama presents merely one of many elements throughout the series that counters any clear-cut gender definitions.

This critical engagement with gender also comes to the fore in the *Knight Rider* segment. This chapter's opening paragraph introduced *Supernatural* as 'a testosterone-charged romp', which underlines the importance of masculinity to the show, a feature shared with *Knight Rider*. All three main characters (i.e., Sam and Dean on the one hand and Michael Knight on the other) are men who can succeed in bar fights, get things done, and drive muscle cars, and the cars are significant parts of their respective masculinities.

John Fiske has argued that Michael Knight's black Trans Am represents "an attempt to close the gap between the penis and the phallus, between the real and the imaginary" (1987, p. 210) and that the car "allows an interpersonal dependency that is goal-centered, not relationship-centered" (1987, p. 263). While I would question Fiske's latter claim due to the buddy-type relationship that emerges between Michael and KITT in the course of the series, the coupling of Knight and the Trans Am contrasts sharply with Dean's relationship with his car, lovingly dubbed 'Metallicar' by *Supernatural*'s fan community. On the one hand, the Impala forges a link to the Winchesters' lost father, for he bought and owned the car prior to Dean. The Impala thus functions as a constant reminder that Dean is 'merely' the son, effectively *widening* the gap between the penis and the phallus in the process. On the other hand, Dean feminizes the car by repeatedly referring to it with female pronouns. Even though Dean stresses 'her' beauty and promises to protect 'her' time and again, the feminization of the car does not establish Metallicar as a replacement for a girlfriend, lover, or even possible wife. Rather, the Impala assumes a maternal role. In this interpretation, the car's interiors represent a womb; a place that promises safety and the illusion of coherence and unity—things Dean yearns for, but which also preclude ego-formation and thus keep Dean from accessing (phallic) power according to the Lacanian model (2001).

Oh, No—a Procedural Cop Show! Audience Power in the 21st Century

In addition to the topic of gender, Dean's depiction as an ardent fan of *Dr. Sexy, M.D.* (while Sam obviously thinks little of the show) underscores the different cultural spheres the two brothers belong to—Dean the blue-collar hero and Sam the academic overachiever who was just about to be interviewed for Stanford's law school when their father disappeared. From this perspective, "Changing Channels" at first seems to cater to certain stereotypes by suggesting that Dean, the somewhat less 'intelligent' of the two who occupies a lower rank on the social ladder, is ready and willing to passively watch whatever is on the tube, whereas Sam more selectively chooses what he watches on TV. However, Dean's fannish obsession with some of *Dr. Sexy*'s most trite and insignificant details implies that he, too, does not just watch anything that is being broadcast; rather, he watches *Dr. Sexy* because he *wants to*.

The viewing behavior exemplified by Dean provides a telling example of why television's 'flow' has recently been re-conceptualized. Traditionally conceived as a fusion of disparate texts into "a current of images and sounds that are in large measure outside our control, where we can barely escape from its powerful fascination" (Buonanno, 2008, p. 31), conceptualizations of the 'flow' have lately focused on "tactics of audience/user 'flows'" (Caldwell, 2003, p. 136). This emphasis on audience agency is made most explicit later in the episode when Sam and Dean find themselves in a police procedural (more specifically, in the world of *CSI: Miami*) and Dean complains: "Oh no... I wear sunglasses at night... I hate procedural cop shows. It's like three hundred of them on television and they're all the freakin' same." In these few sentences, Dean clearly asserts his power as a viewer; that is, the power not to tune in.

Within the context of audience power, it is noteworthy that Dean's apparent addiction to *Dr. Sexy, M.D.* saves the day (at least momentarily), for his insider knowledge of the show's conventions and working principles allows him to understand that Dr. Sexy is not Dr. Sexy, but the archangel Gabriel (still believed to be a trickster at this point) in disguise, for "a part of what makes Dr. Sexy sexy is the fact that he wears cowboy boots, not tennis shoes." Dean's outing as a fan—which he downplays as a "guilty pleasure"—presents just one of numerous shout-outs to *Supernatural*'s own fan community, made most explicit in the episodes "The Monster at the End of this Book" (2009), "Sympathy for the Devil" (2009), "The Real Ghostbusters" (2009), and "Season Seven: Time for a Wedding" (2011). In all of these episodes, *Supernatural* fans are, in fact, depicted in the show's diegesis. In "The Monster at the End of this Book," fans complain about the "trite and craptastic" storylines in online forums. Becky Rosen appears as the (stereo)typical fanfic writer in "Sympathy for the Devil" and as organizer of a *Supernatural* convention in "The Real Ghostbusters," where her knowledge of the show (which, in the storyworld, is a book series whose narrative mirrors the television program's) allows her to help the Winchester brothers. In the final episode mentioned above, fanon effectively turns into canon when Becky sees her formerly unanswered fangirl wishes fulfilled when she marries Sam thanks to a love potion.

Even though one might describe the representation of fans—especially Becky—in these episodes as outright mean at certain points, Dean's fannish rise to heroism presents just one example of how this apparent meanness becomes appreciative of fandom. In addition, Dean's depiction as a fan in "Changing Channels" ties in with the larger *Supernatural*verse, within which the program and several actors have repeatedly taken humor to unexpected self-deprecating levels. In sum, fans' representation in the show thus becomes a tool in forging a bond between the fan community and the show—if the show can laugh at its ridiculous cliché-ridden moments, why shouldn't the fans laugh at some of the more ridiculous aspects of their existence (such as writing and publishing cringe-worthy slash fiction), too?[3] Finally, due to *Supernatural*'s repeated thematization of fandom, one could even argue that the show's appreciation of fandom is turned into practice in "Changing Channels." After all, by creatively interacting with a number of other shows, the episode effectively allows *Supernatural* to assume an active role in contemporary remix culture; a role usually reserved to fans.

Of course, the abovementioned self-deprecating humor capitalizes on fans' knowledge of the show (and its production) and their awareness of the differences between fiction and reality.[4] This awareness is emphasized when

---

[3] Not all (real-world) fans have reacted positively to the representation of fandom in the show. For commentaries on negative fan responses, see Schmidt (2010) and Zubernis & Larsen (2012, pp. 143–174).

[4] At times, Becky's characterization questions the fans' ability to distinguish between fiction and reality. In "Sympathy for the Devil," *Supernatural*'s author, Chuck Shirley a.k.a. Carver Edlund, calls Becky, telling her that he "need[s her] to get a message to

Dean tells Sam that Dr. Sexy even features a ghost. Sam's consternated reaction—"This show has ghosts?"—is certainly humorous, for *Supernatural*, as the show's title implies, has repeatedly featured ghosts; in fact, already the pilot was a ghost story. However, the entire situation's humor is based on the recognition that the ghost in *Dr. Sexy*'s parodic target—*Grey's Anatomy*, that is—was portrayed by Jeffrey Dean Morgan, the same actor who not only played Sam and Dean's father in *Supernatural* but even appeared as a ghost on the program. In this way, the joke is, at the end of the day, not only on *Grey's Anatomy*, but just as much on *Supernatural*.

Welcome to TV Land: Metaleptic Genre-Mixing

Finally, this episode that mixes seemingly disparate genres provides a larger message about genre proper. As Jason Mittell has stressed, genre parodies "highlight the generic assumptions that often go unspoken" (2004, p. 159). Indeed, even though "Changing Channels" primarily lampoons specific genre shows rather than genres per se,[5] these spoofs entail implicit assumptions concerning genres and how the audience at large (which, of course, merely exists as a conceptual construct) categorizes certain shows into specific genres—the laugh track, domestic setting, and somewhat cheesy humor emblematic of sitcoms, the gendering characteristic of medical dramas and action series, the unquestioned weirdness of Japanese game shows for Western viewers, the ridiculousness of commercials proper and the capitalist drives spurring them, and the triteness of standard horror plots. Although "Changing Channels" can be productively interpreted from various perspectives, ranging from enacting Sigmund Freud's notion that "an uncanny effect is often and easily produced when the distinction between imagination and reality is effaced, as when something that we have hitherto regarded as imaginary appears before us in reality" (1990, p. 367) to engaging with postmodernist discourses surrounding the blurring of the boundaries between reality and artifice, reviews of and various online com-

---

Sam and Dean." After initially emphasizing that she doesn't "appreciate being mocked," for she "know[s] that *Supernatural* is just a book," Chuck's insistence that "it's all real" makes her forget her reservations instantaneously and proclaim: "I knew it!"

[5] Even the somewhat 'unreal' Japanese game show Nutcracker has an equivalent in the real world, as a widely circulated clip from *Downtown's "This Is No Task for Kids!!"* demonstrates (see roggenvollkornbread 2007).

mentaries on the episode indicate that what it, in fact, is most successful in is parody.

As such, the episode "foreground[s] the role that genres as cultural categories play in situating texts within larger contexts" (Mittell, 2004, p. 195). Indeed, "Changing Channels" has much to say about the various genres out there in TV land, both in terms of what distinguishes various genre texts from *Supernatural* and the common features they share. Thus, "Changing Channels" suggests that a singular genre show cannot exist in a vacuum. Not only does said program need other genres to define itself, the generic history it is part of, and the generic expectations it draws on, but it is thus also constantly influenced not only by its generic forefathers and siblings, but also shows from other genres, not to mention the maybe most important of all television genres, commercials.

References

Abbott, S. (2011), Then: The Road So Far. In S. Abbott & D. Lavery, *TV Goes to Hell: An Unofficial Road Map of Supernatural* (pp. ix–xvii). Toronto, ON: ECW Press.

Buonanno, M. (2008). *The Age of Television: Experiences and Theories* (J. Radice, Trans.). Bristol: Intellect.

Butler, M. (2009). "Please Play This Song on the Radio": Forms and Functions of Metareference in Popular Music. In W. Wolf, K. Bantleon, and J. Thoss (Eds.), *Metareference across Media: Theory and Case Studies* (pp. 299–318). Amsterdam: Rodopi.

Caldwell, J. T. (2003). Second Shift Aesthetics: Programming, Interactivity and User Flows. In A. Everett & J. T. Caldwell (Eds.), *New Media: Theories and Practices of Digitextuality* (pp. 127–144). London: Routledge.

Caldwell, J. T. (1995). *Televisuality: Style, Crisis, and Authority in American Television*. New Brunswick, NJ: Rutgers University Press.

Calvert, B. (2011). Angels, Demons, and Damsels in Distress: The Representation of Women in *Supernatural*. In S. Abbott & D. Lavery (Eds.), *TV Goes to Hell: An Unofficial Road Map of Supernatural* (pp. 90–104). Toronto, ON: ECW Press.

Carver, C. (Writer), & Beeson, C. (Director). (2009). Changing Channels. In J. Michaels (Producer), *Supernatural*. Burbank, CA: Warner.

Dabb, A., Loflin, D. (Writers), & Andrew, T. (Director). (2011). Season Seven: Time for a Wedding! In T. Aronauer (Producer), *Supernatural*. Burbank, CA: Warner.

Dunne, M. (1992). *Metapop: Self-Referentiality in Contemporary American Popular Culture*. Jackson, MS: University of Mississippi Press.

Elsaesser, T., & Hagener, M. (2010). *Film Theory: An Introduction through the Senses*. New York, NY: Routledge.

Feyersinger, E. (2011). Metaleptic TV Crossovers. In K. Kukkonen & S. Klimek (Eds.), *Metalepsis in Popular Culture* (pp. 127–158). Berlin: Walter de Gruyter.

Fiske, J. (1987). *Television Culture*. London: Methuen.

Freud, S. (1990). The "Uncanny" (J. Strachey, Trans.). In A. Dickson (Ed.), *Sigmund Freud, Vol. 14: Art and Literature* (pp. 339–376). New York, NY: Penguin.

Genette, G. (1980). *Narrative Discourse: An Essay in Method* (J. E. Lewin, Trans.). Ithaca, NY: Cornell University Press.

Klimek, S. (2011). Metalepsis in Fantasy Fiction. In K. Kukkonen & S. Klimek (Eds.), *Metalepsis in Popular Culture* (pp. 23–40). Berlin: Walter de Gruyter.

Kripke, E., Weiner, N. (Writers), & Conway, J. L. (Director). (2009). The Real Ghostbusters. In T. Aronauer (Producer), *Supernatural*. Burbank, CA: Warner.

Kripke, E. (Writer) & Singer, R. (Director). (2009). Sympathy for the Devil. In T. Aronauer (Producer), *Supernatural*. Burbank, CA: Warner.

Lacan, J. (2001). The Mirror Stage as Formative of the Funciton of the *I* (A. Sheridan, Trans.). In A. Sheridan (Ed.), *Écrits: A Selection* (pp. 1–8). London: Routledge.

Lotman, J. (1977). *The Structure of the Artistic Text* (G. Lenhoff & R. Vroon, Trans.). Ann Arbor: University of Michigan Press.

Mittell, J. (2004). *Genre and Television: From Cop Shows to Cartoons in American Culture*. New York, NY: Routledge.

Neale, S., & Krutnik, F. (1990). *Popular Film and Television Comedy*. New York, NY: Routledge.

Palmer, L. (2011). The Road to Lordsburg: Rural Masculinity in *Supernatural*. In S. Abbott & D. Lavery (Eds.), *TV Goes to Hell: An Unofficial Road Map of Supernatural* (pp. 77–89). Toronto, ON: ECW Press.

Paul, N., Helm, H., Fowler, K., Burns, W. (Writers), & Amateau, R. (Director). (1958). Hypnotizing Gracie. In R. Amateau (Producer), *The George Burns and Gracie Allen Show*. New York: CBS.

roggenvollkornbread. (2007, May 12). *Japanese Gameshow* [video file]. Retrieved from http://www.youtube.com/watch?v=dS3tjP6Yh1w

Rose, F. (2011). *The Art of Immersion: How the Digital Generation Is Remaking Hollywood, Madison Avenue, and the Way We Tell Stories*. New York, NY: Norton.

Schmidt, L. (2010). Monstrous Melodrama: Expanding the Scope of Melodramatic Identification to Interpret Negative Fan Responses to*Supernatural*. *Journal of Transformative Works and Cultures*, 4. http://dx.doi.org/10.3983/twc.2010.0152

Siege, J., Weiner, N. (Writers), & Rohl, M. (Director). (2009). The Monster at the End of this Book. In T. Aronauer (Producer), *Supernatural*. Burbank, CA: Warner.

Spigel, L. (1992). *Make Room for TV: Television and the Family Ideal in Postwar America*. Chicago, IL: University of Chicago Press.

Thoss, J. (2011). "Some weird kind of video feedback time warp zapping thing": Television, Remote Controls, and Metalepsis. In: K. Kukkonen & S. Klimek (Eds.), *Metalepsis in Popular Culture* (pp. 158–170). Berlin: Walter de Gruyter.

Tosenberger, C. (2008). "The Epic Love Story of Sam and Dean": *Supernatural*, Queer Readings, and the Romance of Incestuous Fan Fiction. *Transformative Works and Cultures*, 1. http://dx.doi.org/10.3983/twc.2008.0030

Wright, J. M. (2008). Latchkey Hero: Masculinity, Class and the Gothic in Eric Kripke's Supernatural. *Genders*, 47. Retrieved from http://www.genders.org/g47/g47_wright.html

Wolf, W. (2011). Is there a Metareferential Turn, and if so, How can it be explained? In: W. Wolf, K. Bantleon, & J. Thoss (Eds.), *The Metareferential Turn in Contemporary Arts and Media: Forms, Functions, Attempts at Explanation* (pp. 1–47). Amsterdam: Rodopi.

Wolf, W. (2005). Metalepsis as a Transgeneric and Transmedial Phenomenon: A Case Study of the Possibilities of "Exporting" Narratological Concepts. In J. C. Meister, T. Kindt, & W. Schernus (Eds.), *Narratology Beyond Literary Criticism: Mediality—Disciplinarity* (pp. 83–107). Berlin: Walter de Gruyter.

Zubernis, L., & Larsen, K. (2012). *Fandom At The Crossroads: Celebration, Shame and Fan/Producer Relationships*. Newcastle: Cambridge Scholars.

Appreciating Nietzsche in Episodic Drama: The Highbrow Intertextuality and Middlebrow Reception of *Criminal Minds*

Michael Wayne

Introduction

For the majority of its history, from Newton Minow's "vast wasteland" to the anti-TV activist groups who proclaimed the medium a public health concern akin to illegal drug use, television has been a low status cultural form. As television entered the post-network era in the late 1990s, however, this began to change and some critics now assert the cultural significance of televised serial drama has surpassed that of Hollywood film (see Polone, 2012; Wolcott, 2012). Culturally legitimated content, like HBO's *The Sopranos* (1999-2007) or AMC's *Mad Men* (2007-present), is frequently conceptualized as the product of an "artist of unique vision whose experiences and personality are expressed through storytelling craft" (Newman & Levine, 2012, p. 38). In addition, courses addressing HBO's *The Wire*, offered at a variety of elite colleges and universities, attest to the ongoing institutionalization of the medium as a highbrow cultural form (Newman & Levine, 2012, p. 169). Yet, traditional crime dramas produced by major networks are often maligned by critics as "lacking ambition" (see Owen, 2012) and understood by scholars as supporting the hegemonic ideologies of the post-welfare, neoliberal state (see Bonnycastle, 2009).

I begin this analysis with a discussion of televisual intertextuality and argue that the dominant understanding of what I term "highbrow intertextuality"[1] in

---

[1] Here, I define highbrow intertextuality as the tendency for post-network television shows to explicitly make reference to texts associated with more traditionally prestigious cultural forms like fine art, literature, philosophy, film, etc. The explicit verbalization of the allusion that connects a post-network television text to a highbrow cultural text is analytically central. Using *The Sopranos* as an example, the Soprano family's discussion of Nietzsche, initially called "Nitch" (2:7), is considered an instance of highbrow intertextuality in the context of this analysis because both the author and the content of the text being referenced is made explicit for the audience. In this case, Tony Soprano's (played by James Gandolfini) son A.J. (played by Robert Iler) makes explicit reference to the content of *The Gay Science* when he explains to his father

the post-network era assumes a literary relationship between niche text and educated audience. In the following section, I justify the choice to use *Criminal Minds* as a case study by using critical reviews to demonstrate that the show's deployment of highbrow intertextuality lacks the appeal of similar elements in culturally legitimated drama and briefly describe the research methodology used to gather audience reception data regarding this quantiatively popular network show. Next, I use sociological research addressing American middlebrow culture to frame online fan discussions of *Criminal Minds* to highlight the pleasures provided by highbrow intertextuality in episodic crime drama. Lastly, I conclude by noting the use of intertextuality exclusively with reference to literary allusions in culturally legitimated content marginalizes the viewing experiences of network audiences.

Televisual Intertextuality in the Post-Network Era

In the broadest sense, the term "intertextuality" refers to the ways in which the meaning of a particular text is shaped by other texts. Originally coined by Kristeva (1996), contemporary scholars use the term in a variety of contexts for a variety of purposes ranging "from those faithful to Kristeva's original vision to those who simply use it as a stylish way of talking about allusion and influence" (Irwin, 2004, pp. 227–228). In the sub-field of television studies, intertextuality has a long history extending back to Raymond Williams' (1974) work on flow and John Fiske's (1988) exploration of the distinction between horizontal and vertical intertextualities. In describing the emergence of television's second golden age during the 1980s and 1990s, Robert Thompson characterizes "quality TV" as "literary and writer-based" and notes the frequent use of highbrow cultural allusions in shows like Hill Street Blues (1981-1987) and Picket Fences (1992-1996) while asserting that "the classier cultural references... serve to distance these programs from the stigmatized medium and to announce that they are superior to the typical trash available on television" (1997, pp. 14–15). As the post-network era began in the early 2000s, highbrow intertextuality remained central to the medium's increasing cultural legitimacy (Newman & Levine, 2012).

In the recent critical darlings frequently described as "artistic" (Nussbaum, 2009), "difficult" (Martin, 2013), and "revolutionary" (Sepinwall, 2012), high-

---

that Nietzsche's existentialism doesn't deny the existence of God but rather proclaims that God is dead.

brow intertextuality helps a text forge relationships with educated audiences by demanding active viewing (Mittell, 2006) or providing opportunities to demonstrate high levels of knowledge (Lavery, 2006). Film scholar Dana Polan (2009), for example, argues that the use of highbrow allusions in The Sopranos is particularly important in the context of the relationship between Tony Soprano as a working-class mobster and his upper-middle-class psychiatrist Dr. Jennifer Melfi. For example, in "Fortunate Son" (1:1), Melfi likens Tony's experience of recalling his first panic attack while eating cold cuts in his mother's kitchen to Proust's madeleines. The exchange continues:

> Tony: What? Who?
> Melfi: Marcel Proust. Wrote a seven-volume classic, *Remembrance of Things Past*. He took a bite of a madeleine -- a kind of tea cookie he used to have when he was a child—and that one bite unleashed a tide of memories of his childhood and ultimately, his entire life.
> Tony: This sounds very gay. I hope you're not saying that.

According to Polan, the reference to Proust in this scene allows "the viewer who gets the reference" to "both feel superior to Tony and be impressed by his talent at clearing away the verbiage and getting to the core of the situation" (Polan, 2009, pp. 52–53). Discussions of other culturally legitimated television programs conceptualize the function of highbrow intertextuality in similar terms. In his analysis of HBO's The Wire (2002-2008), for example, Erlend Lavik asserts that textual features like "behind-the-scenes cameos and amateur performers playing versions of themselves" can be understood "as trivia that separates those in the know from the rest, and lends the series a ludic spot-the-reference quality" (2011, p. 61). Regarding AMC's Mad Men (2007-present), Jeremy Butler argues the show's intertextuality provides audiences with a similar the opportunity as its "style showcases historical specificity and urges us to engage with it" (2011, p. 69). Like Thompson's (1997) earlier conceptualizations, however, these understandings of highbrow intertextuality in culturally legitimated prime-time drama assume a literary relationship between text and audience.

According to David Lavery, the use of allusions on television, which he defines as "direct or indirect references in a work of art," possess a "kind of literary cache" resulting from their "bookish past" (2006). However, to claim the deployment of literary allusions in The Sopranos and ABC's Lost (2004-2010) implies "a mutual 'fund of knowledge'" that acts "as a testimony to the medium's increasing sophistication," as Lavery does, largely glosses over the different relationships such highbrow intertextuality establishes with post-network audiences. If culturally legitimated cable drama, as discussed above, provides educated audiences with opportunities to demonstrate their intellectual superiority, then references to famous philosophers in a network drama like Lost "can be understood as 'nerd bait'" an attempt to draw audiences into "transmedia" extensions like DVDs, affiliated web sites, videogames, novels, and comic books thereby ensuring that viewers who invest more time with the show (and its related paratexts) are rewarded with more valuable interactions (Clarke, 2012, p. 5). To further explore the variable relationship between highbrow intertextuality and contemporary audiences in other parts of the post-network landscape, it seems useful to ask, how do such textual elements function in content that is not legitimated? What kind of relationship does highbrow intertextuality create with audiences engaging with traditional episodic narratives?

Criminal Minds, Critical Reception, and Fan as Audience

To begin addressing the role of intertextuality outside of culturally legitimated content as it is understood by viewers with literary relationships to televisual texts, *Criminal Minds* is a useful case study for several reasons. Among the episodic prime-time network dramas like those of CBS's *CSI* franchise or NBC's *Law and Order* franchise, one of the ways in which *Criminal Minds* distinguishes itself is through the deployment of highbrow intertextuality at the beginning and ending of each episode. In fact, during the twenty-two episodes of the first season, there are quotations from a wide range of intellectuals, artists, scientists, and authors including Albert Einstein, William Faulkner, Samuel Johnson, Euripides, William Shakespeare, Ernest Hemingway, Carl Jung, Voltaire, and Friedrich Nietzsche. Yet, in the majority of episodes, the references are only one or two sentences long. At the conclusion of the pilot episode, for example, a character provides the following voice-over: "Nietzsche once said, 'When you look long into an abyss, the abyss looks into you'" (1:1).[2]

---

[2] Some episodes include more instances of intertextuality which are typically deployed in the context of a puzzle created by a serial killer who is being pursued by the BAU

Aside from this narrative technique, the show also distinguishes itself from other network procedurals by featuring protagonists that are neither police detectives nor forensic analysts. Instead, they are a team of criminal profilers working for the Federal Bureau of Investigation's Behavioral Analysis Unit (BAU) who travel the country assisting local police departments to identify and capture serial killers. The cast includes many actors with previous network television experience including Thomas Gibson of ABC's Dharma and Greg (1997-2002) as Supervisory Special Agent and BAU Unit Chief Aaron "Hotch" Hotchner and long time network staple Joe Montegna as Supervisory Special Agent David Rossi. Furthermore, unlike many culturally legitimated programs produced by cable channels for niche audiences, the network show Criminal Minds is quantitatively popular. During its sixth season, for example, Criminal Minds reached the top ten with an average weekly viewership above fourteen million (Gorman, n.d.). In 2010, Criminal Minds entered syndication and reruns are shown on multiple cable channels including the A&E Network and ION Television (Albiniak, 2008).

Most importantly, however, Criminal Minds is ideally suited to highlight the relationship between televisual intertextuality and post-network audiences because of the disjuncture between critical and popular reception of the show. Simply stated, critics do not enjoy Criminal Minds. Of the forty-two reviews reviews published in major American newspapers between August 1 and October 31, 2005 (Criminal Minds premiered on September 22), identified by the Lexis-Nexis Academic search engine, all but three of the professional television critics in the sample gave the show mixed or negative reviews. Matthew Gilbert (2005) of the Boston Globe, for example, writes, "Criminal Minds faces an uphill battle to distinguish itself from the many other crime procedurals already on TV, most of which similarly borrow from Silence of the Lambs. It's not a cool-science show, but its crimes blur together with what we already see on the CSI series, and its supporting cast is indistinct." Similarly, New York Daily News television critic David Bianculli (2005) writes, "Sometimes a new show seems so old—so familiar, so utterly recycled—that the term déja vu doesn't come close to describing it. It's more like tréj vu. Criminal Minds, the newest crime drama from CBS, is one of those shows... It's a premise that feels almost insultingly derivative." Alt-

---

team. However, this analysis is primarily concerned with the references that bookends each episode.

hough these complaints might seem mundane, the overwhelmingly negative critical attitude to *Criminal Minds* is significant precisely because many find the show's intertextual efforts to be particularly unappealing. Entertainment Weekly's Nicholas Fonseca (2005), for example, gives his readers the following advice, "Do yourself a favor and read some Nietzsche instead of watching this junk." Similarly, Robert Bianco (2005) of USA Today notes, "The only possibly novel touch is the reliance on quotes from such historical giants as Beckett, Nietzsche, Faulkner and Churchill, men who don't deserve the guilt of this association." According to David Kronke (2005) of the Daily News of Los Angeles, the use of "lofty voice-overs cite epigrams from philosophers and statesmen" justifies the show's "seediness with pseudo-philosophizing." Whether related to the show's episodic narrative structure or its resemblance to other network crime dramas, these evaluations strongly suggust the appeal of the intellectual references in this show differ from similar textual elements in more culturally legitimated content.

To understand the role of highbrow intertextuality in prime-time network drama, this research combines elements of cyberethnography and content analysis to explore the ways in which *Criminal Minds* establishes relationships with viewers. Historically, examinations of American television audiences using traditional methods such as qualitative interviews or ethnography have been complicated by the homogenous nature of production and the medium's association with feminine passivity, laziness, and mass culture (Seiter, 1999, p. 131). However, recent scholarship examining online "fan" communities indicates the opposite (see Gray, 2005; Hills & Luther, 2007).[3] Despite this theoretical and methodological uncertainty, I began monitoring message boards like the "*Criminal Minds* Fan Wiki" (CMFW) and "*Criminal Minds* Fanatic Blog" (CMFB) as well as the official *Criminal Minds* community message boards hosted by the network (CBS.com) and one of the cable channels that syndicates the show (AETV.com) at the beginning of the show's seventh season in the fall of 2011. I discovered that viewers of *Criminal Minds* discuss the show's intertextuality using phrases like "opening quotes," "closing quotes," or "bookend quotes." Using these terms,

---

[3] Although some scholars suggest meaningful differences between analytically active "fans" and passive "consumers" (Abercrombie & Longhurst, 1998, p. 145), comparing the reception of presumably more engaged fans with presumably less engaged general audience members is outside the scope of this research.

I also used Google Search to identify data on websites like Tumblr, Squidoo, and Wordpress. In an effort to address televisual intertextuality within a larger cultural context, during data collection, I cataloged any public information regarding the basic demographics of a given audience member along with their posts. While the amount of available background varies from only a screen-name with a blank avatar to extended autobiographic accounts, and as such, cannot approach the level of nuance typical of traditional qualitative methodologies, these details are particularly useful as they help position *Criminal Minds* fans outside elite audiences such as critics and scholars.

Subjectivity, Morality, and Network Intertextuality

Although the division between highbrow and lowbrow cultures is never "fixed and immutable", as Lawrence Levine observes, sociological research indicates that middle-class orientations to culture predictably vary with socioeconomic status (1988, p. 8). The most common American middle-class taste culture, as literary theorist Janice Radway (1999) describes in her investigation of The-Book-of-the-Month Club during the 1920s and 1930s, is defined by the prominence of individual subjectivity. In particular, this "middlebrow personalism" both requires and supports a worldview in which taste is a reflection of "individual, idiosyncratic selves" (Radway, 1999, p. 283). The importance of critical assessment associated with highbrow cultural forms is mirrored by the significance of individual, subjective assessment in middlebrow cultural worlds and, not surprisingly, much online discussion of *Criminal Minds* is dedicated to viewers identifying what they find most appealing in the text.

In general discussions of the show, audience members frequently reference the value they associate with highbrow intertextuality. On CMFW, rseabrease, a middle-aged white male living in Pennsylvania who describes himself as a "long-time woodworker," explains, "I believe that *Criminal Minds* is the best show on television... The show does not use trite or sarcastic dialogue as is done on other programs such as CSI. I really like the use of quotes from major writers—it adds sophistication and class to the entire scenario." In addition to general discussions, discussions asking viewers to identify their favorite quotes from the series are some of the most popular threads on a variety of fan websites like, for example, the "Favorite

Quotes" forum on CBS.com which has fifty-five topics and more than 1400 individual messages. Posts like this one written by thn0715, a retail employee living in Alabama, are very typical: "My favorite is from 'Seven Seconds' [(3:5)] at the end when Hotch is sitting in his son's room watching him sleep. I can't remember who said it, but it was... 'Fairy tales don't teach children that dragons exist. Children already know dragons exist. Fairy tales teach children that dragons can be killed.'" Highbrow intertextuality is also frequently discussed when audience members claim a particular quote is their favorite part of a given episode. In a discussion of "Mosley Lane" (5:16), ILDRSR, a student living in Colorado whose username is a derivative of the phrase "I Love Dr. Spencer Reid" (played by Matthew Gray Gubler), writes, for example, "**teengirlmoment** OH-EM-EFF-GEE It was perfect. It was awesome. I FRICKEN LOVED IT. My favorite part was how the quote at the beginning was about hope being torture and ended with hope saving all. Ah! I loved it! Ah!" Although fans often include the relevant quote in their post, in some cases, like when it has already been posted by another user on a particular message board, fans commonly assume the content is shared knowledge and simply state a preference for either the opening or closing reference.

In addition to the prominence of individual subjectivity, Radway (1999) also notes middlebrow taste is ideologically based upon the recognition that cultural engagement is a highly variable experience (277) and this is frequently reflected when audience members reference their emotional response to the highbrow intertextuality of *Criminal Minds*. On CMFW, woskxn4848, a young woman from Texas, writes, "Okay boys and girls, I'm pretty new here, but I've found the one thing I love reading are the quotes, the sad ones, the intense ones, the funny ones ..." Similarly, on the CBS forum addressing "Tearjerking lines/quotes," meikat518, a young Asian-American woman in an unspecified white-collar occupation, writes, "...the quote at the ending of 'House on Fire' [4:19] sort of gave a lump on my throat." Such comments are largely in line with Gans' sociological understanding of "lower-middle culture" in which quantitatively popular texts are considered "user-oriented" since they were produced the intention of being entertaining for the audience rather than fulfilling for the creator (110–111). And, one of the most common reasons fans cite to explain the pleasure of *Criminal Minds* is that intertextual references serve as a source of inspiration. On CMFB, for example, crochet95, a medical records clerk with some college education from North Dakota, writes, "I love the quotes. They are one of the many reasons why I love this show so much. They put perspective into life and the show itself... You can take the quotes and put them into your own life... inspiration." Furthermore, viewers like riffjim4069, a "Lowly Defense Contractor" from Dallas whose interests include "Beerin', Bikin', Bassin', Shootin, and VoOmin,'" assert this inspiration generates real-world benefits. In a forum for technology professionals dedicated to CBS shows, he writes:

> Besides serial killing, I find these quotes often apply equally well to marriage, family, and the workplace. For example, I used the following quote ["Without a family, man, alone in the world, trembles with the cold." ~ Andre Maurois] when discussing family commitments with my wife, and I was showered with love and affection. Who would have thought *Criminal Minds* would give inspiration to relationships with family, friends and coworkers.

While riffjim4069 was the only audience member who reports being showered with love and affection, as these examples indicate, the entertainment value of intertextuality is closely related to the practical value of inspiration for many viewers. Yet, in a notable contrast with critics, the lack of context associated with the deployment of these allusions is largely unproblematic. Although audience members frequently refer to the intellectual value they associate with highbrow references, they do so through a middlebrow framework emphasizing individual subjectivity where the ability to appreciate the televisual text does not require preexisting knowledge. Shadow007, for example, an unemployed twenty-six year-old white male from California, starts a thread on AETV.com by writing, "I like how they start & end each show with deep, thought provoking, famous quotes." In the remainder of the post, he simply lists a few of his favorites and their authors. In fact, many audience members explicitly acknowledge that the historical/intellectual context of the references remain unaddressed. On her WordPress blog dedicated to the show, Chrissiemusa, who is studying to be a teacher, notes, "The quotations used in *Criminal Minds* to relate to each case can be both inspiring, interesting, dark, but they are all amazing and delivered extremely well... The quotations used may not be the full versions, they may have been edited or 'slimmed down' for the shows purpose." Most viewers, like Shadow007 and Chrissiemusa, have little interest in using references to demonstrate cultural capital. This is frequently reflected when individuals assert that the inability to "get it" or "be in the know" is unproblematic. On her Tumblr page cataloging the references, Betweenthebarrs, a college student studying psychology, explains her interest in the following terms, "As all you *Criminal Minds* fans know, each episode begins and finishes with a quote. This is a blog dedicated to all those quotes. I often find them inspirational or sometimes i don't quite understand them. But I love the concept of this in the show." Yet, while primarily concerned with the pleasures provided by the text rather than the cultural capital associated with the reference, the pleasure many viewers associate with intertextuality has a distinct moral character.

According to Gans, a central characteristic of drama in lower-middle-culture is the tendency to "express and reinforce the culture's own ideas and feelings" (1999, p. 111). In this cultural context, as media sociologist Todd Gitlin argued of network era television, definitive moral conclusions are particularly important because they encourage the ideological belief that large-scale social problems are "susceptible to successful individual resolutions" (1982, pp. 259–261). Contemporary scholars make similar arguments regarding prime-time network crime dramas. As Hohenstein argues regarding CSI, for example, the "scientific examination of facts leads to clear and concise conclusions" which "offer easy answers to complicated conflicts" in the criminal justice system (67). Among audiences, viewers understand *Criminal Minds*' use of intertextual references in exactly this context. SylviaRolfe, "a webmaster, a writer, and internet marketer and mommy to 5" living in Canada, employs this framework in a Squidoo page dedicated to "*Criminal Minds* Quotes --> Season Two." She writes, "[The ending quote] ties the episode up in a neat little package, and pretty much gives you the moral of the episode right there for you, without you having to decode it and try and figure out what the hidden meaning was." The moral appreciation of intertextuality, however, often extends beyond middlebrow narratives. As Gitlin (1982, p. 259) and Gans (1999, p. 111) both argue, ideologically, narrative resolution also confirms the validity of traditional morality and the institutions that promote such values. Take, for example, Wbisbill, a retired pastor from Tennessee speaking on the behalf of himself and his wife Barbara. On his Squidoo page explaining "Why The *Criminal Minds* TV Show Is So Successful," it is clear Pastor Walt (as he identifies himself) understands the references through the moral binary of good and evil. He writes, "The *Criminal Minds* TV Show is one of our favorite programs. My wife and I DVR it every Wednesday night, and watch it after church... We root for the good guys, laugh at the humor, anticipate the well timed quotes given in each episode, marvel at the insights of the team, and rejoice at the capture of the serial killers." Unlike SylviaRolfe, the value viewers like Wbisbill ascribe to the show's intertextuality is directly related to traditional notions of morality commonly found in lower-middle-culture.

Although many in the *Criminal Minds* audience understand intertextuality through subjective and moral middlebrow frameworks, there are other interpretations. In some cases, individuals find the deployment of particular references problematic and in other instances, audiences members research the source of a particular reference as part of their search for symbolism. In a CMFW forum addressing "Demonology" (4:17), for example, malrescue writes, "About the snow, I started by researching the comments that Prentiss and Rossi made at the end... While reading about both of these references I began reading more about James Joyce... Well, there is a reference to snow in a discussion about one of James Joyce's books... So was the snow in this episode also symbolism?" Although some viewers do indeed relate to the intertextuality of *Criminal Minds* in critical or literary ways, this kind of engagement is uncommon.

Conclusion

Perhaps the differences between professional television critics and quantitatively large audiences of network content in the post-network era is not very surprising. Where the CBS viewer finds inspiration and confirmation of traditional values in stories where the majority of conflicts are resolved at the conclusion of the hour, professional critics see pseudo-intellectual commentary about human nature in a thoroughly unrealistic show where Federal employees have access to a leer jet and successfully stop the non-existent scourge of rampaging serial killers week in, week out. Despite such divergent interpretations, the dominant theoretical understanding of highbrow intertextuality on post-network television as a means by which legitimated content appeals to cultural elites by providing opportunities to demonstrate literary cultural capital cannot be applied to non-elite audiences of quantitatively popular content.

Like film during the 20th century, the increasing status of any cultural form is dependent on the degree to which it develops its own "intellectual viability" (Baumann, 2007, p. 3). And, as Newman and Levine convincingly argue, the increasing legitimacy of post-network era content is only possible with the support of cultural elites who invest "the medium with aesthetic and other prized values, nudging it closer to more established arts and cultural forms and preserving their own privileged status in return" (2012, p. 154). Nevertheless, from a scholarly perspective, it is only by recognizing the ways in which such class-stratified understandings are socially constructed that the increasing legitimacy of post-network television ceases being taken-for-granted. Like the increasingly common arguments regarding the emergence of a new golden age which require an ahistorical conception of television, the association between intertextuality and qualitative superiority in the post-network era ignores the broader context of the medium's increasing legitimacy. By exclusively addressing highbrow intertextuality in legitimated post-network drama, scholars universalize the view experiences of culturally elite audiences while simultaneously marginalizing network audiences by denying the very real middlebrow pleasures viewers associate with traditional episodic content. As such, the contrast between the values fans find in the highbrow intertextuality of *Criminal Minds* and the reasons scholars assume educated viewers celebrate the use of Proust in *The Sopranos* indicates the perpetuation of a status-based hierarchy.

References

Abercrombie, N., & Longhurst, B. (1998). Audiences: A Sociological Theory of Performance and Imagination. Sage Publications Limited.

Albiniak, P. (2008, November 16). *"Criminal Minds," "Numb3rs"* Find Syndie Homes. Broadcasting & Cable.

Baumann, S. (2007). Hollywood Highbrow: From Entertainment to Art. Princeton University Press.

Bianco, R. (2005, September 21). Something is Criminal about Gruesome Minds. USA Today, p. D3.

Bonnycastle, K. D. (2009). Not the usual suspects: The obfuscation of political economy and race in CSI. The CSI Effect: Television, Crime, and Governance, 149–178.

Butler, J. G. (2011). Smoke Gets in Your Eyes: Historicizing Visual Style in Mad Men. In Mad Men: Dream Come True TV (pp. 55–71). IB Tauris.

Clarke, M. J. (2012). Transmedia Television: New Trends in Network Serial Production (1st ed.). Continuum.

Fiske, J. (1988). Television Culture. Routledge.

Fonseca, N. (2005, September 23). *Criminal Minds*. Entertainment Weekly.

Gans, H. (1999). Popular Culture and High Culture: An Analysis and Evaluation Of Taste Revised And Updated (Second Edition.). Basic Books.

Gilbert, M. (2005, September 22). *"Criminal Minds"* Doesn't Offer Much New to Think About. Boston Globe, p. C2.

Gitlin, T. (1982). Television's Screens: Hegemony in Transition. Cultural and Economic Reproduction in Education: Essays on Class, Ideology, and the State, Ed. Michael Apple(Boston: Routledge & Kegan Paul), 202–246.

Gorman, B. (n.d.). 2010-11 Season Broadcast Primetime Show Viewership Averages. TVbytheNumbers. Retrieved January 12, 2013, from http://tvbythenumbers.zap2it.com/2011/06/01/2010-11-season-broadcast-primetime-show-viewership-averages/94407/

Gray, J. (2005). Antifandom and the Moral Text Television Without Pity and Textual Dislike. American Behavioral Scientist, 48(7), 840–858.

Hills, M., & Luther, A. (2007). Investigating "CSI Television Fandom": Fans' Textual Paths through the Franchise. In Reading CSI: Crime TV under the microscope (pp. 208–221). IB Tauris.

Irwin, W. (2004). Against Intertextuality. Philosophy and Literature, 28(2), 227–242.

Kronke, D. (2005, September 22). Crime Shows Push Depravity Envelope. Daily News of Los Angeles, p. U6.

Lavery, D. (2006, January 26). The Allusions of Television. Flow.

Lavik, E. (2011). The Poetics and Rhetoric of The Wire's Intertextuality. Critical Studies in Television, 6(1), 52–71.

Levine, L. (1988). Highbrow/Lowbrow: The Emergence of Cultural Hierarchy in America. Harvard University Press.

Martin, B. (2013). Difficult Men: Behind the Scenes of a Creative Revolution: From The Sopranos and The Wire to Mad Men and Breaking Bad. [S.l.]: Penguin Books.

Mittell, J. (2006). Narrative Complexity in Contemporary American Television. The Velvet Light Trap, 58(1), 29–40.

Newman, M. Z., & Levine, E. (2012). Legitimating Television: Media Convergence and Cultural Status. Routledge.

Nussbaum, E. (2009, December 4). When TV Became Art: Good-Bye Boob Tube, Hello Brain Food. New York Magazine.

Owen, R. (2012, April 15). Tuned In: "NYC 22" -- Uninspired CBS offering has typical cop drama MO. Pittsburgh Post-Gazette, p. TV1.

Polan, D. (2009). The Sopranos. Duke University Press Books.

Polone, G. (2012, September 12). The Main Reason TV Is Now Better Than Movies. Vulture. Retrieved from http://www.vulture.com/2012/09/why-tv-is-better-than-movies-gavin-polone.html

Radway, J. A. (1999). A Feeling for Books: The Book-of-the-Month Club, Literary Taste, and Middle-Class Desire. The University of North Carolina Press.

Seiter, E. (1999). Television and New Media Audiences. Oxford University Press, USA.

Sepinwall, A. (2012). The Revolution Was Televised: The Cops, Crooks, Slingers and Slayers Who Changed TV Drama Forever. What's Alan Watching?

Thompson, R. (1997). Television's Second Golden Age. Syracuse University Press.

Williams, R. (1974). Television: Technology and Cultural Form. Routledge.

Wolcott, J. (2012, May 1). Prime Time's Graduation. Vanity Fair, (May), 148.

The Seed of an Idea and its Cognitive Field: Minding the Gap of Alternate Reality in Flash Forward and Fringe

Inbar Kaminsky

When Fredric Jameson conceived of the postmodern viewer, he defined the viewing task as "impossible", since this viewer is asked to "see all the screens at once, in their radical and random difference" (1990, 31). While television has yet to adopt the multi-screen model, the idea of parallel universes which coexist and at times even simultaneously represented is perhaps the small-screen attempt to point towards the unrepresentable. By employing postmodern science fiction, television shows such as FlashForward and Fringe explore "the finitude of the material and the placidity of the imagination" (Waugh, 1992, 11), essentially embracing the postmodern crisis of language and narrative construction.

Both FlashForward and Fringe introduce a narrative in which the entire world and its human population have become "lab rats", subjects in mass experiments conducted by powerful and yet obscure corporations. In FlashForward, it is the global blackout and a related experiment executed by Dr. Simon Campos and Dr. Lloyd Simcoe, two quantum physicists. In Fringe, it is the Pattern and a mysterious group of scientists who call themselves ZFT. Both shows deal with the unusual phenomenon through the point of view of law enforcement; FBI's Project Mosaic is formed in the first episode of FlashForward and the FBI's Fringe Division is formed in the first episode of Fringe.

The concept of parallel worlds is slightly different in each show but seems to create similar effects of estrangement and anxiety. In FlashForward, the flashforwards themselves become an alternate reality, coexisting in the minds of the individuals alongside the reality they are experiencing in the present. In Fringe, the team that comprises the Fringe Division becomes aware of the existence of a parallel universe, a slightly different version of their prime universe.

However, there is a fundamental thematic difference between the two shows; while FlashForward deals with the power of words and their ability to shape reality, Fringe exhibits a postmodern sensibility, assuming that everything has already been said (or written), nothing is original and words are insignificant in comparison to perception and the ability to manipulate and control it.

In this chapter I intend to explore the thematic differences between the first season of FlashForward and the first two seasons of Fringe, as well the narratological tools that enable each show to create and sustain the concept of parallel universes. In addition, I will discuss the posthuman question and the cultural importance of parallel worlds to post 9/11 American narratives.

Touched by the Word: Flash Forward, Season 1

The underlining fear of all the protagonists of FlashForward is intrinsically linked to their anxiety about narrating, in the narratological sense of unfolding the plot. The reoccurring question of "what did you see", aiming at 137 seconds long flashforward experienced by the entire world in the first episode, is often met with pauses, partial answers, omissions or even blunt lies. For instance, in the "137 Sekunden" episode, FBI agent Demetri Noh lies to his fiancée Zoey about having the same flashforward as she did, when in fact, he did not experience a flashforward during the global blackout, which has been commonly interpreted to mean he has no future.

The "137 Sekunden" episode also provides a powerful allusion that relates to narrator anxiety, when an old Nazi tells FBI Agent Mark Benford that the numeric value of the word Kabala in Hebrew amounts to 137 and therefore, it is somehow connected to the global blackout. This assumption is neither refuted nor corroborated throughout the season, but this kabalistic allusion can easily be linked to narrator anxiety; the Kabala emphasizes the powers of utterance and its ability to create a reality, the most famous example is the Jewish inclination to refer to God as "Hashem" (literally meaning "the name" in Hebrew) and the strict prohibition to pronounce the Hebrew name of God as written in the Old Testament, which has been translated to English as Jahova. In adherence to this principle, the protagonists of FlashForward are constantly faced with the dilemma of whether or not to articulate the narrative of their flashforwards, precisely because they fear its utterance will somehow facilitate its foothold in reality.

Another aspect of narrator anxiety is provided via the Borges allusion in the "The Garden of Forking Paths" episode—infinite possibilities. Borges' "The Garden of Forking Paths" presents a hypertext narrative structure, in which the reader is essentially asked to choose a path among various plotlines and in FlashForward, Dyson Frost, the mastermind behind the global blackout, refers to a map he has drawn of the possible futures as his "Garden of Forking Paths." If the flashforwards only represent a possible future rather than a preordained one, then clearly the characters are right in their concern about narrating the flashforwards, since phrasing the plot of the flashforwards (as opposed to the visual manifestation of the flashforwards) could constitute a choice, possibly grounding the narrative that the flashforwards present.

It is also important to note that throughout most of the show, many of the characters presume that the blackout was either an act of God or simply an anomaly of nature. In the absence of a scientific explanation, it is hardly surprising that the characters resort to (whether consciously or subconsciously) the folkloric belief in the power of words.

Perception is Key: Fringe, Season 1-2

Throughout the first two seasons of Fringe, it becomes apparent that the overarching theme of the series, which also enables the conception of parallel universes, is the supremacy of perception, or as Dr. Bishop puts it the "Bad Dreams" episode, "perception is the key to transformation". For instance, in "The Arrival" episode Dr. Walter Bishop tells his son, Peter, that ideas can be absorbed through osmoses, through proximity of one mind to the other, which is the reason that the man the FBI refers to as "the observer" could read Peter's thoughts.

In "Power Hungry" episode, Dr. Bishop suggests that part of deceased FBI Agent John Scott's consciousness has transformed into the consciousness of FBI Agent Olivia Dunham, Scott's lover and partner, when she tapped into his consciousness in the "Pilot" episode. This serves as a scientific explanation of the phenomenon that Olivia is experiencing; her hallucinations of Agent Scott are in fact mental projections of his consciousness, which her mind is trying to expel from its boundaries.

The process evolves to the extent in which Olivia cannot differentiate between her memories and Agent Scott's. In "Safe" Episode, Olivia mistakes some of Scott's memories to be her own; she is completely convinced that she has previously met the victim in a case she is investigating, but is eventually told be the victim's wife that the events she is referring to only occurred in the presence of herself and John Scott.

In "The Dreamscape" episode, the viewer is presented with the concept of "mind over matter", as Dr. Bishop suggests that the suspicious suicide case they are attempting to solve is in fact a case in which a man had been injected with powerful hallucinatory drugs. These drugs are so potent that they essentially made his mind believe he was being cut and his mind bridged that gap by inflicting the body with these cuts, made from "the inside out".

It is important to note that in "Pilot", "The Transformation" and "The Dreamscape" episodes, the sensory deprivation tank functions as the paranormal equivalent of a 'think tank', only instead of sharing ideas, people share consciousness and tap into someone else's memories, just as Olivia shares consciousness with the deceased Agent Scott, attempting to retrieve some of his memories. These incidents relate to some of Walter's existential comments about the powerful nature of consciousness, which can supersede it material boundaries (the body).

In "The Equation" episode, Dr. Bishop says that "curious minds often conjure up similar ideas", in response to the odd fact that two strangers—Dashiell Kim, a former mathematician who suffered a mental breakdown and hospitalized alongside Dr. Bishop and Ben Stockton, a boy who happens to be a musical prodigy—came up with the same dilemma, Dashiell encounters it as a mathematical formula and Ben encounters its equivalent in musical notes. This phenomenon suggests that ideas are essentially metaphorical entities which can be shared, tapped into by several sources. This reoccurring theme of shared consciousness and shared ideas can be construed as an inherently postmodern commentary about society's inability to generate an original thought, echoing Barthes' comment in Death of the Author—"The text is a tissue of quotations drawn from the innumerable centers of culture"(1977, 146).

In the "Momentum Deferred" episode, it is a bell sound that triggers Olivia's flush of memories from her visit to the parallel universe; even though she has spent several episodes attempting to uncover her memories by talking to colleagues, it is eventually a non-linguistic sound which bridges the gap and enables her to access these memories. Once again, the unrepresentable is looming in the background.

In "Grey Matters" episode, Walter's memory is "materializes", as removed slices of Walter's temporal lobe are accessed using technology; this incident is compatible with Walter's frequent references to the human mind as an "organic computer" and certainly attuned with Fringe's overarching theme of the supremacy of consciousness and its eternal energy. If "God is technology", as it is often suggested in Fringe, than consciousness is its archangel, its vehicle of transformation.

The Cyborg in Everyday Life, or the Post-human Question

The ability of consciousness to transcend its corporeal (and also temporal-spatial) boundaries is an important theme in both shows. While some scholars, such as Katherine N. Hayles, have suggested that the posthuman is still confined to its embodiment and cannot escape it (1999, 372), I maintain that the fundamental assumption—implicit in FlashForward and explicit in Fringe—that consciousness can exist outside of the body is inherently posthuman. The notion of disembodies consciousness presupposes that technology could potentially find an alternative to human corporeality (such as downloading consciousness into a computer) but it also presupposes that consciousness is not an exclusively human phenomenon and can be linked to other organisms.

In FlashForward, as it becomes apparent that the global blackout was a malevolent and premeditated act of a mad scientist, Dyson Frost, the question of technology as a form of posthuman existence is raised, albeit implicitly. If technology can create a flashforward that affects the consciousness of entire human race, then the potential to manipulate and even control consciousness to some extent may evolve into either a synthetic alternative to consciousness or a technological embodiment of human consciousness.

In Fringe, two separate issues arise in relation to posthumanity—non-human consciousness and the creation of human and machine hybrids. The issue of non-human consciousness is illustrated in "What Lies Below" episode, presenting the possibility of a virus endowed with consciousness, which manipulates the infected humans into complying with its survival instinct. Upon infection, Peter defies his own moral boundaries and acts on the virus' overwhelming urge to escape the contained area in order to spread the infection.

Whether it is Nina Sharp's robotic arm, courtesy of Massive Dynamic, or the cortexiphan experiments conducted on Olivia as child, rendering her as "not far removed from the life of a cybernetic organism"(Clarke, 2011, 6), it is clear that the issue of posthumanity is an important element of Fringe. Moreover, the literary and cultural allusion of Dr. Frankenstein as pertaining to Dr. Walter Bishop calls into mind the imagery of a man-made monster— not only made by a man but also made out of man.

The Frankenstein allusion is interwoven with the first two season of Fringe, evident in the "Pilot" episode, as Peter replies to Olivia's description of Walter's past research—"So you're telling me... what? My father was Dr. Frankenstein?". Each additional episode provides a glimpse into Dr. Bishop's past and his ethically questionable techniques, experimenting of children (among them young Olivia) being the prime example, until it becomes clear that prior to his mental breakdown and his seventeen years stay at a mental hospital, Dr. Bishop was the quintessential mad scientist, whose "most recognizable literary forebear is Mary Shelley's Victor Frankenstein" (Clarke, 2011, 17).

Walter's obsession to defy the corporeal boundaries and create a new man works; Olivia is the posthuman product of the cortexiphan experiments, endowed with an expended consciousness which eventually allows her to both perceive and travel to the parallel universe. But like Frankenstein's monster, Olivia's uniqueness is a type of monstrosity in the sense that she cannot fully control it and thus cannot contain her abilities, which are often triggered by an emotional response. In the "Jacksonville" episode, Olivia has to find a way to tap into her dormant abilities in order to perceive the glimmer which objects from the parallel universe project, but she is terrified when she uncovers that as a child she exhibited Pyrokinesis abilities and set an entire room on fire simply because she was scared of that very same glimmer.

THE SEED OF AN IDEA AND ITS COGNITIVE FIELD

Collision or Coalition: The Disharmony of Multiple Futures

While it is beneficial to discuss posthumanity as a phenomenon rooted in a shift of cultural perceptive, since, as Elana Gomel suggests, "the posthuman is plural rather than singular; a process rather than an entity"(2010, 113-114), it is precisely the question of free will, which distinguishes between humanity and posthumanity; the former being inevitably bound by its biology and historicity and the latter being liberated from these very restrictions (Gomel, 2010, 114). In this sense, the protagonists of both shows are very much human; they often grapple with their own cultural preconceptions of contingency versus prophecy.

The tension between free will and destiny intensifies in "The Gift" episode of FlashForward, when FBI agent Al Gough commits suicide in order to prevent the car accident in which he kills Celia, a young mother. The aftermath of the car crash is portrayed in a phone conversation Gough experiences in his flashforward, informing him of her death. From that point on, most of the characters adhere to the symbolic role of Gough's suicide in proving that the future is not predetermined.

This belief is somewhat subverted in the "Course Correction" episode, where Celia is accidently run over by MI6 Agent Fiona Banks, who attempted to save her from being killed. The man who intended to kill Celia has killed others who had managed to avoid the death foretold in their flashforwards. The eerie and tragic unfolding of events signals to the protagonists that the universe constantly strives to "course correct" itself in remaining true to the narrative displayed in the flashforwards.

In the "The Garden of Forking Paths" episode of FlashForward, the viewers are led to believe that Dmitri's preordained future is catching up with him— involuntarily killed by Mark on March 15, 2010—only to realize that Dmitri is saved, and the future can be changed (Ames, 2012, 115). In this very chapter, the allusions to Oedipus as manifested by the Oedipus and the Sphinx painting that Mark's daughter receives from Frost serve as "symbolic references point to the negative consequences that accompany attempts to alter time" (Ames, 2012, 120).

In "The Ability" episode of Fringe, former FBI Agent Loeb tells Olivia that "what was written will come to pass", which then leads her to think of ZFT as a text, subsequently finding a manuscript with the initials ZFT. The manuscript predicts that the advancements of technology, which have led to the discovery of the parallel universe, will eventually lead to the destruction of one of these realities. In another strange loop, Walter, who is fascinated by the manuscript, discovers that it had been typed in a typewriter with an elevated "y", matching his typewriter.

The idea of predestined future is also alluded to in "A New Day in the Old Town" episode of Fringe, in which Olivia wakes up in a hospital muttering a phrase in Greek to Peter, the very same sentence Peter's mother used to say to him before bed—"Be a better man than your father". Both the subtext of this sentence and the fact that it was uttered in Greek suggests an implicit allusion of Sophocles' Oedipus Rex, and the theme of man's inability to escape the preordained fate that has been assign to him by the gods.

However, the quantum tectonic event presented in Fringe's "Jacksonville" episode, in which two identical buildings from the two parallel worlds collide and collapse into one another can be seen as a metaphor. In the absence of a preordained future and in the face of man-made temporal-spatial manipulations, the multiple futures (represented here by the two buildings from two parallel realities) simply merge and demolish one another.

The Narratology of Parallel Universes: The Blog and the Typewriter

There is an important allegorical element to the concept of parallel universes, corresponding with the postmodern perception of multiple meanings, multiple selves and multiple realities. Through the looking glass of postmodernism, the singular perception of the universe is tantamount to the 'grand narratives' of modernism, which no longer provide us with a unifying sense of meaning:

> The purpose of the multiple versions is to illustrate an idea rather than to represent objectively happening courses of events: for instance, that the self cannot be reduced to a stable identity or that all versions of the world are equally valid, because reality is fundamentally unknowable. (Ryan, 2006, 669)

If the "I" cannot be neatly assembled into one coherent unit, than it only stands to reason that the same principle applies to all seemingly unified systems, namely, the projection of one sustainable reality. Both shows betrays such an existential reflection upon the nature of singular identity in a world (or worlds) spiraling out of control. In FlashForward, the global blackout is the glue that binds the collective consciousness of the human race, relaying both an individualized and shared glimpses into the future. In Fringe, as Clarke maintains, "The construct of the two universes also symbolizes the duality of the show's overarching themes: fate and free will, destruction and creation, mind and body, reason and faith" (2011, 116).

Both shows also present a form of embedded narratives that are uniquely related to the parallel universe or the entanglement between the two universes. In FlashForward, the mosaic blog is the narrative depicting the individual accounts of the flashforwards, which often overlap other individual accounts. However, the overlap is never complete, due to the simple fact that even when two people who share the same flashforward are recreating essentially the same story, they are still depicting it from a different point of view as they are two distinct focalizers, inevitably creating a different narrative.

Such is the case of Dr. Lloyd Simcoe and Dr. Olivia Benford; in "White to Play" episode, where the two meet for the first time but Lloyd does not recognize Olivia as the woman from his flashforward since he couldn't have seen her face from the point of view he had experienced, but Olivia instantly recognizes Lloyd. Notably, Olivia does not initially tell Lloyd or her husband Mark about the fact that she has met the man who is supposed to be her lover in the flashforward, marking yet another case of narrator anxiety.

In Fringe, shape-shifters and people belonging to the parallel universe can communicate with their handlers while staying in the primary universe by entering a secret room, where a typewriter and a mirror are placed on a table. In "Night of Desirable Objects" episode, it is the shape-shifter who assumed Agent Charlie Francis' body and in "Over There, Part 2" episode, it is the alternate Olivia. In both cases, the communication is conducted through writing on a typewriter. Upon reply, the mirror indicates that the other typewriter in the parallel universe is "writing itself" and the answer appears typed on the page, "reminiscent of the Alice stories, both with its low-tech, old-fashioned style and the use of a mirror" (Clarke, 2011, 115). And so, while FlashForward remains in the realm of contemporary technology and utilizes the 'global village' created by the internet to compile an international list of flashforwards, accessible to the masses via the mosaic blog, Fringe reverts back to the Victorian tropes of typewriter and mirror, betraying a sense of suspicion towards "new" technology.

A Bird's Eye View: Crows and Observers

In "137 Skunden episode" of FlashForward, Mark discovers that a similar blackout of a smaller scale had already occurred in Somalia in 1991, resulting in the death of thousands of crows. Considering the ominous mythological status of the crow, which is often associated with death, as well as the species' group intelligence, it is hardly surprising that crows come to symbolize the dangerous element of the flashforwards. In addition, the choice of crows also relates to the issue of observation; in essence, the death of the crows symbolizes the absence of a bird-eye view in FlashForward.

The possibility of a unified, global and all-inclusive revelation regarding the flashforwards and the global blackout is therefore abolished, as evident in the last episode of the series, "Future Shock", in which the day that the flashforwards had depicted comes to pass and fulfills only some of the flashforwards, and even those are partially fulfilled. No explanation is offered, the protagonists are just as lost as the audience. Even Mark, the designated hero of the show, is plagued by anxiety upon the discovery that a second global blackout is about to take place and he has no way of stopping it.

In Fringe, the observer effect, referring to the physics phenomenon in which the act of observation changes the behavior of the observed particles, becomes more than just a frequent scientific reference, but rather enacted through the characters of the Observers. The Observers have a human exterior (albeit having notably less pigments and no hair), but they are not human in the sense that they transcend the human temporal-spatial dimension. It is often stated throughout various episodes that the Observers simply show up at important historical events in order to observe them, but none the less, they often influence the course of events.

In quantum physics, the observer effect is applied "when under observation, electrons are being "forced" to behave like particles and not like waves. Thus the mere act of observation affects the experimental findings" (ScienceDaily, 1998). Adhering to this principle, the "Peter" episode of Fringe shows us the pivotal moment in 1985, in which the Observer known as September distracts Walternate (the Walter of the parallel world) who then misses the experimental result that confirms the success of his compound, which could save his son's life. Another observer of this interaction is the grieving Walter, who has just lost his Peter due to the same illness and is watching the missed opportunity from a window into the parallel world. In a twist of double observation, September changes Walternate's behavior through observation but also changes Walter's behavior due to his own observation of this observer effect.

However, these extra-diegetic watchers can also stand for "the technology that is "watching over us" all the time, the various programs that track our locations, our internet behavior, and our shopping habits" (Clarke, 2011, 153), or even the audience—"Fans, like the Observers, transcend time and space in relation to the series, seeing everything, just like the Observers, and remembering even when the main characters may have forgotten" (Clarke, 2011, 171).

The various narratological possibilities embodied in the Observers only serve to emphasize the unpredictable nature of the future, its fluidity and flexibility. Just as the death of the crows in FlashForward symbolizes the absence of observation, the Observers in Fringe symbolize the endless possibilities of observation. In the end, this dichotomy is doomed to fail, as neither the absence of observation nor endless observations enable anyone (protagonist and viewer alike) to predict the future.

The Visual Effect of a "Do-Over": Post 9/11 Television

Jameson remarks that "Science fiction is generally understood as the attempt to imagine unimaginable futures. But its deepest subject may in fact be our own historical present" (2007, 345). It has been suggested that shows such as FlashForward and Fringe have a therapeutic quality, enabling post- 9/11 television viewers to rework their anxieties into fictional narratives, in which individuals do make a difference (Ames, 2012, 114).

Moreover, since both FlashForward and Fringe fits into "the loose category of 'time travel narratives' "(Ames, 2012, 114), it is only fitting to discuss them in relation to the existential question of 'What if', which post-9/11 American culture associates with the terror attack on the World Trade Center—"One thematic motif that participates in such narrative disruption is the "do-over". The last several decades have found this theme increasing in popularity in the American culture realm and it has amplified further since the September 11 attacks" (Ames, 2012, 110).

Post 9/11 television certainly treats the September 11 attacks as a form of collective cultural trauma. Identifying FlashForward as pertaining to the "subgenre of 'trauma sci-fi'"(Mousoutzanis, 2012, 97), enables us to understand the thematic significance of its time-distortion, in which trauma influence the temporal structure, creating a non-liner timeline (Mousoutzanis, 2012, 101). In Fringe, it seems that the post-9/11 effect is one of paranoia and distrust towards authority figures, as it "exposes a society's collective paranoia about an invisible web of clandestine puppet masters" (Clarke, 2011, 1). Notably, one of the first visual manifestations of Fringe's parallel world is the image of the World Trade Center, grandiose and intact:

> The alternate Earth is still our Earth, but different in ways our own world could have been different. Our first clear look at the other world: the twin towers of the World Trade Center standing tall and straight in the sunlight. Visually and emotionally stunning. (Brotherton, 2011, 89)

The compulsion to reenact 9/11 is intrinsically linked to the cultural inability to represent absence; both FlashForward and Fringe deal with the possibility of the annihilation of the human race, it is always looming in the background but cannot be fully articulated precisely due to the incapability of language (both written and spoken) to capture the death of the referent and the destruction of the human archival structure:

> But the burden of every death can be assumed symbolically by a culture and a social memory... Culture and memory limit the "reality" of individual death to this extent, they soften or deaden it in the realm of the "symbolic." The only referent that is absolutely real is thus of the scope or dimension of an absolute nuclear catastrophe that would irreversibly destroy the entire archive and all symbolic capacity, would destroy the "movement of sur-vival" (Deridda, 1984, 28)

The power of science fiction narratives to reflect existential anxieties about the nature of the future or alternate realities is inherently linked to technological capabilities. The provincial time machine has been replaced with particle accelerators, quantum entanglement objects and teleportation devices. The sophisticated and ominous technology displayed in both FlashForward and Fringe enables these shows to discuss the limitations of the human endeavor to become posthuman by transcending their temporal-spatial restrictions and cultural-historical confinements.

References

Ames, M. (2012). The Fear of the Future and the Pain of the Past: The Quest to Cheat Time in Heroes, FlashForward and Fringe. Time in Television Narrative: Exploring Temporality in Twenty-First-Century Programming. Ed. Melissa Ames. Mississippi: Univ. Press of Mississippi, 110- 124.

Barthes, R. (1977). "The Death of the Author". Image – Music– Text. Trans. By Stephen Heath. Noonday: 1988, 142-148.

Brotherton, M.Déjà (2011). New: Not Quite the Parallel Universe Story We've Seen Before on TV. Fringe Science: Parallel Universes, White Tulips, and Mad Scientists. Ed. Kevin R. Grazier. Dallas: BenBella Books.

Derrida, J. (1984). No Apocalypse, Not Now (Full Speed Ahead, Seven Missiles, Seven Missives). Trans. Catherine Porter and Philip Lewis. Diacritics 14(2) Nuclear Criticism ,20-31.

FlashForward. (2009-2010). Create. Brannon Braga and David S. Goyer. Perfs. Joseph Fiennes, John Cho, Jack Davenport. ABC.

Fringe. (2008-2010). Create. J. J. Abrams, Alex Kurtzman, and Roberto Orci. Perfs. Anna Torv, Joshua Jackson, John Noble. Fox.

Gomel, E. (2010). Postmodern Science Fiction and Temporal Imagination. NY: Continuum.

Hayles, K. N. (1999). How We Became Posthuman: Virtual Bodies in Cybernetics, Literature, and Informatics. Chicago: Chicago UP.

Jameson, F. (2007). Archaeologies of the Future: The Desire Called Utopia and Other Science Fictions. London: Verso.

Jameson, F. (1990). Postmodernism, or, The Cultural Logic of Late Capitalism. Duke UP.

Mousoutzanis, A. (2012). Temporality and Trauma in American Sci-Fi Television. Time in Television Narrative: Exploring Temporality in Twenty-First-Century Programming. Ed. Melissa Ames. Mississippi: Univ. Press of Mississippi, 97- 109.

Ryan, M.L. (2006). From Parallel Universes to Possible Worlds: Ontological Pluralism in Physics, Narratology, and Narrative. Poetics Today 27(4), 633-674.

Stuart, Clarke S. (2011) Into the Looking Glass: Exploring the Worlds of Fringe. Toronto: ECW Press.

Waugh, P. (1992). Practicing Postmodernism: Reading Modernism. London: Edward Arnold.

Weizmann Institute of Science. (27 Feb. 1998). Quantum Theory Demonstrated: Observation Affects Reality. ScienceDaily. Web. 28 Oct. 2012. <http://www.sciencedaily.com/releases/1998/02/980227055013.htm>

Breaking Narrative:
Narrative Complexity in Contemporary Television

Oliver Kroener

With regard to cinematic storytelling, narrative complexity has generated scholarly interest for decades, but when it comes to television studies, this topic seems to have been somewhat neglected—at least up until recently. Contemporary scholars and critics seem prepared to label almost any film or television show a "complex narrative," but they have yet to produce a clear description of exactly what this entails.
Based on Thomas Elsaesser's theory of the mind-game film (2009) and Edward Branigan's concept of the disparities of knowledge (1992), I contend that contemporary television dramas such as *Lost* (ABC, 2004-2010), *The Wire* (HBO, 2002-2008), *Game of Thrones* (HBO, 2011-), *Mad Men* (AMC, 2007-), *Justified* (2010-), and *Breaking Bad* (AMC, 2008-2013) employ specific narrative devices (i.e. complex characters, multiple plotlines per episode, flash-forwards, flashbacks, time jumps, and cold opens) that identify them as puzzle narratives. Understanding contemporary television along such lines not only helps us to comprehend how we process narrative information on a cognitive level, but it also helps us to determine what narrative complexity actually means—a topic that has been frequently discussed among TV scholars, probably most prominently by Jason Mittell (2013) in his forthcoming work *Complex TV*.
David Bordwell (2008) has emphasized that every narrative depends on uncertainties and the interplay among characters' versus spectators' knowledge as these obstructive levels of knowledge shape the curiosity, suspense, and surprise the spectator feels when engaging with the story while Edward Branigan (1992) has stated that the disparities of knowledge between the characters and the spectators must be regarded as the foundation for any form of narration. He has distinguished between two fundamental concepts that are required to analyze narration: what is presented and how. While asking what questions reduces a narrative to an object or end result of some mechanism, the more important how questions are con-

cerned with our comprehension of the story and its characters. Consequently, we can differentiate between procedural knowledge (related to how a narrative works) and declarative knowledge (related to what is actually shown on screen). Both of these knowledge systems are simultaneously at work whenever we watch a narrative unfold.

According to Branigan (1992), the disparities of knowledge are fundamental to any form of narration as "narration comes into being when knowledge is unevenly distributed—when there is a disturbance or disruption in the field of knowledge" (p. 66); therefore in a hypothetical universe in which all knowledge is evenly distributed and every observer is all-knowing, narration is not possible. In other words, in order for there to be narration, someone needs to know more than someone else. This asymmetrical relationship between a subject and an object can function on multiple levels as the subject can either be the spectator, the narrator, the author, a character in the story, or someone else entirely. While we can imagine several different scenarios for an asymmetrical distribution of knowledge within a narrative—for example, the spectator could know more than a character in the story, or a character could know more than the spectator—it seems to be impossible for us to imagine a situation in which the spectator knows more than the author.

In all forms of visual storytelling, there are a variety of ways in which a scene can be depicted, all of which result in a different viewing experience for the spectator. For example, according to Branigan (1992), non-character knowledge such as "a musical chord coupled with the expression on a character's face that 'tells' us all we need to know; a 'tell-tale' glance; or, a narrator's whispered commentary on what B must be saying on the telephone to A" (p. 71), factors into how we perceive an event within a story. Because we are sensitive to the ways in which knowledge is conveyed to us, and can be easily overwhelmed by the amount of narrative information we receive, we create hierarchies of knowledge for ourselves. These hierarchies of knowledge help us to make sense of the cluster of information with which we are bombarded whenever we witness an unfolding narrative. One important function of the hierarchies of knowledge is that the higher levels of the narrative are concealed from the spectator. That is to say, certain aspects of the narrative are supposed to be hidden from the viewer in order to delay the end of the story. The concealment of these aspects is possible because the viewer only has access to the diegesis and thus must rely on "'less knowledgeable' agencies (e.g. characters) at appropriate moments" (Branigan, 1992, p. 74), which means that we are supposed to be misled by these less-knowledgeable agencies. Based on the disparities of knowledge, Branigan has defined narration as follows:

> Narration is the overall regulation and distribution of knowledge which determines how and when the spectator acquires knowledge, that is, how the spectator is able to know what he or she comes to know in a narrative. A typical description of the spectator's 'position' of knowledge includes the invention of (sometimes tacit) speakers, presenters, listeners, and watchers who are in a (spatial and temporal) position to know, and to make use of one or more disparities of knowledge. Such 'persons' are convenient fictions which serve to mark how the field of knowledge is being divided at a particular time. (p. 76)

How narrative information is conveyed to the viewer is also an underlying factor in other definitions of narration, but Branigan (1992) has identified it as the single most important aspect, and has placed it in relation to how we emotionally relate to what we see on-screen. Elsaesser's theory of the mind-game film is interrelated with Branigan's definition of narration since withholding knowledge from the viewer to mislead or disorient the audience is a key element of the puzzle narrative. Withholding narrative information enables mind-game films to trick and surprise the audience through unforeseen plot developments, or plot twists at the end of the narrative. When comparing mind-game films to traditional murder mysteries, one key difference is that mind-game films often feature narrative clues that do not add up—although the overarching storyline is still coherent. While early examples of suspense cinema such as the works of Fritz Lang, Alfred Hitchcock, Luis Buñuel, and Alain Resnais can be regarded as the origins of the mind-game film, these narratives usually mislead or disorient the viewer only for the film's duration. In other words, once the film ends, all plotlines have been resolved. For the mind-game film, such is not always the case. Mind-game films purposely leave plotlines unresolved and include clues or symbols in the narrative that often cannot be easily deciphered by the viewer. For example, in a mind-game film, a mysterious letter or a cryptic numeric code could be the key to resolving a plotline or unlocking the higher meaning of the narrative.

According to Elsaesser (2009), recent cinematic storytelling has become more "intricate, complex and unsettling," a trend that cannot only be found in European auteur or art films but also in "mainstream cinema, event-movies/blockbusters, indie films, [and] not forgetting (HBO-financed) television" (p. 19). Mind-game films are discussed among narratologists because, through their use of "single or multiple diegesis, unreliable narration, and narratives, embedded or 'nested' (story-within-story/film-within-film) narratives, and frame-tales that reverse what is inside the frame" (p. 19), they call attention to how the narrative is told. This means we have to distinguish between mind-game film plot mechanics such as, for example, a protagonist who is mistaken about the difference between reality and his or her imagination, and narrative devices that directly affect the arrangement of information within the story. In addition, by applying a variety of features that are supposed to confuse or mislead the viewer, mind-game films alter the relationship between spectator and text. As Elsaesser (2009) has stated:

> Mind-game films at the narrative level, offer—with their plot twists and narrational double-takes—a range of strategies that could be summarized by saying that they suspend the common contract between the film and its viewers, which is that films do not 'lie' to the spectator, but are truthful and self-consistent within the premises of their diegetic worlds, that permit, of course, 'virtual' worlds, impossible situations and improbable events. (p. 19-20)

Elsaesser (2009) has criticized other theorists for regarding mind-game films as a phenomenon that can be regulated by extending already existing narrative theories and thereby treating them like business as usual. Approaching mind-game films from this point of view is trying to solve the puzzle without acknowledging that the author intended the spectator to experience the story in a different way. Besides, attempting to categorize mind-game films into an already existing scheme disregards that our conception of narrative is constantly evolving. In addition, Elsaesser has found that, in contemporary cinema, the contract between spectator and film is not solely based on "ocular verification, identification, voyeuristic perspectivism, and 'spectatorship' as such" (p. 37), but also on the rules that make spectatorship possible in the first place. In calling attention to the rules of the game, these narratives test and challenge the audience and provide them with a different viewing experience. Feature films such as *Run Lola Run* (1998), *Memento* (2000), and *Eternal Sunshine of the Spotless Mind* (2004) have already been discussed with regard to Elsaesser's theory, but the discussion has to be extended to also include contemporary television shows. Although there are several television shows that qualify as puzzle narratives, or at least feature certain aspects of the mind-game film, the AMC show *Breaking Bad* stands out since it employs nearly all trademarks of the mind-game film.

Breaking Bad revolves around Walter White (Bryan Cranston), a fifty-year-old high school chemistry teacher who lives with his wife Skyler (Anna Gunn) and their teenage son Walter Jr. (RJ Mitte) in Albuquerque, New Mexico. He is diagnosed with inoperable lung cancer and decides to team up with Jesse Pinkman (Aaron Paul), a former student of his, to cook methamphetamine (also known as crystal meth) in order to secure a financial future for his family before he dies. Although this basic premise is slightly reconfigured over the course of the show—which currently is in its fifth and final season—this is the initial setup of the series.

At the beginning of the first episode, the teaser fades into establishing shots of a desert: we see cactuses, red rocks, and a shadow crossing over a hill. For the first few seconds there is no sound except for the wind and the birds. Finally, during a long shot of the clear blue sky, the soundtrack sets in as a pair of khaki-coloured pants float in slow-motion into the frame. The camera pans down and follows them on their way to the ground, where they are quickly run over by an old Winnebago RV, and with that, the image switches back to normal speed.

The soundtrack transforms from sparse, ambient sounds into a pulsating rhythm, and all of a sudden we find ourselves in the middle of a chase sequence. The driver of the RV is wearing nothing except for a gas mask and underwear. He frantically glances at the unconscious young man sitting to his right, who is also wearing a gas mask and has bruises on his face. As the driver looks over his shoulder, we see that two bodies are rolling around on the camper floor in what appears to be a mixture of brown liquid and blood. Apart from the bodies, blood-drenched dollar bills and pieces of some sort of technical equipment are also scattered over the camper's floor. The sequence crosscuts between interior shots of the driver and exterior shots of the camper racing down a dusty desert road. As the scene goes on, the cutting becomes progressively rapid, adding to the viewer's sense of confusion. A brief POV shot that puts us in the driver's position suggests that he is barely able to see anything under his gas mask. Consequently, the driver loses control over the vehicle and crashes into a bush next to the main road.

The music stops and for a moment there is complete silence. We are left with the image of the crashed camper, covered in a cloud of dust. The door opens and brown liquid rushes out of it, followed by the driver. He jumps out of the RV, tears off his gas mask, and exchanges it for his glasses. Now we get our first full look at the mysterious driver, who reveals himself to be a short-haired, middle-aged man with a moustache. The driver, still only wearing glasses, underwear, as well as shoes and socks, nervously stumbles around in front of the camper. He throws away his gas mask, mumbles something indistinguishable, and grabs his head in despair. When he recognizes the sound of a siren in the near distance, he becomes even more nervous. A close-up of his face signals that he is desperately searching for a way out of his situation. He puts on his shirt, which, strangely enough, was hung up on a coat hanger attached to the RV's side mirror, and goes back into the camper. The man collects his wallet and a camcorder, and tucks a handgun into the back of his underwear before rushing back outside. He coughs and wretches afterwards, which tells us that he was wearing the gas mask for a reason. Nervously he tries to turn on the camcorder while the image switches from close-ups of him fumbling around with the device to long-shots that emphasize just how bizarre his situation is: in the middle of the desert, a man is standing in his underwear in front of a crashed RV, attempting to switch on a camcorder while frantically saying to himself, "Come on, come on, come on" ("Pilot"). Eventually, the driver succeeds and the image cuts to footage that was supposedly captured by his camcorder. He starts talking into the camera:

> My name is Walter Hartwell White. I live at 308 Negra Arroyo Lane, Albuquerque, New Mexico, 87104. To all law enforcement entities, this is not an admission of guilt. I am speaking to my family now...Skyler. You are the love of my life. I hope you know that. Walter Jr. You're my big man. There are—there are going to be some things—Things that you'll come to learn about me in the next few days. I just want you to know that no matter how it may look, I only had you in my heart. [He turns around, looking for the police.] Goodbye. ("Pilot")

With that, Walter White puts the camera down and places his wallet, open so it shows his ID, next to the camcorder in the dust. Breathing heavily, he grabs his gun, leaves the crash site, and slowly walks towards the main road. The music sets in as the approaching sirens grow louder and louder. Walt stands in the middle of the desert road, his back turned to the viewer, his shirt tucked into his underwear—ready to fight whatever may come his way. With a determined look on his face, he points his gun towards the sound of the approaching sirens and the image fades to black.

This opening teaser is how television audiences were introduced to the show when it first premiered on AMC in January 2008. It functions as an example of narrative complexity in contemporary television as it confronts the audience with a narrative puzzle right from the start. The viewer is thrown into the story without really being able to grasp what is happening. There has been no setup for the initial chase sequence and we have no idea who the driver of the RV is. We also do not know why the driver is only wearing his underwear and is on the run. As a result, the viewer is confused, which is deliberate and becomes a narrative trademark of *Breaking Bad*.

Technically the opening is a flash-forward that triggers the audience's curiosity by raising a number of questions without answering them. In comparison to the show's other cold opens, the pilot's teaser is an extreme example because, at this point of the narrative, we have not been introduced to anything. The setting, the style, and most importantly the main character, are all completely new to us. This is not necessarily the case with *Breaking Bad's* subsequent cold opens, in which often at least one factor—for example, a character or a location—is known to us, and we are only left in the dark as to what exactly is going on at that exact moment.

The pilot's teaser triggers a sense of surprise in the viewer because throughout the entire opening we know less than Walt and only receive fragmented narrative information. We are forced to bring these fragments into a coherent form until later on in the episode, as the events leading up to the RV scene unfold. In that way, the whole opening becomes a narrative puzzle as we try to figure out where the scene takes place, who the driver is, why he is dressed in such a manner, what he did to the men in the back of the RV, and how he got himself in such a situation in the first place. We are bombarded with so much fragmented narrative information that some questions (like, for example, what has happened to the men in the back of the RV) become less important than others (like, for example, who is the guy only wearing underwear and a gas mask). These unanswered questions remain with us throughout the narrative—they linger in our subconscious mind, and with that influence our viewing experience.

Although the teaser ultimately answers who the driver is, the expository confession that Walter White gives still does not provide us with a lot of information. We get to know the protagonist's name, he tells us where he lives, he lets us know that he cares about his family, and he states that he does not admit to being guilty of whatever crime he has committed. At the end of the teaser, we have recognized Walter White as the main protagonist and it has been implied that many narrative events will be focalized through him. While nearly all of the questions posed in the pilot's teaser are resolved within the first episode, in later seasons *Breaking Bad* becomes more experimental by posing narrative questions without providing immediate answers.

For example, the opening teaser of "Seven-Thirty Seven," the first episode of *Breaking Bad's* second season, confronts the audience with a narrative puzzle that functions slightly differently. Similar to other teasers, the cryptic black-and-white opening provides us with only fragmented narrative information. We are given glimpses of a swimming pool and a half-burned pink teddy bear that is missing an eye—yet we do not know how these images will fit into the overall narrative. What sets the teaser of "Seven-Thirty Seven" apart from the pilot's teaser is that it is part of a season-long narrative puzzle. Throughout the second season, several episodes start with opening teasers that allude to the same black-and-white scene featuring the swimming pool and the mysterious pink teddy bear, but each time the scene is rendered in a slightly different way. In addition, as the season progresses, the show begins to add tiny bits of information to these teasers. In "ABQ," the last episode of the second season, the show adds a lot of narrative information to the already known puzzle pieces. For example, later teasers reveal a blurry figure hunching over the pool and two bodies lying in a driveway.

The recurring black-and-white teasers also act as reminders for the audience. They let us know that, although when we see them for the first time they seem disconnected from the main plot, they will at some point factor into *Breaking Bad's* main storyline. In that way, they encourage us to solve the narrative puzzle surrounding them. We are supposed to ask ourselves whose swimming pool we are looking at and guess how the pink teddy bear might be connected to Walt and his family. For example, since at this point of the story Walt's wife Skyler is pregnant, we might assume that the half-burned teddy bear belongs to the yet unborn child, which then automatically would lead us to believe that something horrible is about to happen to the baby. Finally, the season-long narrative puzzle that stems for these black-and- white teasers is resolved in "ABQ."

The series introduces Donald (John De Lancie), the father of Jesse's girlfriend Jane (Krysten Ritter), at the midpoint of season two, but up until the final episode, we know little about him aside from the fact that he is concerned about his daughter because she has a history of drug abuse. In "Phoenix," the penultimate episode of season two, there is a scene in which Donald and Walt coincidentally meet in a bar and have a brief conversation. Shortly after, Walt goes over to Jesse's apartment to collect a bag of money. While Walt is searching for the money, he sees that Jane, after having done heroin, is in danger of choking on her own vomit in her sleep. The expression on Walt's face suggests that for a moment he considers helping her, but then he suddenly changes his mind because he realizes that she has too much influence on his partner Jesse and therefore, it would be wise for him to let her die. Still, even after Jane's death, it is unclear how Donald will exactly fit into the overall storyline.

At the beginning of "ABQ," Donald arrives at Jane's apartment and learns that his daughter has died in her sleep. After watching a scene in which Donald selects a dress for Jane's funeral, we learn that he works as an air traffic controller to which it says in the episode's script: "Now we finally know what Donald does for a living" ("The Writer's Room"). This underlines that the writers intended the scene as a reveal. When the still grief-stricken Donald returns to work, he is unable to concentrate and causes the collision of two airplanes in midair. The episode ends with plane parts and the aforementioned pink teddy bear falling from the sky and landing in the White family's swimming pool. With that, not only has Donald's purpose for the plot been revealed, but, much more importantly, the season-long narrative puzzle has been resolved.

Puzzle narratives often introduce plotlines or narrative clues without resolving them immediately. This alters the way in which we process the narrative on a cognitive level as it requires us to memorize plotlines and narrative clues while we wait for them to come back into play. In "ABQ," the viewer starts putting the clues together when it is revealed that Jane's father Donald works as an air traffic controller. This, in combination with the mysterious teasers and the episode's title, which refers to the airport code of Albuquerque, already hints at the combustive season finale. Apart from these obvious hints, *Breaking Bad* also integrates more subtle clues into the narrative. These clues often seem to follow a specific pattern and with that add more layers to the narrative puzzle. For example, throughout season two, we can find scenes in which pink objects, such as Walt's pink sweater, or the pink blanket that his infant daughter sleeps in, are highlighted. By interspersing such objects among the narrative, the showrunners encourage viewers to find a connection between these clues and the pink teddy bear from the teasers. The scene in which Donald picks out a dress for Jane's funeral is particularly striking since the pillows on his daughter's bed are pink as well and the mural on her wall depicts a teddy bear, implying that her death is somehow connected to the mysterious opening teasers. In addition, Walt's pink sweater and the baby's pink blanket led many viewers to believe that the season would end with Walt being responsible for the death of his newborn child. However, this did not turn out to be the case, which only highlights the puzzle aspects of the show as scattering narrative clues within the story that ultimately do not lead to the resolution of a particular mystery—another trademark of the mind-game film.

Elsaesser (2009) has suggested that instead of regarding narratives as pre-structured schemes, we should consider regarding them as databases that provide us with the tools to form our own narratives, similar to web-browsing or playing videogames. From this point of view, mind-game films or, more generally speaking, complex narratives, become a product of our time because to be modern is to "remain flexible, adaptive, and interactive, and above all, to know 'the rules of the game'" (Elsaesser, 2009, p. 34). The example Elsaesser has discussed in his theory is watching an episode of *Dallas* (1978-1991) versus watching an episode of *The Sopranos* (1999-2007). Whereas *Dallas* is rather linear and repetitive, and thus easy to understand, watching *The Sopranos* can at times become a challenge for our cognitive skills because we have to keep track of a wide array of characters and multiple plotlines per episode. In the case of *Breaking Bad* this is even more applicable as, while watching the show, viewers not only have to keep track of a wide array of characters and multiple plotlines per episode, but are repeatedly confronted with narrative puzzles that often stem from the show's use of flash-forwards, flashbacks, and opening teasers. The finale of *Breaking Bad's* second season exemplifies how contemporary television narratives regulate the flow of narrative information to create a puzzle for the viewer that is anchored in the show's structure, and makes use of the mismatches between the viewer's knowledge and a character's knowledge. *Breaking Bad* proves that while mind-game or puzzle narratives have frequently been discussed with regard to feature films, this phenomenon deserves more attention when it comes to contemporary television as the serial format allows show-runners to create narrative puzzles that are based on the way in which knowledge is distributed, and can evolve over the course of several seasons, which influences how we engage with the narrative on a cognitive level.

References

Bordwell, David. (2008). Poetics of Cinema. New York, NY: Routledge.

Branigan, Edward. (1992). Narrative Comprehension and Film. New York, NY: Routledge.

Elsaesser, Thomas. (2009). The Mind-Game Film. In Warren Buckland (Ed.), Puzzle Films—Complex Storytelling in Contemporary Cinema. (pp. 13-42). Malden, MA: Wiley-Blackwell.

Gilligan, Vince. (Writer & Director). (2008). Pilot [Television series episode]. In V. Gilligan (Producer), Breaking Bad. Culver City, CA: Sony Pictures Television.

Gilligan, Vince. (Producer). (2010). Breaking Bad—The Complete Second Season [Television Series]. Culver City, Ca: Sony Pictures Television.

Gilligan, Vince. (Producer). (2010). The Writer's Lab—An Interactive Guide to the Elements of an Episode [Television series making of]. In V. Gilligan (Producer), Breaking Bad—The Complete Second Season. Culver City, CA: Sony Pictures Television.

Gilligan, Vince. (Writer), & Bernstein, Adam. (Director). (2009). ABQ [Television series episode]. In V. Gilligan (Producer), Breaking Bad. Culver City, Ca: Sony Pictures Television.

Gilligan, Vince. , Roberts, J. (Writers), & Cranston, Bryan. (Director). (2009). Seven Thirty-Seven [Television series episode]. In V. Gilligan (Producer), Breaking Bad. Culver City, CA: Sony Pictures Television.

Mittell, Jason. (2013). Complex TV: The Poetics of Contemporary Television Storytelling. Pre-publication edition: MediaCommons Press.

The Walking Dead and the Truly Monstrous... on Television

Atene Mendelyte

The American television drama series *The Walking Dead* (2010–present) is a much waited breeze of fresh air in the televisual exploration of encountering the monstrous. While cinematic fascination with zombies may be witnessed in a huge number of horror movies, unlike vampires, their doubles in many respects, until lately zombies did not figure as a main topic or/and characters in television series. The zombies that did appear on television were "toned down" (even to a mere comic effect[1]) so as not to make a real threat to televisual perception and character construction. There is a clear reason for that which I shall now explore and in the process of which I hope to explain why the appearance of such a series as *The Walking Dead* is so fascinatingly disturbing and unprecedented.

The main underlying reason is that the format of television series itself is mostly built on a strong linear narrative structure and the continuous development of characters. The monstrous (the truly monstrous) shatters these two pillars of storytelling to pieces: any action is suspended from a quick incorporation into the action chain because it is not clear what sort of an action is appropriate or effective; the character as well as the subjectivity usually attached to characterisation are put into question or simply annulled. In other words, the monstrous as a subject for television series requires a new form, a new "tonality" in storytelling. Here, I mean to render the truly monstrous as a very particular concept since I do not define the monstrous in a Hölderlinian sense as the union of the human and the divine[2] or in a more prosaic sense of that which evokes horror. I intend the monstrous to mean quite the opposite—the annulment of the human.

---

[1] For example, the humorously figured zombie girl in the British television series *Being Human*. (2008–present)
[2] Friedrich Hölderlin describes "the monstrous" thusly: "The presentation of the tragic rests pre-eminently upon this, that the monstrous—how the god and man pair themselves, and the power of nature and what is innermost in man become one in wrath—grasps itself through the limitless becoming one through the limitless division that purifies." (Hölderlin, 1992, p. 315)

The Non-monstrosity of Vampires

Why then vampires so largely populate the television screen if the monstrous is so difficult to narrate and televisualize? The answer is rather simple: the vampire is not the manifestation of the (truly) monstrous, despite having been and still being regarded as such[3]. Vampires function differently from zombies and their functioning is not unlike that of human characters. While older, filmic vampires may appear more "monstrous" figuratively (remember Friedrich Murnau's *Nosferatu* (1922)), I would argue, it is not only that today's culture and imagination tended to "tame" the beasts and to anthropomorphise the monstrous but that vampires were in principle culturally accomodatable from the very beginning, from their very inception.

The key symptom of this accommodatability is the fact that vampires possess logos, reason, language and all what it entails. They may be reasoned with, albeit they may rip one's neck open in a split of a second. But as they are intelligent creatures, nothing stops them from dwelling in the world of the human. Nothing stops them from falling in love with humans precisely because of their humanity. Nothing stops them from trying to "reform" like human drug addicts do. It becomes quite clear that vampirism is often a metaphoric depiction of the human as a subject and slave to his/her drives[4]. In certain regards, vampires are much like superheroes: they are much more resilient and are not subjects to disease or decay.

In these respects, vampires are the extensions of the human and do not stand for complete alterity. Or, in psychoanalytic terms, they are the reversed obscene subjects[5] that challenge the law and in this challenging only

---

[3] To point out but one of many examples, political theorist Mark Neocleous writes: "On the other hand, there is the idea that this duty must involve challenging the power of the undead. This second dimension is based on the understanding that some entities retain the powers of the living, or develop even greater powers, after death. In this case it is the vampire, but the point is true of the monstrous in general, for one of the fundamental characteristics of monsters is said to be that they are somehow undead." (Neocleous, 2005, p. 1) My aim is precisely to counter all such notions of "the monstrous in general" and explain how different forms of it emerge within televisual or filmic experiences.

[4] This metaphorical dimension is very explicitly explored in Abel Ferrara's film *The Addiction* (1995).

[5] The obscene subject is a Žižekian variation on Lacanian psychoanalysis: "[B]ehind the statement of the moral law that imposes on us the renunciation of enjoyment, there is always hidden an obscene subject of enunciation, amassing the enjoyment it steals. The superego is, so to speak, an agency of the law exempted from its authority: it does itself what it prohibits us from doing. [...] To get an idea of what a social

confirm it, confirm that the foundational morality and the most common forms of human subjectivity are what being human means, which vampires oppose but secretly crave for. The vampiric nostalgia for the human is also the nostalgia for the human law (in the sense of logos, the Symbolic). Nothing monstrous in that. The truly monstrous begins, perhaps, with Marquis de Sade—that fascinated Jacques Lacan so intensely—and his type of hero whose aim is to kill someone as a signifier and a subject. Even in such cases where the town, the state or the world in general is overrun by vampires like in Steve Niles' *30 Days of Night* (2002) or Michael and Peter Spierig's *Daybreakers* (2009), the vampires establish their own equivalents of human power relationships. To put it more emphatically, the chaotic state of nature does not ensue; one state is replaced by another subverse (fascist) state, i.e. one signifier is replaced by another in which binary dialectics prevail.

Thus, as a subject for television series vampirism does not require a change in format: narrative and character development may easily be adapted to this new type of a superhero or a supervillain. Hence, the classical and reiterating stories of *Buffy: the Vampire Slayer* (1997–2003), *True Blood* (2008–present), *The Vampire Diaries* (2009–present) or even the children's television series *Young Dracula* (2006–2008, 2011–present). Just like their human counterparts, vampires become friends and foes, lovers and enemies, human champions and human killers. Also, human temporality is a prison from which vampires are seemingly free; yet they remain its prisoners. Subjects to humanity's historical change (motivated by the fact that their survival depends on their adaptive capabilities) they do not create an alternative temporality.

To make an even more drastic but no less valid association, vampire series and vampire protagonists as a unified phenomenon is related to the popularity of and fascination with psychopathic and criminal characters. Such long spinning and hugely popular series as *Oz* (1997–2003), *The Sopranos* (1999–2007), *Dexter* (2006–present), *and Boardwalk Empire* (2010–present) are but a few such examples. To a less literal degree many of the protagonists from the aforementioned series also depend on their killing to

---

agency functioning like the superego would be like, one has only to recall bureaucratic machinery with which the subject is confronted in Kafka's great novels [...]; this immense apparatus is penetrated with obscene enjoyment." (Žižek, 1995, pp. 159–160)

survive and forego much of the same psychological drama and moral dilemmas. Vampire, psychopath, and criminal series are all parts of one cultural phenomenon: the fascination with the fringes, the possible outskirts of society that may test the social structure from without or within. However, as I have mentioned before, these characters serve to re-establish the norm, confirm the cultural standards rather than obliterate them. It is uncannily much like the function of gossip which serves to confirm what is the right conduct of behaviour by exploring its violations: to lull one into the reassertion of the rules by taking pleasure in an illusory transgression.

The Monstrosity of Zombies

Zombies are a different matter altogether. They do not belong to the system of logos; there is no ego, no subject to speak of. These creatures are the personification of the ultimate abject[6] as destructive rotting flesh, able to bring chaos and death to the whole realm of the human. While people do tend to see the allure of vampirism in the possibility of eternal life and youth—hence, my earlier comparison of vampires to superheroes—I would claim that no one would usually be fascinated with the possibility of becoming a zombie. The thought itself evokes a visceral reaction against simply because there would be no "me" to speak of. A zombie is not and in principle cannot be a subject. It is just flesh. Zombies do not establish any form of communication, any exchange system of relations amongst themselves or with humans; they are a dangerously active, moving mass of intensity. Also, distressful is the following reversal in which identity ("the soul") becomes finite and the rotting flesh (despite being in a state of constant decay) becomes infinite. A zombie is an ontological paradox. It is a crystallization of the horror of flesh transcending the soul.

Here human (historical, biological) temporality is unhinged: whenever zombies appear, they destroy any existing milieu and in its place they erect a state of chaos, of post-history, of anti-temporality. Any historical progress, in its traditional sense, becomes impossible. Humanity is forced to assemble into nomadic, tribal, military groups and it is only the question of time before

---

[6] "According to Julia Kristeva, the abject—that 'pseudo-something' which is neither subject or object, a 'pre-object' which cannot yet be recognized as an 'other' for a 'me'—disrupts all borders and rules, disturbs any identity or location, and both terrifies and fascinates as it collapses the distinctions between inside and out, sacred and defiled, life and death." (Joyrich, 1996, p. 114)

it is going to disassemble as a way of life altogether. I also strongly disagree with the prevailing interpretations of zombie movies as metaphors for capitalism as hunger, lack, and desire (the main operative principles of capitalism) are human notions; they involve a subject that can be interpellated, infused with a need, made to become an addict. One of such interpretations is cultural theorist Judith Halberstam's understanding of the monster and the Gothic in general:

> [T]he ability of the Gothic story to take the imprint of any number of interpretations makes it a hideous offspring of capitalism itself. The Gothic novel of the nineteenth century and the Gothic horror film of the late twentieth century are both obsessed with multiple modes of consumption and production, with dangerous consumptions and excessive productivity, and with economies of meaning. (Halberstam, 1995, p. 3)

Since zombies are not subjects in any strict sense of the word their craving for human flesh is not a need or an addiction; it is akin to a reflex, a spasm completely void of desire. Unlike vampires, zombies do not *desire* the human; neither do they gain any *pleasure* from it.

Film as a medium, understood very simplistically for heuristic purposes, is more of a unified whole, of a punctual event when juxtaposed to the sequantiality and seriality of television series. Therefore, zombie horror movies do not oppose the operative logic and the aesthetic demands of the medium in the case of film. The encounter with the monstrous is an instant that may be disruptive just like the event in Alain Badiou's sense[7], as that which creates a possibility of a new world by interrupting the rule. But it nevertheless operates as a point, a pulse, a rupture. By saying that film forms more of a whole than television series I do not mean that a film in question necessarily must make a holistic sense, must all fall into a unified perceptual image. Instead, a film tends to operate punctually, while series diagrammatically draw a dotted line entailing the possibility of an infinite addition and reverberation.

The monstrous does not seem to be easily if at all transferrable to the serial structure of television series. Such a seriality requires continuity, alteration between action-reaction, tension-calm, problem-resolution circuits in char-

---

[7] "[T]he event, which brings to pass 'something other' than the situation, opinions, instituted knowledges; the event is a hazardous [*hasardeux*], unpredictable supplement which vanishes as soon as it appears[.]" (Badiou, 2001, p. 67)

acter and narrative construction. Television series are the true inheritors of the Aristotelian structure of storytelling and the neo-Aristotelian ideal of the three unities of time, space, and character. This all again hinges on the presupposition of a subject which is precisely what gets destabilized by the introduction of the zombie, of the monstrous into the system. The system transforms into the reaction-reaction, tension-tension, problem-problem module. There is no constant to keep the traditional narrative flow running, i.e. the zombie as the truly monstrous is like Badiou's event in that it interrupts the rule, creates a new world and thus functions punctually (like a film) and not serially (like a drama series). Thus, theoretically *The Walking Dead* should not work as a series. Yet it does.

Therefore, an affective uncomfortability after the watching of every single *The Walking Dead* episode keeps lingering: the episodes are permeated by a consistent tension which does not dissipate even during the most simple and domestic moments. For instance, when the sheriff and his new found allies sneak into a police station to get some ammunition and to take a shower (most of the buildings have no running water anymore), their childish frolicking in the water is overshadowed by a constant danger. Zombies can come from anywhere, anytime. When the sheriff's wife and his best friend (both believe the sheriff to be dead) go away into the forest for their romantic rendezvous, the act of lovemaking is again under the constant danger of a zombie attack. Moreover, the woman is first spooked by the appearance of her lover as she does not know whether it is him or one of the walking dead that is coming from behind the bushes. It is symptomatic of the general liminality that suffuses the series: the distinction between the living and the dead, between the loved one and the completely, monstrously other is metastable.

The scene is also suggestive in other ways as the intercourse gains some animalistic aspects—further indicators that zombies initiate a state of nature from within as well as from without. Here sexuality has more to do with the instinct than the still culturally prevalent nineteenth century notions of romantic (courtly) love. By implication, culture is a product of leisure, a hobby, a make-belief that one has no time for under extreme stress. This is precisely what is so interesting in the series taking the monstrous for its subject: the space becomes universally infected with tension and suspense. There simply are no moments of calm or rest, no safe haven. The series actualizes, makes explicit what is otherwise existent but rejected by the protective ego, i.e. the constant multiple danger under which humanity lives. The encounter with the monstrous fragilizes[8] the human. What changes the most in the series is not the action structure itself (characters do love, argue, go on quests, save and abandon each other, etc.) but the perceptual and affective colouring thereof, its timbre.

The Televisual Encounter with the Monstrous

The serialized monstrous has further consequences for the visual and aural style of television series making, one of the main features of which is the looming silence and the prominent lack or reduced presence of background music, both diegetic and extradiegetic, which translates into the absence of significant emotional cues. Background music came to more and more prominence in the television series production, quite possibly due to the growing popularity of video clips and the MTV style montage as evidenced in *True Blood* or *The Vampire Diaries*. The famous opening credit sequence of *True Blood* even works as a stand-alone video clip. However, *The Walking Dead* deviates from this tendency which is not a random aesthetic configuration but an imperative of the subject matter.

For example, the absence of emotional cues is further foregrounded when a husband's act of shooting his zombified wife is not preceded by any moral, emotional or other considerations. His oscillation, hesitation and weakness in the moment of action are more pregnant with significance than any explanations, explicit character motivations could be. It is simply the one single zombie he has to kill as the implications are exceedingly large. The idea of a loved one's body monstrously transformed is more complex a phenomenon than a return of the memory of a deceased relative in the process of mourning or the actualization of this memory as some ghostly, spectral presence in a haunting. In these cases the loved one's body is gone and yet in a persistent idea of Cartesian dualism his or her "essence" and presence remain.

The transformation of the wife's body into a zombie denies this metaphysical dualism and the existence of an essence. No subjectivity dwells in a body that comes back as destructive flesh, an animated expression of what

---

[8] The notion often used by art theorist Bracha Lichtenberg Ettinger to describe the effects/affects of a meeting with the Other.

befalls a body when it dies (corrosion and decay that insist on being seen) and it cannot be accepted by an existing subject. The husband has to kill his wife (or, rather, her shell) so that his wife (as a subject) could live. The arrival of the-wife-as-a-monster destroys the protective bubble of an ego. As long as this shell walks, it negates the validity of the illusion of a consistent, reified, unified, and substantial personality. When this monstrosity is put to rest the normal process of mourning can begin. It follows that the true death of the wife is not her actual death but her transformation into the monstrous since society and its subjects have a place and function for the dead but they cannot accommodate what denies the notion of humanity *per se*.

Another outstanding scene illustrating the suspension of action is the one where the sheriff is preparing to put to rest the incapacitated, half-bodied torso of a zombie in a park. The sheriff silently walks in the empty park, nicely lit by the afternoon sun and beaming green grass—in all respects an idyllic visual moment. When he finds the zombie he was searching for—after all he knows that in its condition it cannot have had travelled far—the sheriff and the camera stare at the crawling, gnawing at air torso on the green, sunlit grass. This is a moment of idyllic beauty and horror, both at the same time. The very contrast can only be experienced in silence, without any emotional cues as the main characteristic feature of the series is exactly the perceptual uncertainty that the scene evokes.

Even the subsequent act of pity, the shooting itself comes as a surplus, as something extraneous to the moment, like a remnant from another world—a morality. This stand-alone status of the scene is akin to the Deleuzian purely optical or sound situations of the time-image which is rarely the feature of mainstream cinema let alone television series and therefore is so much more effective:

> The purely optical and sound situation gives rise to a seeing function, at once fantasy and report, criticism and compassion, whilst sensory-motor situations, no matter how violent, are directed to a pragmatic visual function which "tolerates" or "puts up with" practically anything, from the moment it becomes involved in a system of actions and reactions. (Deleuze, 1989, p. 19)

Even though the scene has its place in the chain of actions and reactions, even though it is supposed to be an act of pity and the sign of the sheriff's finding his place in the new world, it still comes as a surplus to the chain of action: the two operate on two different perceptual dimensions, the one being narrative, the other purely aesthetic/sublime (or anti-aesthetic/sublime). This way the stress is put on the moments of inbetweeness, on the action before action: the man's hesitation before shooting his wife, the sheriff's stumbling through the ravished urban landscape before meeting other living humans, etc. The aforementioned tension as a constant emotional timbre of the series reaches its climax in moments like these. Therefore, the choice of the initial focalizer as the sheriff that awakes after a coma into a completely changed apocalyptic world is so brilliant. His dizzy consciousness stumbles through the abandoned hospital as if through a dream. All he finds are the indexes of the fight that must have happened: the locked up zombies, the half-eaten human body, and the huge numbers of corpses lying on the ground outside the hospital. The last image is visually and culturally resonant with the images of the Holocaust which morally ambiguously yet significantly connects the abjected bodies of the Jews and the abjected corpses of the zombies[9].

The Falsification of Reality

The protagonist has to induce the world in which he now dwells from these indexes. He has to establish what has happened, what is happening and what his place within this world is. In other words, the human is not a constant; its meaning and function changes depending on the world in which it emerges. It is reminiscent of famous linguist Ferdinand de Saussure's structural notion of language: the value of a signifier does not depend on what it

---

[9] Interestingly enough, Judith Halberstam observes a certain resemblance between the imagery of the Jew and the vampire in her study of the monstrous: "Dracula [...] condenses the xenophobia of Gothic fiction into a very specific horror—the vampire embodies and exhibits all the stereotyping of nineteenth-century anti-Semitism. The anatomy of the vampire, for example, compares remarkably to anti-Semitic studies of Jewish physiognomy—peculiar nose, pointed ears, sharp teeth, claw-like hands—and furthermore, in Stoker's novel, blood and money (central facets in anti-Semitism) mark the corruption of the vampire. The vampire merges Jewishness and monstrosity and represents this hybrid monster as a threat to Englishness and English womanhood in particular. In the Jew, then, Gothic fiction finds a monster versatile enough to represent fears about race, nation, and sexuality, a monster who combines in one body fears of the foreign and the perverse." (Halberstam, 1995, p. 14) However, despite alluding to the same phenomenon *The Walking Dead* operates differently: it does not polarize the distinctions but undermines them.

denotes, what it refers to but on its relation to what surrounds it[10]. The character has to induce his meaning within this universe which is so much more problematic because the zombies as the monstrous do not simply reverse or mess up the pre-existing structure but annul it.

The emphasis on the sheriff's physicality (after his comatose state he is weak, barely mobile and badly suffers from thirst) foregrounds the topicality of the human flesh as well. From the very beginning the series appears as a contemplation on the body: the body with a mind is but one possibility. It calls to mind philosophers Baruch Spinoza's and Gilles Deleuze's famous question: what does a body can? Subjectivity is but one of the potentialities of the body. The zombie world falsifies the human, the protective ego and molarized identities. Here it is instructive to speak about Deleuze's concept of the powers of the false as "[i]n modern cinema, the narrative (or 'storytelling') aspect no longer represents 'reality', but concentrates on showing how the act of narration falsifies reality itself. This is why the central focus of narrative in modern film is what, after Nietzsche, Deleuze refers to as the 'powers of the false.'" (Kovacs, 2000, p. 161) The cinematic image has the potential of creating fake but real universes that in turn uncover the falsity of the "real" world(s).

Consequently, the powers of the false destroy the transcendental Good vs. Evil divide where only the subjective and contextual good and bad remain. The rigid world of morality shatters, only individual ethics can prevail as: "Morality, consisting in the formulas and automatisms of consensus community, treats all relations as internal, encoded, and predetermined. But ethics experiments in external relations, in encounters, events, and processes whose outcome is not determined in advance but invented during the actualization of a virtual event, the realization of a possible event." (Canning, 2000, p. 345) The sheriff awakes into a world as the encounter with the monstrous. There is, perhaps, no better illustration of a falsifying current passing through a particular image of the real (a plane of consistency) than this. The initial quest of the character is to learn how everything that he knew about the world and himself does not work in this new reality; it is the process of unlearning.

---

[10] See Saussure, 2006.

The falsification of the real (morality, values, norms, traditions, i.e. reified cultural essences) is perhaps especially threatening for the American spectators (the series is after all American!) where the fear of uncertainty is particularly salient. Nevertheless, the zombie itself is not an object of fear. Psychoanalytically, the uneasiness that the watching experience induces is linked to anxiety, an objectless distress. Because it is not the monster itself that is frightening but the implications of its existence, its falsification of the human. It turns to dust everything on which the notions of society and the self are built, i.e. undoes the metaphysical stability of these categories. The threat of death is nothing compared to the destruction of the self as a subject and a signifier. In the structuralist sense, zombies are not de-structive but anti-structive; they do not simply destroy the signifying structure, they invalidate it: where there was structure, there shall have never been one! This is the reason why I disagree with literary scholar Jeffrey Jerome Cohen's rendering of the monster as a complete cultural product. Cohen eloquently remarks:

> The monster is born only at this metaphoric crossroads, as an embodiment of a certain cultural moment—of a time, a feeling, and a place. The monster's body quite literally incorporates fear, desire, anxiety, and fantasy (ataractic or incendiary), giving them life and an uncanny independence. The monstrous body is pure culture. A construct and a projection, the monster exists only to be read: the *monstrum*[11] is etymologically "that which reveals," "that which warns," a glyph that seeks a hierophant. (Cohen, 1996, p. 4)

My conception of the truly monstrous as extrapolated from *The Walking Dead* evidently stands opposed to the notion of the monstrous as a crystallization of cultural norms, fears and otherness. The truly monstrous invalidates the symbolic, the cultural, the human. However, it is more constructive to simply stress the distinction between the monstrous and the truly monstrous: the truly monstrous body is pure post-culture and a-culture.

Coda

The fascinating aspect of such a series as *The Walking Dead* is the fact that theoretically it should not work as a series. The encounter with the monstrous as a subject matter and as a dominating perceptual effect op-

---

[11] Emphasis in the original.

poses televisual narrative structure and temporality in its punctual and disruptive nature. Yet it does work due to the slight reconfigurations of the main elements in the television drama narrative construction: the extension of suspense to encompass all of the space-time, the constant deconstruction of characters (as opposed to the traditional construction and development), and the concentration on the moments of in-betweeness or even the appearance of such purely visual and sound situations, detached from the chain of action and reaction as the previously discussed scene in the park. In other words, the serialized monstrous brings with it a new audio-visual and narrative style. The remaining question is what does the appearance of this phenomenon in the broader context of mainstream television entails, what does it symptomatize? Deleuze once noted that one does not

> criticize television for its imperfections, but purely and simply for its perfection. It has found a way of producing a technical perfection that is the very image of its complete aesthetic and noetic emptiness. [...] *Dallas* is completely empty, but a perfect piece of social engineering. [...] To say television has no soul is to say it has no supplement, except the one you confer on it as you describe the weary critic in his hotel room, turning the TV on once more, and recognizing that all the images are equivalent, having sacrificed present, past, and future to a flowing time. (Deleuze, 1990, pp. 74–75)

That is to say, the typical television series have no lines of flight or falsifying currents, no powers to affect or deterritorialize—the powers that, as I have tried to show, The Walking Dead possesses. I thus must finish this article with a paradoxical conclusion that The Walking Dead "(re-) ensouls" television.

References

Badiou, A. (2001). *Ethics—An Essay on the Understanding of Evil*, (P. Hallward, Trans.). London, New York: Verso.

Canning, P. (2000). "The Imagination of Immanence: An Ethics of Cinema". In G. Flaxman (Ed.), *The Brain Is the Screen*, (pp. 327–364). Minneapolis, London: University of Minnesota Press.

Cohen, J. J. (1996). "Monster Culture: Seven Theses". In J. J. Cohen (Ed.). *Monster Theory: Reading Culture*, (pp. 3–25). Minneapolis, London: University of Minnesota Press.

Deleuze, G. (1989). *Cinema 2: The Time-Image*. (H. Tomlinson and R. Galeta, Trans.). Minneapolis: University of Minnesota Press.

Deleuze, G. (1995). *Negotiations*. (M. Joughin, Trans.). New York: Columbia University Press.

Halberstam, J. (1995). *Skin Shows: Gothic Horror and the Technology of Monsters*. Durham, London: Duke University Press.

Hölderlin, F. (1992). *Sämtliche Werke, Volume II*. Munich: Hanser Verlag.

Joyrich, L. (1996). *Re-Viewing Reception—Television, Gender, and Postmodern Culture*. Bloomington: Indiana niversity Press.

Kovacs, A. B. (2000). "The Film History of Thought". In G. Flaxman (Ed.), *The Brain Is the Screen*, (pp. 153–170). Minneapolis, London: University of Minnesota Press.

Neocleous, M. (2005). *The Monstrous and the Dead: Burke, Marx, Fascism*. Cardiff: University of Wales Press.

Saussure, F. de, (2006). *Course in General Linguitics*, (R. Harris, Trans.). Peru: Open Court Publishing Company.

Žižek, S. (1995). *An Introduction to Jacques Lacan through Popular Culture*. Massachussetts: The MIT Press.

Television Cosmo-Mythologies:
The Return to Mythological Naratives in Television Fiction, from *The Prisoner* to *Lost*

Raquel Crisóstomo Gálvez, Enric Ros Zofío

Introduction

It might look paradoxical at first glance —and more so within a context of postmodernism— but the most remarkable creative deed a globally acclaimed television series like *Lost* (ABC, 2004-2010) has achieved is perceiving the prevalence of a particular universal need: that of returning to our origins. And it has carried this out by proposing a lucrative contemporary extension of the grand mythological narratives. Nearly four decades before, the pioneering *The Prisoner* (ITV, 1967-1968) already displayed such existential concerns by placing a troubled archetypal hero in a solipsist mental scenario, the Village —doubtless the herald of its successor, the Island. Initially conceived as a mainstream product, the show created by Jeffrey Lieber, J.J. Abrams and Damon Lindelof rapidly brought in the code of laws of cosmogony, hence addressing a pre scientific view of the world within an unavoidable moral dimension. Thus, the show has become a token of a succession of narratives –the *Oresteia*, the Dantesque narrative or Hesiod's *Theogony* being a few examples of it— in the form of Cosmo-mythologies, that is, as attempts to explain, both philosophically and poetically, the foundations of the Universe and the destiny (its inevitable end) of humankind. Combining adventure stories with cosmogonic speculations, the show emphasizes the admonition of a potential end of the world, generally envisaged as a series of catastrophes resulting from a clash between the forces of good and evil. Just as *The Divine Comedy* was eight centuries before, *Lost* is a true theological story that emerges as a symptomatic witness of the collective concerns and impulses of contemporary viewers; an audience ready to leave the comfort of the naturalist narrative in order to dive into the depths of 'mystery' and of its revelation.

From *logos* to *myth* in contemporary television

We call a myth a narrative symbolic construction with a psychological moral force deeply rooted in the collective conscience of human beings. Its allegorical strength develops through a series of narratives that appeal to the ancestral nature of primeval images. Thus, its validity transcends both time and space. In Lévi-Strauss's words, "myth is language, functioning on an especially high level where meaning succeeds practically at 'taking off' from the linguistic ground on which it keeps rolling" (Lévi-Strauss, 1987: 233).[1]

With the help of myths, humankind has attempted to understand and guide both its existential and emotional needs. After all, a myth is "a fable taken seriously"[2] (Compte-Sponville, 2001: 353). Mircea Eliade reminds us that "for the past fifty years at least, Western scholars [...] unlike their predecessors, who treated myth in the usual meaning of the word, that is, as 'fable', 'invention', 'fiction', they have accepted it as it was understood in archaic societies, where, on the contrary, 'myth' means a 'true story' and , beyond that, a story that is a most precious possession because it is sacred, exemplary, significant. [...] Today, the word is employed both in the sense of 'fiction' or 'illusion' and in that familiar especially to ethnologist, sociologists, and historians of religion, the sense of 'sacred tradition, primordial revelation, exemplary model'".[3] Thus, here a myth will be understood as a fictionalized narrative that preserves and reveals in itself a fundamental truth; a narrative resulting from an apparently false discovery that nonetheless materializes over an indisputable truth and typically incorporates elements of incomprehensiveness, ineffability and elusiveness.

The lines many postmodern television series are following today allude to an urge to revisit this kind of mythological narrative, that is, fictional tales that appeal to the vestiges of truth as well as to a strong need for answers. And these can be obtained through either the construction of particular mythologies—like in the cases of *Battlestar Galactica* (Sci Fi, 2003-2009) or *Fringe* (FOX, 2008-2013)—or the resurgence of certain mythological elements belonging to a range of cultures and related unconventionally to one

---

[1] Translation by Claire Jacobson from: Lévi-Strauss, Claude, *Structural Antropology* (New York: Basic Books, 1963), p. 210.
[2] Except for Eliade and Lévi-Strauss, all translations are mine.
[3] Translation by Willard R. Task from: Eliade, Mircea, *Myth and Reality* (New York: Harper & Row, 1963).

another—as it occurs in *Game of Thrones* (HBO, 2011–) or in *True Blood* (HBO, 2008–). In the latter, for instance, not only the myth of the vampire is resurrected, but also those of other creatures like maenads, werewolves or fairies. In other fictions, such as *Once Upon a Time* (ABC, 2011–), characters belonging to children's classic stories—including Snow-white, Red Riding Hood and the like—blend in with literary personalities such as Dr. Frankenstein or the Mad Hatter, from *Alice in Wonderland*. And in cases like *American Horror Story* (FX, 2011–), an *ad hoc* microcosm shaped as a mansion contains a series of topoi, creatures and characters from the horror genre tradition as well as a spectrum of some of the most gruesome cases in American noir history, like that of the Black Dahlia or the student nurse mass murderer Richard Speck.

But the best instances of complex, coordinated narrative structures developed around mythological tales (bringing together cultural and literary references as well as those of our own imaginary) are the aforementioned *The Prisoner* and *Lost*. And their merit is not so much having managed to reunite and organize a diversity of elements from cultural artefacts and other mythologies into their very own mythology, but remarkably having been able to organize all these elements so as to raise the question of a contemporary necessity of obtaining answers; the necessity of the revelation of a numinous narrative that turns them not only into mythological and teleological tales, but also into theological ones.

The two shows belong to thoroughly distinct eras of the history of television but coincide in its contemporaneity in many different aspects, such as the aim of organizing their narratives within isolated environments, the search by their respective main characters of their own identity, and most remarkably the need for a mythology that enquires about the chief mysteries. *The Prisoner* pioneered in this Cosmo-mythological trend of television fiction by setting itself up as what Robert J. Johnson termed Quirky-TV. In his essay *Quality Goes Quirky* (Thompson, 1996: 149), the television analyst and historian stresses the significance of a series of fictions that belong to the *Television's Second Golden Age*—such as *Picket Fences* (CBS, 1992–1996), *Northern Exposure* (CBS, 1990–1993), *American Gothic* (CBS, 1995–1996) or *Wild Palms* (1993)—and that, drawing on the momentum *Twin Peaks* (ABC, 1990–1991) provided for them, proposed a delusive approach to an imagery that the audience was likely to recognize, therefore altering the laws of a conventional logical narrative. But even before the arrival of ultraterrestrial—if genuinely American—locations such as those of Twin Peaks, Roma (Wisconsin) or Trinity (North-Carolina), the Village already appeared as a dystopian scenario and a metaphysical settlement: an unintentional sketch for the forthcoming the Island. In the era of post-TV, *Lost* corroborates its allegorical nature by creating a mythological universe as complex and intricate as to become "the mythological starting point of current television fiction [...], so we see *Fringe*, *American Horror Story* or *Alcatraz* as variations of the narrative paradigm initiated by Lieber, Lindelof and Abrams" (Carrión, 2012: 24); a paradigm around which multiple narrative structures can be combined: "castaway stories, war and guerrilla narratives, fantasy and science fiction, conspiracy theories, technical and philosophical hypothesis, utopias, religious tales and The Beyond" (Carrión, 2011: 170).

Both *The Prisoner* and *Lost* share a structure divided into three Aristotelian categories that coincide almost perfectly with the Dantesque outline. Firstly, the katabasis—or descent into the underworld—into the Island in *Lost* (Crisóstomo, 2013: 162) and into the Village in *The Prisoner* suggests for the two "an Orphic journey [...] in the search of plenitude, that is, in the search of Heaven. Hell and Heaven go side by side as symbolic images of the great dichotomies: death and beauty, ending and birth, destruction and creation, pain and pleasure..." (Argullol, 2000: 103) Secondly, there is a process of anagnorisis—or discovery by a character of their own identity— that calls for a space allowing a transition towards both identity and the sacred; a transition to the spiritual and the numinous. This stage is generally conceived in isolated locations that enhance the esoteric[4] ambiance and work as Dantesque purgatories (that goes for both the Island and the Village). Finally, a third stage brings in the heroic catharsis, epitomized here by the closure of the theological narrative. As Rudolph Otto points out (Otto, 1996:16), it reveals the numinous—what turns knowledge into usage—and often brings about the decease of the hero, as it does in the case of *Lost*.

Katabasis: the postmodern underworld

Literary theorists like Roland Barthes, Terry Eagleton, Umberto Eco, Harold Bloom, Richard Rorty, Michael Riffaterre or Antoine Compagnon (Aparicio

---

[4] In the etymological sense of the term, from the Greek ἐσώτερος: inside, from inside, interior, intimate.

Maydeu: 476–477) have repetitively insisted in the necessity of regarding a great proportion of our contemporary narratives as mere 'artefacts', that is, as *texts within texts* defined by complex circular systems of literary quotes. Determined to forge ahead and to keep a permanent dialogue with the traditions at the same time, these works both follow pathways already taken (and often forgotten for a long time) and create new ones. Televisions shows like *Alias* (ABC, 2001–2006) (through the works of the DaVincian Rimbaldi) or *Fringe* (with its manuscript of *The First People*) have assembled the essence of this idea so as to incorporate it in their narratives, thus increasing the value of their own mythologies. At the same time, behind the compulsive process of literary namedropping carried out by *Lost* there is much more than an inspired attempt to interact with the fandom or even to give status to a product presumably considered lowbrow. The volume of references collected by its creators contributes to the creation of a sort of *supertale* generously framed by a genealogy of myths, with the Holy Scriptures and the Grand Narrative at the top. Similarly, the *Book of Exodus*, Homer's *Odyssey*, Xenophon's *Anabasis* or Virgil's *Aeneid* describes a series of journeys in a lucrative combination of adventure and symbology. It is certainly not a coincidence that the title in Xenophon's work means literally "expedition into the depths". And perhaps for this reason, the creators of modern television dystopias[5] propose blatantly an escape from the *logos* and a re-examination of the very origins of poetics with the secret purpose of questioning what Paracelsus termed the 'Mysterium Magnum' (Harper, 2013: 222), that is, the core of human existence. All these contemporary fictions stage a return to the prodigious and the inscrutable by displaying a great symbolic journey similar to the pre-Renaissance pictorial and literary image of *The Ship of Fools*. Doubtless, the crew of the Oceanic Flight 815 from Sydney to Los Angeles, composed of a series of current social archetypes, perform a thorough self-examination that queries an existentially confused (postmodern) viewer.

Time and again, literatures of adventure and journey—from Odyssey's madness to Ishmael's suicidal fury in Moby Dick—have underlined the desperate nature of the traveller, who jumps into the sea in search of liberation after corroborating his 'continental' failure (just as Desmond Hume's (Henry

---

[5] The best example of television dystopias is, in fact, Channel 4's *Utopia* (2013).

Ian Cusick) decision of boarding the 'Elisabeth'). For most of the time, the Island is for the survivors a space of intimacy—the shelter of both the warrior and the solipsist—as well as the eternal place where they secretly wish to return in order to find the primordial core ("We have to go back!", cries out Jack Sephard (Matthew Fox), lost once again in the continental land). And the flashbacks in the show are doubtless the best evidence of the disastrous failure of the plane's crew in that sort of Hell on Earth. Similarly, *The Prisoner*'s celebrated prologue shows how the troubled secret agent played by Patrick McGoohan quits his job at the British Secret Intelligent Service with the intention of running off and, eventually, of finding some improbable paradise. Instead, Number Six wakes up in the Village, an isolated community that does not even appear in the maps; a nightmarish holiday village conceived as a genuine non-place that, just like the Island in *Lost*, becomes a chronotope: a location displaced—both in space and time—from the reality we are acquainted with (such as the parallel universes in *Fringe* or the seaside town Storybrook in *Once Upon a Time*). As Jill Franks points out, islands are metaphors of the ego (self). Reversing John Donne's famous statement ("No man is an island") one could establish that every human being *is* in fact an island, one separated by the self from the others and, simultaneously, connected to them by what Freud called the "oceanic feeling" (Franks: 12) (and what Jack Shepard realizes when he puts into words his "Live together or die alone").[6]

All this could explain why *Lost* starts out as a show of contemporary Crusoes, the members of a community that needs to be organized from scratch in a sort of New Paradise. Jack Sephard, initially the protagonist, personifies a genuine *homo oecomenicus*, the one in charge of leading the fate of a new civilization. But soon enough, that optimistic driving force breaks down and all that is left is a dystopian scenario that reveals "the impossibility of the Island"—particularly after the discovery of the failed experiment carried out by their predecessors, the Dharma Iniciative—and the impossibility of a continental world already challenged by the Valenzetti Equation.[7] The Paradise nostalgia felt by the members of the crew of the Oceanic Airlines plane rapidly gives way to fright and grief in a world now conceived as

---

[6] First season finale.
[7] In the show, the equation developed by this mathematician predicts the number of years until humanity extinguishes itself.

a torment in permanent expansion and from which escaping is no longer an option. Perhaps this is why the traditional solar hero that Jack represents at the beginning develops into a bearded personification of self-pity, whereas other characters like John Locke, ready to acquire liberation through the magic and the primitive, benefit from a second, unexpected chance.[8] The descent into the underworld is both in *The Prisoner* and *Lost* an abyss for their respective characters; men and women now uprooted from the common world and forced to wander about territories beyond time and space— like the labyrinth of the Marienbad hotel or the corridors of Overlook hotel— that make them reconsider their identities as well as their very own existence.

Anagnorisis: identifying the hero in the television purgatory

Both *Lost* and *The Prisoner* kick things off with an initial *peripateia*, developing the plot of the hero in an unexpected manner, turning it into *sermo mythicus*, the mythical narrative. In the case of *Lost*, two events function as flashpoints: the incident, in 1977, in which a volume of energy 30.000 times higher than the energy contained in The Orchid station was released in The Swan station (Terry and Bennett, 2010: 160); and the Oceanic 815 plane accident in the dramatic present of the series. Precisely that *peripateia* is what allows the heroes to be relocated in a new scenario, a primary territory (Ros, 2011: 61) that will eventually let the anagnorisis in. Thus, the moment of self-recognition by the heroes takes place somewhere far from society, the world-as-we-know-it, and time itself.

The Island and the Village are spaces in which the reverse of the norm prevails. In these almost oneiric places, social laws are different from those the survivors are used to. They represent an escape from everything that is previous and the possibility of a fresh new start: a second social and indentitary opportunity. There, the hero is allowed to reformulate his own self and his old identity exists nowhere but inside his memory. He is not judged for past crimes, only for present actions. He is given, as it were, a *tabula rasa*.[9] Neither the Island nor the Village contain moral categories of good and

---

[8] For John Locke, this second chance is represented firstly by the miraculous healing of his paralysis and secondly by his 'resurrection' by his alter ego Jeremy Bentham.
[9] It is not a coincidence that 'Tabula Rasa' is the name of the third episode of the first season of *Lost*. Also the name of the pilot episode of *The Prisoner* is 'Arrival'.

evil, for they are nothing but territories of recommencement, completely detached from the *other* world: in fact, the previous lives of the plane crash survivors in *Lost* are only revealed to the audience through flashbacks; and, in the case of *The Prisoner*, the loss of the sense of identity is radicalized to the extreme of enumerating the residents ("I am not a number, I am a free man!", claims the protagonist rebelliously), therefore falling into a sense of alienation and dystopia typical from Orwellian realities. Both locations are neutral and have a particular identity and purpose; both are inescapable unless some guidelines are followed (the coordinates in the case of *Lost*, handling the information requests of Number Two in *The Prisoner*); and both are remote—for the Village has no tongue, currency or nationality[10] and the Island is an actual island. This last circumstance requires inevitably a security system that is also present in both cases: it is the black smoke in *Lost*, rightly termed 'Cerberus' for the fandom, and the big white vigilant balloons in *The Prisoner*.

This kind of cosmos allows a return to the origin, whether it is via the recovery of the Rousseaunian cultural idea of the noble savage (special mention to the character Danielle Rousseau in *Lost*) or through conceptions like those of ideal societies (portrayed in Othersville, a 'holiday resort' for retired spies within *The Prisoner's* the Village). In any case, both locations operate as new limbos that favour a return to the primeval core and epitomize the need for an intimate place; a place to return to the primitive as well as to a state of natural innocence/wisdom. All this is well characterized by the bottle cork[11] in the Island and by the discovery of Number One's identity in *The Prisoner*.

Many television series typify the necessity to go back and reset,[12] a typically postmodern sentiment that rests on the rupture the 9/11 disaster brought about. Some of them reveal an apocalyptic footprint that, nonetheless, allows the presence of a hope of redemption (*Carnivàle*, HBO, 2003–2005); and some leave room for conciliation, represented by instances like the im-

---

[10] During the first episode of the show, the protagonist asks for a map so as to locate the Village but only general topography (the sea, the mountains, etc.) can be distinguished.

[11] The notion, suggested in the sixth season of *Lost*, that the Island is in fact a bottle cork of the whole world coincides with Juan Eduardo Cirlot's idea of islands as "metaphysical moments of force" (*Dictionary of Symbols*).

[12] In the Hatch, a sequence of numbers has to be entered to reset the station's timer and avoid catastrophic consequences.

age of the eclipse in *Heroes* (NBC, 2006–2010), the darkening sun in *Jericho* (CBS, 2006–2008) or by *Fringe*'s black holes.

In the cases here analyzed, these spaces appear as limbos that bolster the possibility of redemption, which is how the hero is, eventually, able to reach anagnorisis. In a more literal sense, they are purgatories where each character expiates one's sins: Sayid (Naveen Andrews) makes amends to those he has tortured by sacrificing himself for his friends, and Benjamin Linus (Michael Emerson) pays for his pride with her daughter's decease. Similarly, it is significant that the monster in *Lost* kills Mr. Eko (Adewale Akinnuoye-Agbaje) after he refuses to repent for his sins of the past. These places are also inhabited by souls that are obedient to external will (lost souls whose very own existence is suspended): these are the residents of Otherville or the Village as well as the isolated whispers and apparitions by the deceased in the rainforest of the Island, almost as if they were trapped in a temporal funnel (Argullol, 2011)—an interregnum of the living and the dead (Pintor, 2005: 2). These souls have surrendered to the loss of identity and refused to carry out the process of self-recognition that the hero will eventually implement, which is why the brainwashing scenes of Karl (Blake Bashoff) in *Lost* and Number Two in *The Prisoner* are of major importance.

In both shows, anagnorisis is reached at the very end: through the acknowledgment, by Jack Shepard, of his condition of hero in *Lost*; and with Number One's discovery of his own identity in *The Prisoner*. And, of course, by the escape of both the Island and the Village. This return to the origin is reached progressively and parallel to the solution of a large number of queries (what the Island or the Village is; who Jacob and Number One are) that are, in fact, ways of reaching an understanding of the hero and his condition, thus favouring the arrival to the paradise: the church at the end of *Lost* and the escape from the Village in *The Prisoner*.

But any act of self-recognition is also a burden. There are signs in the Village in which the message "Questions are a burden to others; answers a prison for oneself" can be read; and McGoohan himself says that "each man is a prisoner unto himself" (Goodman, 2002). Māyā taking off her veil gives access to her hidden identity. By removing her mask[13] she shows her primitive self, just as the ape does when it finds Number Six behind the first

---

[13] From Latin (not Classical): *mascus*, *masca*, or 'phantom'.

mask and finds itself behind the second one. And this is also how John Lock sees and recognizes the heart of the Island in 'White Rabbit',[14] acknowledges his own destiny and recovers from a loss of faith after his accident. Once he is dead, his identity forks and develops into a Doppelgänger.

In all these cases, the process of self-knowledge is a demand for the abandonment of science and a requirement to embrace faith—even for Jack Shepard, the man of science par excellence in television fiction. Both the church in *Lost* and the surrealist "psychedelic circus" (Woodman, 2005: 945) in the last episode of *The Prisoner* (a paranoiac fantasy (Pinto, 2009:4)) represent the access to the truth only by means of spirituality. And as far as *Lost* is concerned, the presence of a particular mythology of the Island is a requisite to understand its core (that cork-device) in the episode 'Across the Sea'.[15] The unsettled desire of (inner and absolute) knowledge is sublimated by the attainment of the 'numinous' (or fiction's eternal search for the mythical roots).

Catharsis: television fiction as theological narrative

To be sure, the recovery of the religious sentiment in postmodern television fiction adheres to a context of general crisis in the core of our civilization, that is, the suspension of belief in the 'myth' of rationality. At the end of the fifth season of *Lost*, the unexpected Daimonic appearances of Jacob (Mark Pellegrino) and The Man in Black (Titus Welliver) become a statement of the aspirations of creating a supra-human exemplary narrative in the fashion of a moral warning. The members of the crew happen to be mere 'avatars' of an ancient war between Good and Evil as described in most religious texts. They are puppets of the 'man behind the curtain'[16]—the magician behind Māyā's veil or even behind the masks of Number One and John Locke. A similar case is that of the ill-fated[17] *Carnivàle*, whose opening sequence already stresses the symbolic nature of what is about to come. The fortune-telling cards of The Sun and The Moon represent the young Ben Hawkins (Nick Stahl) and Brother Justin Croew (Clancy Brown) and their

---

[14] Episode One, Season Five.
[15] Episode Fifteen, Season Six.
[16] Episode Twenty, Season Three.
[17] The show was cancelled after the end of the second season and its creator could not develop the other four he intended to complete.

respective vicissitudes. Furthermore, the presence of Joseph Stalin, Vyacheslav Molotov and the members of the Ku Klux Klan in one side and of Jesse Owens, Babe Ruth, President F. D. Roosevelt or the Bonus Marchers in the other characterize the two opposites of Creation—an unalterable Anthropos divided into Eros and Thanatos. After all, the recovery of the mythological element in this new Golden Age of television aims to carry the audience into an inevitable moral recap.

In the Canto II of *The Divine Comedy*'s Purgatorio, Dante discerns a white light in the sky that turns out to be a boat guided by an angel. The boat lands on a beach and more than a hundred souls alight from it the same way the traumatized survivors of the Oceanic Airlines flight get off the plane eight centuries later. It is not hard to connect the Island with the Purgatory (and the main characters of the show with the Negligent, the Late repentants who died before receiving rites): a territory located half-way between Heaven and Hell so beautifully described by Emanuel Swedenborg or by William Blake in *The Marriage of Heaven and Hell*. It is the same place John Milton called Limbo of Vanity in his *Paradise Lost*, and where God and Satan fought for the last time the same way Jacob—He who protects the Island, according to Linus—has confronted The Man in Black from time immemorial. "One of these days, sooner or later...I'm going to find a loophole (to kill you), my friend".[18] The supernatural elements of the Island—from the presence of black smoke to its changing temporary nature—reinforce the idea that it is a 'sacred' space[19] ruled over by exceptional laws different from the natural ones. Thus, the Island is conceived as a 'hierophany' in the sense of the termed given by Mircea Eliade (Eliade, 2010: 147): a manifestation of the sacred.

In Rudolf Otto's words, the sacred "always manifests as a power different from that of natural forces". The constant allusions, in the two shows, of the presence of daimonic figures like Jacob or Number One take us back to the arcane narratives of Luther's 'Living God' with which Otto worked in his analysis of the religious experience. He presents an overzealous God/Leader (the antithesis of Erasmus's God/Philosopher) who appears, choleric, as the merciless embodiment of a power at the service of reveal-

---

[18] 'The Incident': Fifth season finale.
[19] Similarly, the seaside town Storybrooke is presented as a magical place in the second season of *Once Upon a Time*.

ing the eternal disagreement between human egotism and divine purity. In the case of *Lost*, this attitude is represented in a Janus-like manner between the two brothers: on the one hand, The Man in Black portrays a choleric destructive deity to be restrained behind a circular shield of ashes; on the other hand, Jacob performs as a developer and a benefactor. As far as *The Prisoner* is concerned, the God-as-Leader appears as an omniscient, unrestrained, authoritative ego. Thus, one might regard these modern dystopias as updated samples of literature of religious experience; a particular genre that, as Aldoux Huxley pointed out in *Doors of Perception*, has an apocalyptic nature and employs catastrophic horror as a cautionary warning for Humanity.

Conclusion

To be sure, the return of *fascinans* proposed by the new television fictions is the result of a sentiment of crisis. After all, the revelation of the *Mysterium Tremendum* witnesses the failure of the human project, in contradiction with the regenerative spirit of a nostalgia of The Paradise. The aforementioned struggle between Good and Evil is generally solved in scenarios almost extradiegetic that convey intimacy: the Red Room in *Twin Peaks*, Number One's psychedelic room in *The Prisoner* or the new church in which all religions converge, escape dogma and stress the spiritual in the final episode of *Lost*. Destruction and Rebirth, Hell and Heaven, the Sacred and the Profane are only a few of the fascinating dualities invoked in these fictions that are built up as patchworks from other texts and that conjure high and popular culture, *logos* and myth, television of 'attractions' and world view.

References

Argullol, R. (2000). *La atracción del abismo*. Barcelona, Spain: Destino.
Argullol, R. (2011). El embudo del tiempo. *El País*, 03/13/2011.
Campbell, J. (1992). *Las máscaras de Dios. Mitología creativa*. Madrid, Spain: Alianza Editorial.
Carrión, J. (2011). *Teleshakespeare*. Madrid, Spain: Errata Naturae.
Carrión, J. (2012). "La isla, la casa y el pueblo" *La Vanguardia*. 06/20/2012, 24–25.
Cirlot , J. E. (2007). *Diccionario de símbolos*. Barcelona, Spain: Siruela.
Comte-Sponville (2001). *Diccionario filosófico*. Barcelona, Spain: Paidós.
Crisóstomo Gálvez, R. (2013). The Mystery Box: narrativa matrioska e hipermediática en JJ Abrams. *Trípodos*, 31, 159–170.
Eliade, M. (1991). *Mito y realidad*. Barcelona, Spain: Labor.
Eliade, M. (2010). *Mitos, sueños y misterios*. Barcelona, Spain: Kairós.
Franks, J. (2006). *Islands and The Modernists: the allure of isolation in art, literature and science*. North Carolina, United States: McFarland & Company.
Goodman, R. (2002). "On the Trail of the Prisoner: Roger Goodman Talks to Patrick McGoohan. " CD Interview.
Harpur, P (2013). *La tradición oculta del alma*. Mas Pou, Vilaür, Spain: Atalanta.
Lévi-Strauss, C. (1987). *Antropología estructural*. Barcelona, Spain: Paidós.
Murray, M. A. (2009). *Island Paradise: The Myth. An Examination of Contemporary Caribbean and Sri Lankan Writing*. Amsterdam-New York: Editions Rodopi.
Otto, R. (1996). *Lo santo*. Barcelona, Spain: Alianza Editorial.
Pintor, Iranzo, I. (2005). Los desnudos y los muertos: la representación de los muertos y la construcción del otro en el cine contemporáneo: el caso de M. Night Shyamalan. *Formats*, 4, 1–23.
Pintor Iranzo, I. (2009). Melancolía y sacrificio en la ciencia ficción contemporánea. *Formats: revista de comunicació audiovisual*, 5, 1–10.
Ros, E. (2011). *It's not tv. Las series de ficción en la era pos-TV*. Barcelona, Spain: Fundación Taller de guionistas.
Terry, P. y Bennett, T. (2010). *Enciclopedia oficial de Perdidos*. Barcelona, Spain: Random House Mondadori.
Thomson, R. J. (1996) *Television's Second Golden Age. From Hill Street Blues to ER*. New York, United States: Syracuse University Press.
Woodman, B. J. (2005), Escaping Genre's Village: Fluidity and Genre Mixing in Television's The Prisoner. *The Journal of Popular Culture*, 38, 939–956.

Breaking Bad, a Character-Based Formula

Rodrigo Mesonero

Introduction

Chemistry is essential for life. Oxygen, hydrogen, nitrogen and several other elements create everything in the universe, from solid to liquid, from rational to inert. Among them, carbon is the essential element that can be found in 95% of the known chemical substances.

If carbon is essential in chemistry, good characters are essential in narrative. A narration can be built from the character or from the plot (Chion, 1994: 96). In the first case, when the story is character driven, the interest of the narrative is centered in the decisions and changes that the character suffers when confronting a series of circumstances (Sánchez-Escalonilla, 2001:131). Breaking bad is a character-based series released in 2008 and created by former The X Files (Chris Carter, FOX, 1993-2002) screenwriter and producer, Vince Gilligan. Its last eight episodes will be broadcasted before the end of 2013. The series tells the story of Walter White, a depressed chemistry teacher who decides to experience the dangerous side of life when he turns 50 and is diagnosed with lung cancer. He will become a methamphetamine cook and distributor assisted by Jesse Pinkman, a former student of the high school where Walter teaches. Along five seasons, Walter will fight for power and recognition while he tries to survive the rival traffickers and not to be discovered by his brother in law, a DEA agent.

Breaking bad is considered one of the best tv series in all times[1] and has become a cult show as it introduces an outstanding character in an outstanding context. Walter White's ambition and selfishness sets the most uncomfortable and direct dilemmas to the audience. In opposition with other shows like *The Sopranos* (HBO, David Chase, 1999–2007) or *The Wire* (HBO, David Simon, 2002–2005) where crime is sweetened with likeable characters with understandable desires, *Breaking bad* shows a main char-

---

[1] The fifth season is been rated 99 over 100 by critics on the website metacritic.com. This has allowed *Breaking bad* to enter the Guiness Book of Records as the best rated tv series ever (Guiness World Records, 2013, www.guinessworldrecords.com).

acter whose actions and goals cannot be justified in too many cases, even by the hardcore fans.

Following this, the chapter's aim is to analyze the most important element of *Breaking bad*'s formula, the main character. To do so, it's been used an analytic descriptive methodology. The series has been analyzed episode by episode to understand the character's motivations, development and functions. Key authors regarding narrative, television and philosophy have been used in every segment of the chapter. This analysis is intended for connoisseurs of the series.

From Walter to Heisenberg, story of a transformation

Breaking bad is a character driven narrative with Walter White in the center of interest. Walter White is a multidimensional[2] being whose worries, longings, frustrations, desires and fears are the engine to make things happen. The show is not about a chemistry teacher that decides to turn into a drug pimp but is rather the story of a man who decides to make a radical change in his life to try and make the difference. Walter's actions directly affect the ones that surround him, from his assistant Jesse to his wife, son, siblings in law, criminals, kids, random plane passengers... Walter's dimensions drive him towards becoming Heisenberg, his criminal *alter ego*, a monster capable of anything to get his objectives.

Vince Gilligan defines *Breaking bad* as the transformation of Walter White from Mr. Chips into Scarface[3] (Popcorn Taxi, 2012, www.popcortaxi.com). Walter's kindness and innocence are characterized by the treatment that other characters give to him. At home as well as at high school or with his brother in law he is treated as a weak, fearing and unable to speak his mind or make a point of authority character. Walter is a loser at all levels.

---

[2] A character's dimension means contradiction. A character can be brave or coward, secure or insecure, wise or stupid, etc. depending on the situation. (McKee, 2009: 452). The dimension of the character make the narration more interesting as it allows a deeper understanding of the human behavior showing it in all its complexity.

[3] Mr. Chips, Charles Edward Chipping, is the main character of the novel *Goodbye Mr. Chips* written by James Hilton and published in 1934. The novel presents a timid high school teacher that can finally open to others after meeting his wife Katherine. Mr. Chips is all kindness, transparent in his personal and professional life. Toni Montana a.k.a. Scarface is the main character of the movie *Scarface* (Brian de Palma, 1983) which portrays a Cuban illegal immigrant that creates a drug-based empire using his terror, betrayal and murder as main arguments.

As Walter, Mr. Chips is a loser whose wife is the engine of change. The difference is that in Hilton's novel the change is positive and in *Breaking bad* is negative. Skyler is the dominant figure of the family and Walter is the last in the chain of command. This is perfectly represented in the first familiar scene of the pilot, *The beginning of the end*, when Walter is unable to face his wife while his teenage son does because of the vegetarian bacon Skyler has decided to serve as breakfast. This simple action reflects the complex relationship that will drive the show.

In an interview given to the radio program *Opie and Anthony*, Bryan Cranston, the actor that plays Walter, comments that he tried to represent the character to be as invisible as possible, from the mustache, almost inexistent, to the clothes, all pale tones. His social relations are limited to his family, including Hank and Marie, siblings in law. Walter doesn't like his job as a high school chemistry teacher but he's passionate with chemistry. He was part of the team that got the Nobel Prize Award in 1981.

Walter's characterization will suffer a huge evolution throughout the five seasons of the series. This arc is represented in the transformation of Walter into Heisenberg, his dark *alter ego*. Heisenberg show up when Walter is unable to confront the challenge. His creation takes place in the pilot episode, *The beginning of the end*, and the sixth of the first season, *Crazy handful of nothing*, and happens as follows:

> Awake: When Jesse asks Walter why a man of his age decides to break the law, Walter simply answers that he is awake. This is the first sign of Heisenberg's appearance.
>
> Characterization: Walter shaves his head due to chemotherapy. When he goes to have breakfast, Walter junior tells him that he looks like a bad guy.
>
> Verbalization: Tuco asks Walter who is he when he goes to claim the money that had been stolen to Jesse. Walter, after a moment of doubt, answers that his name is Heisenberg. Walter takes the name from the real chemist Werner Heisenberg who formulated the principle of uncertainty in 1927.
>
> Action: Because of Tuco's negative to giving him back the money, Heisenberg drops a homemade explosive that blows the place up without killing anybody. Tuco gives the money and closes a distribution deal with Walter after the strength demonstration of Heisenberg.

Where Walter paralyzes, in the confrontation, Heisenberg is in his element. In the sixth episode of the first season Walter sets the rules: Jesse is in charge of the streets and Walter of the chemistry. At the end of the episode and throughout the rest of the series it is shown that Heisenberg is the one in charge of the streets. It will be in episode seven of the fifth season, *Say my name*, when Heisenberg finally becomes complete when a scared rival drug dealer recognizes Walter as the dangerous lord of crime Heisenberg. The transformation arc of Walter into Heisenberg is summarized in the following table:

Table 1 - The transformation arc of Walter into Heisenberg.

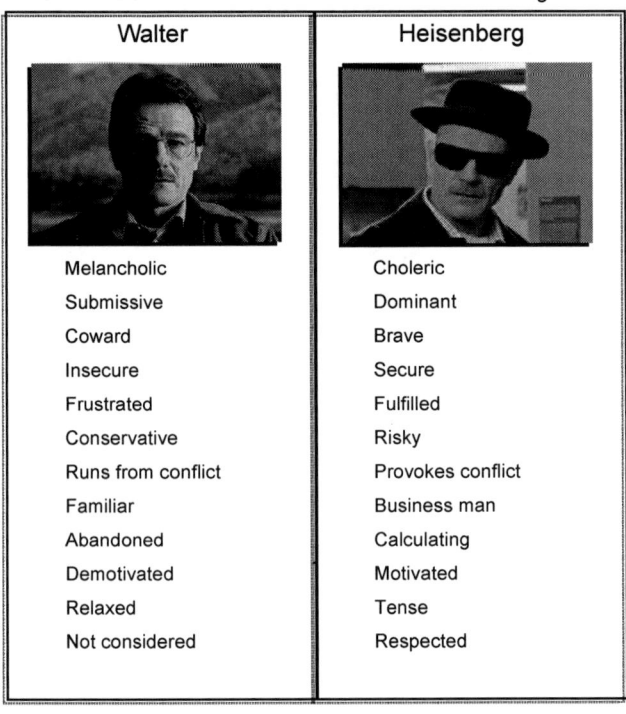

Walter	Heisenberg
Melancholic	Choleric
Submissive	Dominant
Coward	Brave
Insecure	Secure
Frustrated	Fulfilled
Conservative	Risky
Runs from conflict	Provokes conflict
Familiar	Business man
Abandoned	Calculating
Demotivated	Motivated
Relaxed	Tense
Not considered	Respected

Dimensions of Walter White
(Self-elaborated)
(Pictures: *Breaking bad*, 1x01: *The beginning of the end* y 2x07: *Negro y azul*)

Walter's actions not only suppose his damnation but also open the gates of hell to all those who surround him, whether they are familiars, friends, partners or absolute strangers. Skyler is the secondary character that most directly affects Walter's actions. As said before, she is Walter's engine for change. She controls the family, her husband included, and when Walter

starts making decisions of his own, helped by Heisenberg, Skyler won't accept it. She is the reason why Walter goes deeper and deeper in is collapse. The moment of the series that better illustrates this fact is when Walter decides to quit cooking methamphetamine after killing Crazy8 in episode three of season one, *...and the bag is in the river*. Walter has tasted the dark side and he doesn't like it but will be forced to return to make more money to pay the cancer
treatment that Skyler has almost forced him to take. Skyler keeps on pushing, conscious or unconsciously, until there is no trace of his husband.

Jesse's transformation arc evolves along with Walter's but in reverse sense. Characterized as a useless drug addict, Jesse evolves into a mature, intelligent and scarred adult who deserves salvation but can't because Walter is constantly dragging him down. As Virgil in Dante's *Divine comedy*, Jesse longs for salvation but can't. Jesse guides Walter through the underworld of drug and crime in Walter's first steps as Virgil did with Dante in his visit to hell.

Walter's concerns

Among other proposals, the theorist Phil Parker proposes a list of seven possible themes[4] that can be contained in any narration[5]. Moral of individuals, pursuit of pleasure, fear of death and desire for approval and recognition are the four themes held in the stories of change, power and drug that display *Breaking bad*.

Moral of individuals

The freedom of the individual leads to the need to create a regulatory framework that distinguishes right from wrong. This framework can come from natural, divine or human law and serve to establish the social coexistence rules.

---

[4] The theme is what the story is really about (Parker, 2003:142). The themes satisfy the psychological huger that the audience have in a conscious or unconscious way (Vale, 1996: 167). The different themes treated by a narrative are visions of life that the author wants to refute or confirm (Sánchez-Escalonilla, 2001: 58).

[5] The seven themes proposed by Parker are: Desire for justice; Pursuit of love; Moral of individuals; Desire for order; Pursuit of pleasure; Fear of death; Fear to the unknown or what cannot be known and; Desire for approval and recognition.

The world's founding myths often start with a moment of chaos—realm of evil—from which the divine order creates a natural and spiritual order of living things and objects that inhabit the earth. What distinguishes man from other beings is freedom, the ability to choose between options. Natural law is generalizable to animals and plants but individualized to man as he lives in free will and knowledge. According to Saint Augustine, man should handle that freedom guided by God because creation comes from nothing and only a Supreme Being can overcome this absolute void (Safranski, 2010: 31). Mainlander denies that the nature of the transcendent divine principle can be known and states the "death of God" concept later used by Nietzsche (Volpi, 2007: 49). Mainlander doesn't deny the existence of a creator god but claims that the impossibility of conceiving its nature in a scientific mode causes the estrangement of man.

Contemporary Western society turns its back to the divine laws as questions the ones dictated by men. The discomfort of postmodern man places the individual at the center of their own existential emptiness. Right and wrong depend on the aim of the actions. Moved to audiovisual, no matter that James Bond kills dozens of innocent as long as he gets to catch the villain. If the other's life is not sacred, what is then? Nothing, because life is only chemistry. As defined by Walter White in episode three of season one,... *and the bag is in the river*, there is nothing in man but chemistry, elements that create reactions and components when combined.

There is no room for mystery. Soul cannot be condemned because it does not exist. Without a spiritual framework governing the individual's behavior, only the material, tangible and applicable empirically is left. The condemnation of those who do not meet the natural precepts given by the divinity to man has yield to the individual's moral relativism able to justify their decisions in pursuit of a selfish and immediate good.

If the divine law does not govern morality of individuals, nor does men's. Beyond regulating the individual value systems, laws often assume the barrier separating the boring everyday life of the exciting transgression. In the seventh chapter of the first season, *A no rough stuff type deal*, the question of the legitimacy of the laws of man raises. Walter and Hank smoke illegal Cuban cigars and drink alcohol. Walter speaks of the relativism of the law because what they are smoking is illegal at that moment and drinking alcohol was illegal during Prohibition. Hank says that the forbidden fruit tastes better. Walter concludes that the law is relative and does not serve to make moral principles but passing standards. That is how Walter justifies his criminal acts.

This historic moral relativism raised by Karl Marx plans on *Breaking bad* as a reflection of contemporary society. *Breaking bad* projects the failure of Western social model in which work and family are presented as a source of dignity and social stability. The American dream disguised free will, raised from the theological principles, under the guise of the principles of work, sacrifice and family. The individual is free to choose, can get to be anyone, provided they do not escape from the normality and moral validity standards. And outside these ranges is where the disenchantment of the XXI century is drawn.

The moral question posed in *Breaking bad* focuses on elucidating the positioning of right and wrong. Having two mediocre jobs and a family that does not respect you is good and feeling full of life and professionally respected is bad? Everything is relative.

Moral principles condemn Walter for cooking methamphetamine but understand and support Marie for being a kleptomaniac. Hank, the lawman, shows the moral relativism of the rules hiding the excesses of his wife -as seen on episode three of the fourth season, *Open house*—while pursues his life for catching Heisenberg. Perhaps the yardstick of what is morally right is adapted according to whether they apply within or outside the family. So Skyler shows in episode three of the third season, *IFT*, when she explains to her lawyer that she cannot sue Walter because that would end with her family. Skyler, a character of strong moral convictions, relativizes before taking a step concerning her public image. And this is the moral space, the showcase of the public. Never mind the acts themselves but what others say.

The innocence of children seems to be the last bastion of what morally unquestionable in the series. An adult is free to mark his own rules, to offend and destroy as long as it does not affect children. Then society will align itself to morally condemn the offender. *Breaking bad* scans the space of innocence through the death of three innocent children: Thomas, the infant drug dealer; the immature and naive Gale and; the boy killed by Todd in the desert.

A fourth case that endangers an innocent death is Brock, the son of Jesse's girlfriend. In chapter twelve of the fourth season, *End times*, Walter poisons the boy and makes Jesse believe that Gus did it. Walter's purpose is to turn Jesse against Gus so he kills his enemy. This cold manipulation of Walter does not end with Brock's life but shows the amorality of the central character of the series, capable of anything just to achieve his goals.

Breaking bad moves between thin moral principles trying to be a reflection of our society. Walter, encouraged by Heisenberg, goes beyond and is an example of can happen if we don't put limits and coexisting rules in society.

Fear of death

Sigmund Freud defended that the fear of death or thanatophobia responds to unresolved childhood conflicts that the individual cannot express consciously. He added that we cannot be afraid of death because we have never experienced it (Freud, 1953: 304–305). The *Regret theory* of Adrian Tomer and Grafton Eliason (Tomer, 1994) differs from Freud's theories and claims that the origin of anxiety and fear comes when people evaluate the quality or the meaning of life. This vital balance is stressed and anxiety increases the closer to death the individual is situated.

The anxiety generated by the fear of death is presented as a key issue in the book *The denial of death* by Ernest Becker, who points that most of the acts and social rituals focus on relieving this fear (Becker, 2003). The Pulitzer awarded author claims that the foundation of society is to overcome the widespread fear in varying proportions to death. The *Terror management theory* completes the idea of Becker stating that the individual self-confidence helps reduce anxiety and fear of death.

The *Edge theory of death anxiety* says that fear levels are maintained at moderate levels during the individual's normality, allowing to enjoy life without the constant fear that enunciate existentialists like Becker (Kastenbaum, 2000: 153–155).

The role of religions in managing the fear and anxiety of death is too broad as to attempt to address it in the present study. Many religions offer the possibility of an eternal life of happiness if the precepts marked during life are met. In this case the fear and anxiety arise when the believer is aware that death shall entail deprivation of eternity or positive transformation.

The fear of death usually results in two vital attitudes: existential angst or vitalism. The first causes the search without results for the meaning of life. This pessimistic view of life creates individuals with low levels of energy which distress is reflected in passive attitudes. The pain and uprooting are constantly present in their minds. Vitalists, on the other hand, are people who decide to take full advantage of life before it runs out. Aware of the finitude of being, they find the meaning of life in making every moment worthwhile. The memories and experiences are the meaning of life.

Breaking bad proposes an atheist character who lives in existential angst caused by work and family frustration. Walter thinks that there is no more of life than what he has. The series begins when Walter turns 50 plunged into midlife crisis or in the process of individuation as philosopher Carl Jung defined. Individuation is the ultimate expression of individuality, one in which the person reaches self-realization, he becomes the deepest and true I. (Jung, 2002: 477).

Lost, Walter begins the series in search of authenticity, the real sense of life. The announcement of death makes Walter wake of his angst—see pilot episode, *The beginning of the end*, when Jesse asks Walter why he suddenly decided to become a bad guy and he simply answers: *I'm awake*—. The fear that the character always had to make mistakes—see episode eight of the second season, *Better call Saul*—turns into vital desperation after his cancer diagnosis.

Walter always has had fear in his life, fear of choosing and fear of being wrong as he states to Hank in episode eight of the second season. Death produces a cathartic effect on the character. The diagnosis of inoperable lung cancer is taken by Walter as a death sentence, as the beginning of the end as titles the pilot episode. As already explained, the diagnosis means Walter's breakage with his "normal" life and the appearance of Heisenberg. It can be said that the death of Walter is the birth of Heisenberg.

Death is present throughout the series, being shown as moments of reflection and vital balance. An example of this is the ninth episode of the second season, *4 days out*, in which Walter and Jesse are stuck in the desert all weekend because the caravan where they have cooked methamphetamine is damaged. During that time both characters have a near-death experience and Walter repents of all the evil that his new outlook on life as a criminal is causing around: *All I ever managed to do is worrying and disappointing and lie. Oh, God, all the lies... I can't even keep them straight in my head anymore...* Repentance near death defined by Tomer and Eliason appear to Walter for what he has done instead for what he has not.

The pursuit of pleasure

The Greek philosopher Epicurus postulated a materialism that denies the providence and the immortality of the soul (García Gual, 2004: 269). Lost the fear of death and of the gods, Epicurus advocated the pursuit of pleasure as a natural principle as the pleasant state assumes the absence of pain, anxiety, boredom, etc. The Epicurean pleasure is at an intermediate point between the purely intellectual pleasure advocated by Plato and Aristotle, the exclusively physical raised by cirenian hedonism and the spiritual one emerged from the Christian God (Cassadesús Bordoy, 2007:10).

Theodore Millon structures all aspects of personality in the relationship of three polarities: the goals of existence, replication strategies and primary survival modes. The first is based on the balance between the pursuit of pleasure and avoidance of pain (Millon, 1981).

Breaking bad presents a character who has developed his life with fear of pain and death. Walter developed his life constrained in his own insecurity until, immerse in a midlife crisis, decides to adopt an epicurean vision of life. This is Heisenberg's philosophy, a character born from death and whose main goal is to enjoy life like never before done by Walter.

The pleasure of breaking the law makes sense itself not for the fact of being performed. To show how far man is from God, from virtue, Saint Augustine gives an example of his life equating pleasure to evil. When he describes a passage of his life in which he stole some pears, the saint says that "*I didn't even want what I was about to steal, but for the simple pleasure of stealing*" (Saint Augustine, 2002: 34). In the seventh episode of the first season, *A no rough stuff type of deal*, Walter and Skyler have sex in the back sit of their car. Skyler is wondered why was that so good. Walter follows Saint Augustine and answers that sex was so good because they were breaking the law, not because neither of them was particularly inspired.

While Plato relates the concepts pleasure-good as something inseparable, Socrates separate them stating that good implies the stability of possession while the pleasure is temporary (Villacañas, 1991:331). Walter's pursuit of pleasure is oriented to momentary pleasure rather than the long-term good.

Walter does not measure the consequences of his actions in the long term but does what suits him at the time no matter if it causes pain in the medium or long term. The series is full of examples that illustrate how the pursuit of immediate pleasure of Walter does not carry any good. This applies from the first decision to cook methamphetamine—which satisfies immediate desire to experience the danger but that causes bad to himself and to those around him—, to the train robbery with methylamine in the fifth season—which supposes the immediate pleasure to become the chief of methamphetamine in the area but kills a boy. Far from being associated with the good, the pursuit of pleasure leads Walter to evil.

Desire for approval and recognition

Hegel pointed that the individual can only achieve self-awareness as long as is recognized by other (Hegel, 1998: 388). This self-knowledge provides the individual spiritual fulfillment through relationships with others. The shift of consciousness to self-consciousness only occurs in a two ways direction in which two consciences recognize each other. This mutual recognition creates the spirit.

In *Breaking bad* the desire for approval and recognition is seen as one of the main motivations for Walter's transformation. In episode six of the fifth season, *Buyout*, Walter explains to Jesse why he will not leave the business of methamphetamine despite having more money that he can spend in a lifetime. Walter explains how cheaply he sold his shares in *Grey matter*, the company he founded in college with Elliot and Gretchen. This company is worth millions today but is not only that why Walter feels remorse for the decision but by the lack of recognition of his work. This becomes clear when Walter finishes his explanation saying that he is not in the drug or money business, but in the empire business. Walter wants to create an empire so that others recognize him as someone important, the winner he has never been. As Vince Gilligan explains, it's all about power and recognition because if you are Jesse James and no one knows, it is not the same (Popcorn Taxi, 2012, www.popcorntaxi.com).

To Hegel, the process is based on the combination of the notion of ourselves and the state to which we aspire and its achievement supposes the integrity of the being (Taylor, 1975: 137 and 153). In episode twelve of the second season, *Phoenix*, Walter complains of having money and not being able to tell anyone. The character needs recognition of others to feel that the actions taken reach plenitude and define him. In the fourth episode of the fourth season, *Shotgun*, Walter cannot stand listening to Hank praising the work of Gale as a methamphetamine cook assuming he was Heisenberg. Drunk, Walter suggests that Gale was not a master brain of chemistry but a follower. Again, Walter is frustrated and incomplete due to the lack of recognition for his work. Finally, episode seven of the fifth season, *Say my name*, is a recognition of Heisenberg, that is, Walter's desired self-awareness when the drug dealer with whom he is negotiating speaks out his name recognizing him as the dangerous and talented man who killed Gustavo Fring and cooks the blue metham-phetamine. In that moment Walter is completed as an individual achieving self-consciousness for the first time as he finds another that recognizes him only as Heisenberg, without any trace of the strengths and weaknesses of the original Walter.

This recognition process developed between Walter and Gustavo but in a dysfunctional way. The second wants to be recognized in Walter but he refuses. In episode eleven of the second season, Gus tells Walter that they cannot work together because they are not equal because Walter trusts in Jesse, a drug addict, and he does not. When the employment relationship between the two is established, Gus wants to be recognized in Walter again but again he refuses. This occurs in episode eleven of the third season, *Abiquiu*, when Walter tries to persuade Gus not to make the same mistakes as he did and learn how to be rich. Gus wants to recognize Walter as an equal, someone who can fill the space left by his professional partner Max, killed years ago by Hector Salamanca. In this case, the notion that Gus has of Walter does not match with the one that the latter has of himself. Walter does not have the notion of himself an equal to Gus, but someone superior. Walter's desire for recognition and its achievement will bring the destruction of himself and his family.

Walter, Heisenberg and Ozymandias

"I did it for me. I liked it and I was... really... I was alive". With these words Walter finally confesses to Skyler, in the last episode of the series, his real motivation for becoming a drug kingpin. Walter's actions, defined by anger, selfishness, antipathy, duality and ambition, define a postmodern character. His existence is only possible after a radical break or coupure (Jameson,

2003:1) that will bring the unpredicted, surprising and the uncovered aesthetic (Habermas, 2008: 110). Postmodern characters despise the traditional family values to embrace materialism (Lyon, 1997: 132).

Walter is a character with no possible redemption as is shown at the series finale. He dies self-satisfied but only after realizing that his actions will never been understood by his family or society. As a postmodern representation, Walter is a character whose behavior is neither forgotten nor eradicated (Bauman, 2007: 45). Only death can set him free.

Werner Heisenberg's Principle of uncertainty states that it is impossible to determine the position and velocity of a particle at the same time. Just the mere act of observation modifies the situation and momentum (Heisenberg, 1949: 13–46). This theory points the impossibility of knowing reality as the mere observation alters the true nature of objects.

The principle of uncertainty is been used to feed the postmodern malaise: how can we life in a world we cannot understand? But this uncertainty can be applied to Walter, a.k.a. Heisenberg, to define a character that is unpredictable, not only in his ability to raise hell but also when changing his heart and showing humanity when all seems to be lost.

In the final series episodes Walter sacrifices himself and his earned prestige to make sure his family will get the money to cover their expenses for life. Walter won't take credit for it, as Skyler and Walter Junior won't ever take anything from the former head of the family, and it will be Elliot and Gretchen who give them the money as an altruist contribution to compensate Walter's terrible impact on the family. He also shows humanity and forgiveness when he saves Jesse in the final gunfire that kills Jack and the rest of the gang.

But these noble acts don't only show humanity in Walter but also hope and submission. Walter accepts being disowned by his family as he finally understands that he has done terrible things just to satisfy his ego. With Jesse, not only he saves his life but also lets him free. These shows Walter as a functional father to Jesse, who listens and respects the choices of his now mature symbolic son.

As a conclusion, Breaking bad portraits a postmodern main character who, at the end, understands that life is about self-realization but also caring for the ones you love. The series shows family as the center of social interaction and its destruction only brings death and destruction. Walter could have done any bad and get away with it until he caused Hank's death. After that, there is no way back.

At the end we finally have the answer to the question formulated in episode 3 of season 1,... and the bag is in the river, what is that 0,111950 per cent of human components that Walter and Gretchen cannot break down? It was the soul, as she pointed to a disbelief and bigheaded young Walter. It turns out that all the series was set to demonstrate that there are factors in the human being that cannot be rationally controlled. Science is helpless before human essence. That was what Walter had to learn. And he did, too late.

References

Agustín, S., (2004). Las confesiones. Madrid. Ediciones palabra.
Alighleri, D. (1993). Divina comedia. Madrid. Cátedra
Bauman, Z. (2007). Miedo liquid. La sociedad contemporánea y sus temores. Barcelona. Paidós.
Becker, E. (2003). La negación de la muerte. Madrid. Kairos.
Campbell, J. (2010). El héroe de las mil caras: Psicoanálisis del mito. México: Fondo de Cultura Económica Ciudad de México.
Cassadesús Bordoy, F. (2007). Epicuro y el epicureísmo. Madrid. E-exelence. Online edition, available in: http://books.google.es/books?id=5P4afmAni1UC&printsec=frontcover&dq=Epicuro+y+el+epicure%C3%ADsmo&hl=es&sa=X&ei=XJ-DUazNObD7AaO2IDwAw&ved=0CDMQ6AEwAA#v=onepage&q=Epicuro%20y%20el%20epicure%C3%ADsmo&f=false. [Consultation: February, 27th, 2013].
Chion, M. (1994). Cómo se escribe un guión. Madrid. Cátedra.
Freud, S. (1953). "Thoughts for the Times on War and Death". The Standard Edition of the Complete Psychological Works of Sigmund Freud, Vol. 4. London. Hogarth Press.
García Gual, C. (2004). Historia de la filosofía antigua. Madrid. Editorial Trotta.
Habermas, J. (2008). El discurso de la modernidad. Madrid. Katz editores.
Hegel, G., Willhelm, F. (1998). Phenomenology of the spirit. India. Shri Jainendra Press.
Heisenberg, W. (1949). The physical principles of the quantum theory. United Stated of America. Dover Publications Inc.
Jameson, F. (2003). Postmodernism or the cultural logic of late capitalism. United States of America. Duke University Press.
Jung, C. G. (2002). Recuerdos, sueños, pensamientos. Buenos Aires. Seix Barral.
Kastenbaum, Robert (2000): The psychology of death. New York. Springer Publishing Company.
Lyon, D. (1997). Postmodernidad. Madrid. Alianza editorial.
McKee, R. (2009). El guión. Madrid. Alba Editorial
Millon, T. (2011). Disorders of personality. New Jersey. John Wiley & Sons Inc.
Parker, P. (2003). Arte y ciencia del guión. Barcelona. Robinbook.
Safranski, R. (2010). El mal. Barcelona. Tusquets editores.
Sánchez-Escalonilla, A. (2001). Estrategias de guión cinematográfico. Barcelona. Ariel
Taylor, C. (1975). Hegel. United States. Cambridge University Press.
Tomer, A. (1994). "Death Anxiety in Adult Life: Theoretical Perspectives", in Neimeyer, Robert (ed.), Death Anxiety Handbook. Washington. Taylor & Francis.
Vale, E. (1996). Técnicas del guión para cine y televisión. Barcelona. Gedisa.
Villacañas B., José L. (1991). Los caminos de la reflexión. Historia de la filosofía I. Murcia. Universidad de Murcia.
Vogler, C. (2002). El viaje del escritor. Barcelona: Ediciones Robinbook.
Volpi, F. (2007). El nihilismo. Buenos Aires. Siruela.
Breaking bad [DVD]. VV.DD. Seasons 1, 2 y 3. Madrid: Sony Pictures, 2012. 12 DVD

Breaking bad [DVD]. VV.DD. 4th Season. Madrid: Sony Pictures, 2012. 4 DVD
Breaking bad [DVD]. VV.DD. 5th Season. Madrid: Sony Pictures, 2012. 3 DVD

www.popcorntaxi.com
www.avclub.com
www.guinessworldrecords.com

Representing Occupations in Media and Audience Perceptions of TV Series

Valentina Marinescu

Introduction

Our everyday lives are conditioned by the mass media. Media texts and images have become important factors creating identities, moulding attitudes and constructing images of the world. Television is a major source of factual information, opinion and analysis which impart knowledge, influence the understanding of issues by their readers and may also act as advocates for the recipients of news items. A smorgasbord of items is offered but most people will never watch all of television programs. Mass media are less likely to therefore grab attention on low salience stories unless presented in a manner designed to attract attention (Neuman et al., 1992).

If mass media are reconstructing the social world, as Mohan suggests (2010), then the image we have about one society in a given moment of time is also the result of this reconstruction. Also, orientation of media coverage—the negative or positive, attraction or aversion, favorable or unfavorable orientation—has been an important feature of commentary on the performance of mass media in open societies (Gunther ,1998). In other words, the way in which television represents reality structures how most audience members interpret reality and events and can help to frame public opinion (Jeon, Haider-Markel, 2001).

The article deconstructs the ways in which various audiences' members understand the representation of occupations in TV series. "Are the ways of representing various occupations in TV series consistent with the "definitions" of those occupations at the level of Romanian audience's member or not?"—This is the research question at which I search to offer an answer in the present study.

Theoretical framework

The theoretical framework of the present article is based on the thesis from Social Cognitive Theory and Cultivation Theory.

As Social Cognitive theory states, people have a set of cognitive capabilities that guide their actions (Bandura, 2002). These capabilities include a symbolizing capability, a selfregulatory capability, a self-reflective capability, and a vicarious capability. The symbolizing capability allows humans to create cognitive models based on their experiences. Humans use these models to guide future behavior. Because of their self-regulatory capability, humans can self-direct their actions. People can predict possible consequences of their actions from their relevant cognitive models, and can set goals and plan actions. The self-reflective capability refers to humans' ability to evaluate their judgments and thinking. People have an idea of what normal thoughts and behaviors are considered and can compare their own to these standards. According to Bandura (2002), cultures could not function if humans solely learned through direct experience; the process would be too tedious and time-consuming. Instead, humans can learn by vicariously observing others' actions and their consequences. People can learn from more than just observations of other humans and their actions; people can also observe and learn through media representations. As McQuail (2005) summarizes, the basic idea is that we cannot learn all or even much of what we need to guide our own development and behavior from direct personal observation and experience alone. We have to learn much from indirect sources, including the mass mediall (McQuail, 2005, p. 493). In addition, observational learning from the media occurs through symbolic modelling (Bandura, 2002). People learn behaviors from models of actions shown in the media. This process occurs through four subfunctions: attention, retention, production, and motivation (Bandura, 2002). Attention refers to the selective nature of human observation; a person has to become aware of the modelled behavior in order to learn it. In addition to attention, retention is also a necessary part of modelling; in order to be influenced by observations, people have to remember them. Humans extract information from a model and restructure it into rules and conceptions for memory representation (Bandura, 2002, p. 127).

Following retention, the third subfunction of observational learning is the production of the behavior. Production occurs when symbolic conceptions are translated into appropriate courses of action (Bandura, 2002,p. 129). People do not produce actions once they learn them, however; the final sub-function of motivation is necessary to perform an action.

In sum, social cognitive theory distinguishes between acquisition and performance because people do not perform everything they learn (Bandura, 2002, p. 129). People become motivated to perform an action from the anticipatory rewards or punishments associated with the behavior.

Cultivation research focuses on the comparison of perceptions across the different viewership levels. Heavy viewers of television perceived the world to be more violent than light television viewers (Gerbner, 1998; Gerbner, Gross, 1976; Shanahan, Morgan, 1999). Light viewers rated the world as more violent only in certain situations, such as after recently watching a violent episode (Littlejohn, Foss, 2008; Shanahan, Morgan, 1999). Despite the history of using cultivation theory to predict perceptions of violence, the theory can be used to observe perception differences between viewership levels of any television genre. At the core of cultivation theory is the idea that regularly viewing a specific behavior, point of view, or act on television will have an effect on a viewer's perception of that behavior, point of view, or act in real life (Gerbner, 1998; Hammermeister et al., 2005; Hether et al., 2008; Hetsroni, Tukachinsky, 2005; Morgan, Shanahan, 2010). Mass media scholars are now regularly studying different TV genres with cultivation theory and their results show the importance of it in fields as various as health communication, e-literacy and communitarian development (Finnegan, Viswanath, 2002; Morgan, Shanahan, 2010).

Elements of methodology

To answer at the general research questions ("Are the ways of representing various occupations in TV series consistent with the "definitions" of those occupations at the level of Romanian audience's member or not?") I conducted a set of thirty interviews with members of the audience who have one of the following occupations: professor, lawyer and policeman. The internal structure of the sample was a simple one: ten respondents were policemen, ten of them were professors and ten were lawyers. The interviews were made in March–April 2013 in Bucharest.

Analysis of the results

"What were the main reasons for which some (that is, professors, policemen and lawyers) members of the audience watched TV series that present occupations similar to their one?" At the first sight, for all groups of respondents, the main reason to watch this series is to entertain in free time. Despite this general image, at a closer look, some differences among the three groups of respondents emerged. Thus, the professors were the only who watched the TV series which dealt with their profession only for fun, for entertainment. At the same time, lawyers and policemen had more various reasons to consume TV series about their occupation: to learn something new from the plot or characters, to make comparison with the activities of their peers from other countries.

> Lawyer 1: I watched this TV series to see how it is the law system in the United States and how it is the law applied in the case of different situations.
>
> Lawyer 4: I watch it because I like this type of TV series and also, to be sincere, the plot and characters are part of my daily conversation at the work-place because I persuaded also my colleagues to watch it.
>
> Policeman 5: First of all those series are very interesting. They show you the way in which the Police from other countries is functioning. You can make the comparison between what is going on in Romania with the way in which police is functioning in UK, with a strong respect for the law, and in US, where the accent is put on the laboratory analysis and computer techniques.
>
> Policeman 9: I watch it during the week-end, in my spare time. I like very much this TV series due to the stress which is put on the details, those being of maximum relevance in order to solve the case.

"Professionalism", "interesting scripts", "good actors" are the most frequent common elements of the TV series' scripts that are most appreciated the respondents. The difference notices in this case is, again, between the professors,on the one hand, and the lawyers and the policemen, on the other. Thus, the Romanian professors were the only respondents who couldn't refer to the script and general human values presented in the TV series dealing with the teacher-student relationships and they are the most vivid critiques of such TV series. On the contrary, the Romanian lawyers and policemen could deeper assess TV series about law and criminal activities, making comments regarding the actors, the human values found in the script, the *mise-en-scene* and they were less critique about the TV series they watched.

Lawyer 6: What I like the most at this TV series?!!....i think I like the most the way in which the actors perform the roles, the fact that this is a psychological TV series with a logical plot and which is somehow inspired from real life. The strong points are the style of presenting the plot, the way in which actors act and as weak points I could stress to the fact that sometimes the plot is not inspired from reality, that sometimes some things are exaggerated and you can understand very easy who is the killer.

Policeman2: The TV series' plot is very interesting, it is very well structured, There are presented a lot of cases from the police-world and the ways in which the policemen solve them. An the main actor is acting very well, he is very well suited for this role. In the TV series there are presented not only cases but also the teamwork that is specific to the police.

Professor 8: It can be assess that if a student watch this TV series he or she will judge the school in a wrong way because the accent is put on extra-school activities.

The combination between the fictional character of the specific cases presented in TV series and the high level at which occupations are presented in those drama is the main characteristic emphasized by the respondents at the question: "In what degree do you assess that the TV series resemble to your every-day activity in Romania?".

Lawyer4: These TV series were made according to the US law system. As such, the deals between parts in law-suits play an important role and this new way of law-suits is implemented now in Romania.

Policeman9: I think that this TV series is not similar with what is going on in Romanian police. In Romania there are no judiciary system involved in criminal investigation-such is the case in the TV series. For this reason many confound the Police with the Court. You will never see an attorney making criminal investigation—this is the job of a policeman.

Discussion

The purpose of this article was to deconstruct the ways in which various audiences' members understand the representation of occupations in TV series.
The TV series genre is one type of fictionalized television programming that not only contains elements of other genres, but is the fusion of several genres. As was the case for many dramatic genres that came before, the TV

series genre has developed its own blueprint for success. I assess from the beginning that TV series are worthy of investigation as their impact on contemporary society are undeniable. Although the TV series can be entertaining and engaging, they are significant because of their potential to inform and persuade the viewers regarding controversial but important topics. This was the the case of my research project where the results showed that the respondents had recognized cultural artifacts as presenting either fictious or heavily dramatized accounts of real incidents and never equated the reality with the fiction.

Social cognitive theory posits that people can learn behaviorsb from observing others performing the behavior in the media or in other contexts (Bandura, 2001). Cultivation theory posits a positive relationship between televisionviewing and perception of social reality, with viewers developing a view of socialreality similar to that presented on television (Gerbner, Gross, Morgan, Signorielli, Shanahan, 2002). The analysis of the empirical data analysed demonstrated that the main elements motivating respondents' viewing of television series related to their own occupations are learning something new and enabling comparison with the activities of their peers from other countries.

In the end I have to agree with Gabbard (2001, p. 265) who states that media like television and film occupy a region between reality and illusion. As Gabbard (2001, p. 268).suggests, this realm is known as a "play space", a psychological space between fantasy and reality and between one's inner and external worlds. In the case of the research project the respondents who watched TV series related to their own occupation were susceptible to adopt new definitions of reality, and to adjust their value systems as the result of this type of consumption.

References

Bandura, A. (2001). Social cognitive theory of mass communication. *Media Psychology*, 3: 265–299.

Bandura, A. (2002). Social cognitive theory of mass communication. In J. Bryant and D. Zillman (eds), *Media Effects: Advances in Theory and Research* (2nd ed), pp. 121–153. Hillsdale, NJ: Erlbaum.

Christen, C.T., Kannaovakun, P., Gunther A., C. (2002). "Hostile Media Perceptions: Partisan Assessments of Press and Public during the 1997 United Parcel Service Strike." *Political Communication*, 19(4): 423–36.

Finnegan, J. R., Viswanath, K. (2002). Communication theory and health behavior change. In K. Glanz, B. K. Rimer & F. M. Lewis (Eds.), *Health Behavior and Health Education: Theory, Research, and Practice.* (3 ed., pp. 361–388). San Francisco: Jossey-Bass.

Gabbard, G. (2001). Psychotherapy in Hollywood cinema. *Australasian Psychiatry*, 9(4): 365–369.

Gerbner, G., Gross, L. (1976). Living with television: The violence profile. *Journal of Communication*, 26 (2): 172–201.

Gerbner, G. (1998). Cultivation analysis: An overview. *Mass Communication & Society*, 1(3/4): 175–194.

Gerbner, G., Gross, L., Morgan, M., Signorielli, N. (1981). Health and medicine on television. *New England Journal of Medicine*, 305: 901–904.

Gunther, A. C. (1998). The Persuasive Press Inference: Effects of Mass Media on Perceived Public Opinion, *Communication Research*, 25(5) :486–504.

Hammermeister, J., Brock, B., Winterstein, D., Page, R. (2005). Life without TV? Cultivation theory and psychosocial health characteristics of television-free individuals and their television-viewing counterparts. *Health Communication*, 17(3): 253–264.

Hether, H. J., Huang, G. C., Beck, V., Murphy, S. T., Valente, T. W. (2008). Entertainment-education in a media-saturated environment: Examining the impact of single and multiple exposures to breast cancer storylines on two popular medical dramas. *Journal of Health Communication*, 13: 808–823.

Hetsroni, A., Tukachinsky, R. H. (2006). Television-world estimates, real-world estimates, and television viewing: A new scheme for cultivation. *Journal of Communication*, 56(1): 133–156.

Jeon,Y, Haider-Markel, D. P (2001). Tracing Issue Definition and Policy Change: An Analysis of Disability Issue Images and Policy. *Policy Studies Journal*, 29 (2): 215–37.

Littlejohn, S. W., Foss, K. A. (2008). The media. In S.W. Littlejohn & K.A. Foss, (Eds.), *Theories of Human Communication* (pp. 285–314). Belmont, CA: Thomson Wadsworth.

McQuail, D. (2005). *Mass communication theory: An introduction* (5th ed.). London: Sage.

McQuail, D. (2010). Processes and models of media effects. In D. McQuail (Eds.), *McQuail's Mass Communication Theory* (6 ed., pp. 453–476). Thousand Oaks,CA: Sage.

Monhan, B. A. (2010). *The shock of the news: media coverage and the making of 9/11/*, New York University Press.

Morgan, M., Shanahan, J. (2010). The state of cultivation. *Journal of Broadcasting & Electronic Media*, 54(2): 337–355.

Neuman, W. R., Just, M. R., Crigler, A. N. (1992). *Common Knowledge-News and the Construction of Political Meaning*, University of Chicago Press.

Shanahan, J., Morgan, M. (1999). *Origins. Television and its viewers: Cultivation theory and research*. Melbourne, Australia: Cambridge University Press.

Homeland: War on Terror Revisited

Marc Perelló-Sobrepere

Introduction

Homeland (Showtime, 2011) is an American political thriller created by Howard Gordon and Alex Gansa. The two have previously worked on other action-oriented series: Gordon was involved in the series *24* (FOX), and Gansa worked on *Numb3rs* (CBS), both of them having generated great ratings. They also teamed up on another renowned series: *The X-Files*. With such a track record between the two, the industry anticipation for *Homeland* had been very high ever since the first drafts were unveiled, and the series, which holds three action-packed seasons already, has certainly lived up to expectations. *Homeland* boasts a soft, modern and intelligent narrative structure. The series follows Carrie Mathison, a Central Intelligence Agency operations officer played by the actress Claire Danes. In the first episode, an asset warns Carrie that an American prisoner of war has been turned over by al-Qaeda. Back in the United States, Carrie is introduced to Nicholas Brody, a U.S. Marine Sergeant portrayed by Damian Lewis, who had been reported missing in action in 2003. Brody is received in the United States as a hero, and his return is depicted as an unprecedented victory that will collaterally benefit the culture of Homeland Security. Soon after the events, Carrie begins an unapproved operation to control every step Brody makes and find out whether or not he is the man that turned to al-Qaeda. The tense relationship between Carrie and Brody drives the story forward, using extremely current issues such as political communication, surveillance, security, freedom and propaganda.

Complex storylines for dense characters

Carrie Mathison is depicted as a young, unstable and subversive officer. She is on her early thirties and unengaged, which turns her into a workaholic. The blurry, if not entirely non-existent, line between her personal and professional life becomes essential for a vibrating narrative structure. As the series develops, we learn that Carrie failed to predict the 9/11 attacks. Because of this, she becomes obsessed with the possibility that Brody might be a terrorist himself. Her mind is full of psychological demons, thus her past marks the delusional character of her present. As a result, she ignores recommendations and protocols, and conducts, at her own risk, unauthorized missions. Carrie's rebellious side may be understood as a result of the progressive bureaucratization of contemporary society: due to an excess of rules and protocols, some people tend to overlook legal regulations in order to achieve individual and group purposes. As the story develops, we also learn that Carrie suffers of a bipolar disorder. Her mental status—and the way she deals with it—becomes a key factor in the development of her personal and professional life. The disorder has made her a lonely person, and her loneliness will work against her—bringing her on the verge of suicide. These three characteristics—youth, rebellion and illness—add up for a very intense character that appeals to broad audiences.

In his turn, Nicholas Brody is an equally complex character. At the beginning of the series, the sole piece of information that the spectator learns about Brody is that he is a US Marine that was captured in 2003 by the troops of Abu Nazir (an al-Qaeda high-rank leader) and has now been rescued and returned home safe. He is soon marketed as a national hero and receives offers and praise from governmental officials. The story of Brody as a war prisoner is something that we slowly learn throughout the episodes, as well as how he turned to al-Qaeda and why. After reuniting with his family, Brody finds himself in the middle of thought-provoking situations. His wife Jessica has been maintaining a regular relationship with one of his best colleagues, Mike. Jessica will hide this information, but Brody will eventually find it out. His daughter Dana has turned into a beautiful teenager, with all the good and bad sides to that. She is very supportive of Nicholas because she knows about her mother's lover and feels sorry for her father. Nicholas's son Chris, who was very young when his father left for Iraq, is also a teenager now. He has grown well under Mike's considerable influence. Since Brody barely spends time with Chris, the boy will maintain a strong relationship with Mike. The convolution of these bonds will result in many uneasy circumstances all through the first season, where we see how a fragile Brody is almost unable to recover the sympathy for his family.

For the second year of the series, the family paradigm changes as they need to stay together (or appear to do so) when the Vice President of the

United States, William Walden—depicted as the one responsible for the war on terror—will engage in the presidential race confirming Brody as his potential running mate. Walden will be unaware that he is joining forces with his enemy until it is too late to reverse his fate. In this sense, Brody's past becomes essential to understanding everything that is going on in his mind: how he acts and why he does it. The method that the writers chose to acquaint us with Brody's past is through flashbacks, a recurrent element in contemporary storytelling (e.g. *How I Met Your Mother*, *Family Guy*, *Lost*) used to unveil, create and resolve certain plot acts that otherwise would remain unknown or unfinished (Kenny, 2004). These sequences also introduce a great number of guest characters that almost necessarily create more issues that they resolve (Smith, 2007), which is the case in *Homeland*. As the series develops, we learn that at some point of his captivity, Abu Nazir stopped torturing Brody and asked him to be his son, Issa's English tutor. The young boy will eventually be killed by a drone attack near his school, and Brody will swear to Nazir to avenge him by murdering the sole responsible of the attack, the Vice President William Walden. With the drone storyline, *Homeland*'s writers draw yet another parallelism with the most up-to-date reality, as drone attacks are currently one of the most discussed war topics (Ahmed, 2013; Benjamin, 2013).

Since their initial meeting, Brody and Carrie become obsessed with each other, entering a dangerous territory with unexpected consequences. Carrie trusts him half the time and distrusts him the other, eventually initiating a prohibited relationship with him. The forbidden love motif is actually recurrent in the literature of all époques: Oedipus, Romeo & Juliet, Madame Bovary, Lolita, and more recently, the love triangle between Edward, Jacob and Bella in the Twilight saga. In *Homeland*, the passionate bond between the protagonists becomes a key element in the structure of the series. While love is a conventional topic, *Homeland*'s writers provide the spectator with unpredictable plot twists and other narrative elements that make their love come out as utterly fresh. Interestingly enough, every time that Carrie and Nicholas attempt to set the bases of a possible relationship something happens and plans suddenly change. We will further explore plot twists and their attractiveness in this political thriller.

The contradiction that exists in Carrie—she loves the man, whom she suspects (and later knows) is a terrorist—is a theme present in every episode.

There is one episode in particular, the fourth of the second season, when Carrie arrests Nicholas in an unexpected ending. One minute before the ending credits, Carrie and Nicholas share a moment of truth at a hotel room. Brody says: "I've had a pretty good run so far"—in a clear attempt to intimidate Carrie and act as if he could continue his plans without the CIA knowing. Immediately after, Carrie follows with a demolishing sentence: "You're a disgrace to your nation, Sergeant Nicholas Brody. You're a traitor and a terrorist, and now it's time you pay for that". Brody is arrested immediately after their brief conversation. During the detention, Carrie's has a deeply emotional and convulsive look on her face. She knows that she did the right thing, but a part of her still refuses to admit that Brody is a terrorist. This fact is also common in modern narrations.

Brody's story has been compared to that of Ulysses in the Odyssey, and the thin line between heroes and terrorists (Cuadrado, 2013). We believe that another comparison may serve as well: Brody as the character V from *V for Vendetta*. After all, Brody's commitment is born from his determination to seek revenge for the death of a friend. Also, when stating his reasons for doing what he does, Brody mentions domestic terrorism as his country's main enemy, in accordance with V's views on current governments and societies. In this regard, one may notice how the most successful characters in contemporary television series, even if they are generally well-meaning, also exhibit small doses of bad behavior and sparks of insurgence— Gregory House in FOX's *House M.D.* is a good example of this. The imperfect depiction of humans, as opposed to the traditional flawless hero conception, is even edgier in cable series, e.g. Walter White in AMC's *Breaking Bad*. *Homeland*'s narrative is no stranger to this, as all the main characters must often act outside the law in order to accomplish their purposes.

A glance at various reviews of the show reveals that *Homeland*'s characters and narrative structures have aroused disputes among supporters and opponents. On one hand, some critics see the show as too left wing, and classify it as anti-American propaganda. On the other, the show is also perceived as right wing and imperialist propaganda. The reason behind these two completely different approaches is found in the storylines. *Homeland*'s plot is focused in the battle between the CIA and al-Qaeda. The scripts are written with a certain degree of ambiguity, showing the spectator both the victories and the defeats from each side, with terrible consequences for everyone involved. Hence the show can hardly be regarded as a patriotic one, or be classified in the left-right binomial. It simply exposes flawed characters in a flawed war. In this sense, it is not new that the media industry, particularly cinema and television, produces stories that raise moral concerns relying on ambivalence and without resolving them. In this type of productions, the audience will always have the last word (Dant, 2012). Interestingly enough, *Homeland* is reportedly Barack Obama's favorite show (Ahmed, 2013; Lee, 2013).

Overall, the main fictional characters of *Homeland* appear to be thoroughly developed. Quite deservingly, Clair Danes and Damian Lewis have received a good amount of critical recognition. For her portrayal of Carrie Mathison, Danes has been awarded the Primetime Emmy Award for Outstanding Lead Actress in a Drama Series, and twice with the Golden Globe Award for Best Actress in a Television Series Drama. She has also won the TCA Award for Individual Achievement in Drama, the Critics' Choice Television Award for Best Drama Actress, the Satellite Award for Best Actress in a Television Series Drama (also twice), and the Screen Actors Guild Award for Outstanding Performance by a Female Actor in a Drama Series. Lewis has also received great praising for his portrayal of Nicholas Brody. He has received the Primetime Emmy Award for Outstanding Lead Actor in a Drama Series, the Golden Globe Award for Best Actor in a Television Series Drama, and the Satellite Award for Best Actor in a Television Series Drama. Such a large collection of awards indicates the skill of Danes and Lewis performing as Carrie and Nicholas, and simultaneously recognizes the sophistication of their characters and the well-structured plots.

Narrative as seen on cable television

Most series in America are offered to the big-four networks: CBS, ABC, NBC, and FOX. Historically, these stations have had no competition in terms of ratings and production budget when compared to cable channels, so every producer in town wanted to work with them. More recently, however, high-budget TV movies and series, as well as new documentaries and reality shows, have challenged the previous assumption. Nowadays, it is common to find cable programs among the overall top rated television networks almost every day. This has created a new scenario where some producers sell their drafts directly to cable networks, so that they can have greater creative control over their stories, without the influence of executives and advertisers. *Homeland*, however, almost ended up in a big network. Alex Gansa, one of the show creators, admitted that the show was initially presented to national channels, but they rejected it. In the initial draft of the show that was presented to them, Carrie was a straight-laced CIA officer. However, when the show was picked up by Showtime, the creators felt a greater freedom to turn Carrie into the flawed character that we know of. While it is impossible to think what could have happened if Carrie had ended up as a prudish agent, it could be argued that her imperfect character has become the backbone to the series narrative structure. Cable networks and their shows are famous for depicting the dark side of their characters in an elegant manner: *Mad Men*, *Game of Thrones*, *Magic City*, *Breaking Bad* and *Sons of Anarchy*, among many others, serve as an example. Actually, it has been asserted that television owes most of its innovation to digitalized cable systems, whose subscribers have tripled to 30 million between 2000 and 2005 (Ashby, 2012).

Developing a cable show certainly guarantees producers more freedom in the series development. But more than that, it allows them to pursue more changeling and ambiguous storylines in which the line between good and evil is often blurred in favor of the audience's perception. This is precisely the case for *Homeland*. The spectator is shown two sides of the story: that of Carrie and the CIA, and that of Brody and al-Qaeda. The show creators said in an interview that they do not try to favor one side of the story, but rather ask the question and let the people come to a conclusion on their own. According to the main plot points in *Homeland*, the CIA can either be seen as the savior of the United States, who protects its people, or as a savage organization that uses drones to conduct selected killings with enormous collateral effects. Similarly, Brody can be seen as a traitor to his nation and his cultural roots, or as a loyal man who promises to revenge the death of a child and maintains his objective all through the events while remaining an American soldier. This ambivalent portrayal of war on terror would hardly ever make it to the air on a national television as their executives, advertisers, and other lobbyists would appear with a long list of issues regarding the ambiguous narration. The reason why such a storyline can exist at a cable network is that the external pressure on the producers and writers is far less.

Another one of the many possibilities in cable series is that of upending the usual television narrative structures, and *Homeland* does it very often. A plot twist can happen in a matter of seconds, drifting completely from the first minutes of the episode and ending the story in a way that was not expected at the beginning. Considering the massive amount of television (and cinema) that a single person watches on average every year, finding a series that still has surprising elements is like finding a treasure. The narrative structure of *Homeland* is unique in that it provides the spectator with many nerve-wracking scenes, where the tension is supported with flawless dialogue. The series also has a refined soundtrack driven by jazz music, which is Carrie's favorite. She listens to jazz whenever she feels sad and alone, which is quite often. The Dixieland music is also present in the opening sequence, which alternates artistic shots of the protagonists and real footage of political officials, and blends it all with a minute long jazz piece.

Jason Mittell (2004, 2012) has extensively studied various narratives in contemporary television genres. One of his many conclusions is that complexity is a key factor in current narrative structures, and we certainly agree with his view. Cuadrado (2013) goes further and divides the complexity of contemporary series in two directions: horizontal and vertical. Horizontally, complexity resides in the plot, the characters and their storylines. Vertically, the complexity is accumulated in different layers and refers to universal narrative structures and fictional spaces. We believe that Cuadrado's explanation suits *Homeland* the best. As we previously explained in this chapter, the plot twists in *Homeland* happen in almost every episode. The moral ambivalence of the characters and the ambiguity of the situations, as well as its moral and ethical repercussions, enhance the complexity in *Homeland*. In this sense, Richardson (2008) reminds us that narration is not just a matter of enjoyment, but it is also "deeply consequential" for our social and political lives. The 9/11 attacks, for instance, developed a strong aesthetic debate on morality and narrative imperatives (Banita, 2012)—we will get back to this point later.

With all its structural elements combined, *Homeland*'s narration flows as smooth as a bird's feather falling from the skies. In conclusion, we may assert that *Homeland*'s development and narrative structure is built in layers. Each episode peels a layer and as it does, the storylines add complexity: more characters are involved; the usage of flashbacks becomes a key factor; and the plot arcs interact to a greater degree. Compare it with the Earth's layers: the deeper you dig, the more complicated it becomes. In this regard, *Homeland* may be understood as a journey to the core of the United States values in contemporary times.

Homeland Security in Society and Media after 9/11

The term homeland means native land, and as such, is a perfect title for the plot that Gordon and Gansa created. In the series, the protagonists clash in their views on how their nation should face counter terrorism. It must be noted that, in everyday language, "homeland" is rarely used as a single word. In Europe, where nationalism has a greater history, the variants "motherland" and fatherland" are more widely used than "homeland" itself. In the United States, the word is often used in the phrase Homeland Security. The term gained popularity after the September 11th attacks. The United States then engaged in an unprecedented domestic and international fight against terror, mostly focused on preventing new attacks, and particularly targeting al-Qaeda. Following the attacks, the US Congress approved the Homeland Security Act in 2002, which later promulgated the United States Department of Homeland Security in 2003. As a consequence, the American politics drove the country through many counter terrorism strategies that affected both its domestic and international policy-making (Aldis, Herd, 2007).

All the decisions and actions taken under the Homeland Security umbrella are contained in what is known as the post-9/11 culture. On a sociological level, this affected the field international relations like no other event in history. Authors Tulloch and Blood (2012) assert that after 9/11, the Unites States "wrote off the rest of the world as a reliable partner". In a similar way, some authors criticize that the war on terror supported by the actions of George W. Bush, Colin Powell and Tony Blair, among others, has contributed to the "devastation in the name of freedom and democracy" (Brady, 2012). They have also been accused of transforming terrorism into "an instrument that reaffirms the state", while pushing an "idealized, highly rhetorical and ideological" national security discourse (Campos, 2007). This new geopolitical path had—and has—an enormous influence on media productions, which tend to reflect Homeland Security affairs as realistically as possible (Quay, 2010). As a consequence, it has been stated that the American media turned to uncritical and patriotic propaganda (Holloway, 2008). Speaking of visual media in particular, many American series have since 9/11 included in their plots storylines that deal directly and indirectly with national counterterrorism. These productions have revived the Cold War feeling but with different antagonists. The communist storylines decreased in favor of those related to Islamism. Birkenstein, Froula, Randell (2010) note that while the industry was at first reluctant to dramatize the events of 9/11, it ended up producing several films directly or indirectly related to it. For instance: *Bowling for Columbine, United 93, World Trade Center, Lions for Lambs, Body of Lies, The Hurt Locker,* and *Zero Dark Thirty*. Simultaneously, many television series also dealt with counter terrorism in the aftermath of 9/11: *CSI: NY, Law & Order, The West Wing, The Wire, The Unit, Strike Back, 24,* and *Homeland,* among others. Some authors have criticized the endeavors of the media industry to portray counter-terrorism as a simplistic "us against them" narrative (Schopp, Hill, 2009) and also for prompting the principle of liberalism in every plot (Keniston, Quinn, 2008). Author Timothy Melley (2012) has similarly described the post-9/11 series as a "geopolitical melodrama" being itself a legacy of the Cold War. While Melley admits that the post-9/11 series have inspired a major debate on issues like torture and cruelty, he also criticizes the "victimization" and "narcissism" of the US in the plots.

With similar arguments, author Richard Jackson noted that the television narrative regarding counter terrorism resembles that of the Administration when defending the Afghanistan and Iraq wars, presenting these countries as having oppressed populations, needing the help of a hero—the US military—to help them to be freed (Jackson, 2005). In this regard, author Walid El Hamamsy, critical of what he calls the "US imperial narratives", defines the series *24* as a "cultural therapy". Hamamsy notes that "although Bauer [the protagonist of 24] faced a wide range of domestic and international terrorists, the stories invariably turned on the personal psychologies of the American characters, thus reinforcing the clash of civilizations" (Hamamsy, 2013: 192). Similarly, author Akbar Ahmed (2013) has criticized the tendency of the war on terror to put a lot of various religious conceptions into a single sack, therefore affecting the public opinion views of Islam. He asserts that the war on terror. As portrayed by the media makes the mistake of imposing cultural values on situations that are driven by a very different context. While the storylines of some of the aforementioned productions may have actually fallen on the side of America, we believe that *Homeland* deserves recognition for allowing its audience to have a critical approach to the war on terror and doing this in a very ambitious and clear way like no other production has done before.

One of the most interesting aspects of the media imaginary in the post-9/11 era is that Russia is not an enemy anymore. While a few Russian officers depicted as the bad guys still have a prominence in some recent productions (e.g. 8th season of FOX's show *24*), their conception as *eternal* enemies seems to be buried. In order to depict Cold War arguments, the productions have to travel back in time. A good example of this can be found in the FX series *The Americans* (2013). The show is based in the Cold War period, in the early 1980s. The series follows the undercover life of two Soviet KGB officers who pose as a 20th century traditional American married couple in the suburbs of Washington D.C. in a long-term mission to spy on the United States. The show has also been compared to *Homeland* for its plot-twist and the involvement of governmental characters. Nowadays and in real life, the American and Russian governments have actually been collaborating for a long time—in spite of their different socio-political views, which remain alive. For instance, in July 2013 Russia agreed to grant asylum to Edward Snowden, a former CIA technician who unveiled massive amounts of information on US surveillance programs. While Russia will not extradite him to the United States (as demanded by the White House), Snowden had to agree to stop releasing information that could damage the US as a condition imposed by Russian officials. After his reveal, Snowden claimed to have released the secret information because he was an American patriot, and as such he considered his actions crucial for the preservation of the principles of freedom. The thin line between being a hero and being a traitor is something that is usually decided quickly by the prevailing law. In this sense, many officials within the United States, as well as a part of the American public, have already considered Snowden a traitor. Nevertheless, Snowden has also received the praise of many American and international individuals, even at a political level, claiming that his actions may be promoting a better, more efficient inner democracy in his nation and hopefully worldwide. One thing is true: Snowden's actions have prompted a revived interest in the threat of surveillance as hasn't been seen since

George Orwell published his opera magna *1984*. The book became an instantly scholarly favorite and was largely studied in the second half of the 20th century. Now, thanks to Snowden, *1984* is experiencing renewed interest and has even appeared in the 2013 bestseller chart on Amazon. As for Snowden's fate, only time will tell.

Final notes

Homeland depicts the evolution of the United States imaginary after 9/11. The war on terrorism that began as a patriotic response to radical and extremist terrorists has now turned into a crude examination of homeland security policies. The show created by Howard Gordon and Alex Gansa challenges the traditional genres and narrative structures in television. The storylines evolve into a multi-genre space, were more complex stories can be carried on while exploring various issues at a time. For instance, a current political thriller does not only feature issues in the realm of politics, but has a transversal approach involving communications, sociology, psychology, economy, and other disciplines. The multiple layers of the flawed characters are also a key factor in *Homeland*'s narrative. They do not only add spice to the story, but also demand the maximum involvement of the audience. In fact, it is quite difficult to find successful straight-laced characters anymore, at least as protagonists, probably because humans are certainly not flawless. Both the main leads of the Showtime series, Carrie and Brody, act outside the law in order to meet their objectives, alongside the many consequences thereof. Without their rebellion and determination, the show would be meaningless. The insightful complexity of the characters and the sophistication of the storylines make *Homeland* a one-of-a-kind show. In a more sociological respect, it must be noted that the post-9/11 shows created the collective thought that war on terror was an urgent need, and that there was no alternative (Croft, 2006). Furthermore, it has been noticed that while committing to liberty and democracy, the American government might be morphing into an image of its antagonists (Tanguay, 2013). Similarly, it has also been suggested that the counter-terrorism discourse and language, and what derives from it, may make society end up worse off than when it started (Jackson, 2005). In this regard, we believe that the surveillance programs initiated by many worldwide governments after the 9/11 attacks are based on the inefficient assumption that everyone is equally suspicious, a situation that must be redirected in order to preserve the principles of liberty and freedom. It is our concern that the critiques to the post-9/11 culture previously reflected in this text come to prove that the debate on Homeland Security is a living discipline with many approaches, and that there is room for further progress and development.

References

Ahmed, A. S. (2013). *The thistle and the drone how America's War on Terror became a global war on tribal Islam*. Washington, D.C.: Brookings Institution.

Aldis, A., & Herd, G. P. (2007). *The ideological war on terror worldwide strategies for counter-terrorism*. London: Routledge.

Amoore, L. and M. de Goede (Eds.) (2008) "Introduction: Governing by Risk in the War on Terror", in *Risk and the War on Terror*, pp. 5–19. London: Routledge.

Anderson, T. (2008). *"24, Lost, and Six Feet Under: Post-traumatic television in the post-9/11 era"*. Denton, Texas. UNT Digital Library. http://digital.library.unt.edu/ar k:/67531/metadc6137/. Accessed July 13, 2013.

Ashby, L. (2012). *With amusement for all: a history of American popular culture since 1830*. Lexington, KY: The University Press of Kentucky.

Banita, G. (2012). *Plotting justice: narrative ethics and literary culture after 9/11*. Lincoln: University of Nebraska Press.

Benjamin, M. (2013). *Drone warfare*. London: Verso.

Birkenstein, J., Froula, A., & Randell, K. (2010). *Reframing 9/11 film, popular culture and the "war on terror"*. New York: Continuum.

Brady, S. (2012). *Performance, politics, and the war on terror: "whatever it takes"*. Houndmills, Basingstoke, Hampshire: Palgrave Macmillan.

Campos, J. H. (2007). *The state and terrorism national security and the mobilization of power*. Aldershot, Hants, England: Ashgate.

Croft, S. (2006). *Culture, crisis and America's War on Terror*. Cambridge: Cambridge University Press.

Cuadrado Alvarado, A. (2013). "Ulises y el héroe terrorista: mito y modernidad en la serie *Homeland*". In *Área Abierta*, 34(1), 2013, pp. 27–42.

Dant, T. (2012). *Television and the moral imaginary: society through the small screen*. Houndmills, Basingstoke, Hampshire: Palgrave Macmillan.

Dant, T. (2012). *Television and the moral imaginary: society through the small screen*. Houndmills, Basingstoke, Hampshire: Palgrave Macmillan.

Grandío, M. (2011). "Riesgo y trauma en la ficción televisiva estadounidense post 11-S: el caso de Heroes". In *ZER*, 16–31, 2011, pp. 51–67.

Hamamsy, W. (2013). *Popular culture in the Middle East and North Africa: a postcolonial outlook*. New York: Routledge, Taylor & Francis Group.

Holloway, D. (2008). *Cultures of the war on terror. Empire, ideology and the remaking of 9/11*. Montreal: McGill-Queen's University Press.

Jackson, R. (2005). *Writing the war on terrorism: language, politics and counter-terrorism*. Manchester: Manchester University Press.

Keniston, A., & Quinn, J. F. (2008). *Literature after 9/11*. New York: Routledge.

Kenny, R. F. (2004). *Teaching TV production in a digital world*. Westport: Libraries Unlimited.

Lee, N. (2013). *Counterterrorism and cybersecurity total information awareness*. New York: Springer.

Melley, T. (2012). *The covert sphere: secrecy, fiction, and the national security state*. Ithaca: Cornell University Press.

Mittell, J. (2004). *Genre and television: from cop shows to cartoons in American culture*. New York: Routledge.

Mittell, J. (2010). *Television and American culture*. New York: Oxford University Press.

Quay, S. E. (2010). *September 11 in popular culture: a guide*. Santa Barbara: Greenwood.

Richardson, B. (2008). *Narrative beginnings theories and practices*. Lincoln: University of Nebraska Press.

Schopp, A., & Hill, M. B. (2009). *The war on terror and American popular culture: September 11 and beyond*. Madison, NJ: Fairleigh Dickinson University Press.

Smith, G. M. (2007). *Beautiful TV*. Austin: University of Texas Press.

Tanguay, L. (2013). *Hijacking history: American culture and the war on terror*. Montreal: McGill-Queen's University Press.

Tulloch, J., & Blood, R. W. (2012). *Icons of war and terror: media images in an age of international risk*. New York: Routledge.

Understanding Health
in Grey's Anatomy Television Series

Bianca Mitu

Introduction

Due to the globalization phenomenon people have an open access to information. As well as many other concepts used in the humanities and social sciences, *globalization* is a term that has been discussed in various ways. As Klein (2002) states, globalization is a term used to explain the phenomenon of a world becoming interconnected. Globalization became one of the key debates of the 1990s, producing a huge body of criticism within, and between, the fields of sociology, economics, international relations, communications theory or cultural studies.

When it comes to the television's effects on people, there are several theories about television use and its effects, both positive and negative, each of which stem from two equally opposing hypotheses. The first hypothesis, referred to as the cultivation theory, operates on the premise that it is the quantity of television programs that people consume that has the most significant influence on people's beliefs and behaviours irrespective of the specifics of content.

The cultivation theory implies a commonality in messages across the programming spectrum that along with an increased exposure to TV programs is able to reinforce these messages, good or bad and therefore is able to falsely cultivate people's beliefs and behavioural norms. An example of the cultivation theory would be the widespread goodies versus baddies scenario that exists in many guises throughout television fictional narratives, fostering across many generations the expectation that the good and the truth will always win and prosper and the bad will always be defeated. However, complications usually arise when the good and bad characters are less simply defined and thus the focus shifts onto how the characters from both sides, good or bad, solve their problems and deal with the consequences of their actions. If the central characters across a number of television programs are seen to express inappropriate beliefs and use inappropriate behavior to solve their problems or are seen to go unpunished for various acts of violence, the cultivation theorists argue that people will interpret this behavior as normal and adjust the concepts of reality accordingly (Signorielli, Morgan, 1990).

The second hypothesis is conversely grounded by the non-analogous nature of television and argues that behavioural effects are cultivated by the specifics of the chosen content consumed by the people. This content-based hypothesis forms the basis for the majority of effects studies, although some researchers have attempted a combination of both theories. However despite the vast quantity of extensive studies regarding television effects undertaken by researchers utilizing varied research designs, a clear conclusion has yet to be achieved. Moreover, the research findings can be gathered into three main areas:

- Studies that certify that there is no discernible association between people's behaviour and media consumption.
- Studies that assert that there is a negative conjunction between the two and therefore people become more aggressive as a result of watching television.
- Studies that certify that there is a positive conjunction between the two and consequently people are not influenced by watching television.

Starting from these considerations the present study aims to answer to the following questions: Are television series influencing people's understandings of health? What does it mean to be healthy in the medical television series? The article will also provide an evidence of the most important Romanian medical magazines, television shows and television series and will investigate Romanian people's perception of health in Grey's Anatomy television series.

Communicating Health

The problem of finding a definition for the concept of communication created over time many controversies among researchers. In the recent decades this concept has become the object of many scientific disciplines. Taking into consideration that the subject of this article is related to communication we think it is necessary to clarify, in short, the concept of communication and also highlight the conjunction between communication and health.

The concept of "communication" seems very affordable, but only when it comes to describing it we begin to realize its versatility and ambiguity. Therefore, we will not risk a general definition, but we will attempt a description, an approach to the concept from different perspectives. Any communication process has some characteristic structural elements:
- the existence of at least two partners;
- the ability of the partners to deliver and receive signals in a specific code;
- the existence of a channel for the transmission of the message. The communication process rises as a result of the relationship of interdependence which exists between all these structural elements.

When it comes to health communication the interdependence of these basic structural elements is required and considered essential for the effectiveness of the communication process. Trying to approach the relation between communication and health it is easy to assume that communication bears a great importance on people's health because it can:

"- increase knowledge and awareness of a health issue, problem, or solution
- influence perceptions, beliefs, attitudes, and social norms
- prompt action
- demonstrate or illustrate skills
- show the benefit of behavior change
- increase demand for health services
- reinforce knowledge, attitudes, and behaviors
- refute myths and misconceptions
- help coalesce organizational relationships
- advocate for a health issue or a population group"

(Thomas, 2005: 4)

Trying to find a definition for health communication, Thomas (2005) states that "health communication encompasses the study and use of communication strategies to inform and influence individual and community decisions the enhance health. It links the domains of communication and health. Health communication encompasses the study and use of communication strategies to inform and influence individual and community knowledge, attitudes and practices with regard to health and healthcare. The field represents the interface between communication and health and is increasingly recognized as a necessary element for improving both personal and public health. Health communication can contribute to all aspects of disease prevention and health promotion (2005: 1–2). Furthermore in his study Thomas concludes that health communication is a process able to take place at different levels of impact such as: the individual, the social network, the organization, the community, the society as a whole. Therefore he states that "if the process of communication is effective it can:

- "improve the health outcomes of acute and chronic conditions
- reduce the impact of racial, ethnic, disease-specific and socioeconomic factors in care
- improve the effectiveness of prevention and health promotion"

(Thomas, 2005: 4)

Health and the Media

Romanian media has known a constant development especially after the end of the Communist Regime in 1989. After 24 years of democracy Romania has more than 300 television programs. Analyzing the Romanian media landscape we have tried to realize a top of the best publications dedicated to health. The publications were classified taking into consideration the number of views as shown by the following table.

Table 1: Classification of the Romanian Health Magazines

No.	Romanian Health Magazines	Number of views
1.	Taifasuri	63007
2.	Slab sau Gras	46338
3.	Sana	41282
4.	Tonica	33486
5.	Farmacia Ta	31806
6.	Psihologia Azi	22590
7.	eMedic.ro	15766
8.	Universul Terapiilor	15536
9.	Magazin Terapeutic	13639
10.	Infoterapii	12936
11.	Revista Romana de Reumatologie	11391
12.	Psihiatru.ro	11157
13.	Viata Medicala Romanesca	11101
14.	Info Medica	10200
15.	Chirurgia	9794
16.	Stetoscop	9353
17.	British Medical Jurnal	9245
18.	Viata Stomatologica	8375
19.	Medic4All	8316
20.	Bioetica	8274
21.	Pharmakon	6424

Source: www.reviste.ro

Besides more than 21 publications dedicated to health and healthcare and the importance of being healthy, Romania has more than 14 medical television shows. The most popular are to be revealed by the following table.

Table 2: Health and Lifestyle Romanian Television Shows

No.	Tv Show	Tv Channel
1.	Ce se întâmplă doctore?	ProTv
2.	Sport, dietă și o vedetă	Prima tv
3.	Ai grijă de tine!	Realitatea TV
4.	Trăiește sănătos!	Antena 2
5.	Sănătatea în bucate	Digi 24
6.	Stil de viață	Publika TV
7.	Dreptul la sănătate	Focus TV
8.	Noi să fim sănătoși	Giga TV
9.	Tinerețe fără bătrânețe	Digi 24
10.	ABC-ul sănătății	Speranta TV
11.	Sănătatea întâi de toate	NeptunTV
12.	Doctor Oz	EuforiaTV
13	Mișcare, sănătate și frumusețe	TvH2.0
14.	Sănătatea ta	Sănătatea TV

Besides all these health television shows, Romania has one online radio station, Sanatatea FM and one online medical television, Sanatatea TV—sanatateatv.ro. Taking into consideration the empirical evidences we can easily notice that health has become a constant preoccupation for the Romanian media. Either we think of health myths, health advices or lifestyle, health is considered an important and attractive issue.

Health and TV Series

Lately besides medical magazines and medical television shows, Romanian people also choose to watch medical television series. This study focuses on the most viewed medical TV series and investigates Romanian people's perception of health in *Grey's Anatomy* television series. In order to investigate all these different aspects, a quantitative audience research was conducted, using a structured questionnaire. The survey was conducted in January 2014 and used a sample of 550 regular TV series viewers of all ages, Romanian people who watch medical TV series. Only 450 responses were valid for the present study, representing 41% men and 59% women.

According to the results of the survey, from all the medical television series broadcasted by the Romanian televisions, Romanian people choose *Grey's Anatomy* TV series (73%), *House M.D.* (18%) and *Private Practice* (8%).

Figure 1: Most viewed medical TV series

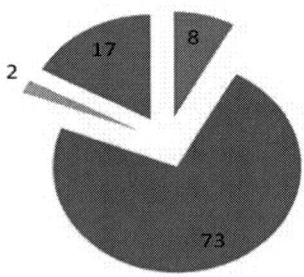

The main reasons for watching *Grey's Anatomy* are the dynamics of the interpersonal relationships of the main characters (64%), gathering information about health problems (21%) and curiosity (15%).

Figure 2: Reasons for watching Grey's Anatomy

- Interpersonal relationships
- Gathering information about health problems
- Curiosity

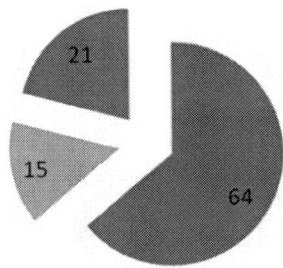

Although people consider themselves fans of *Grey's Anatomy* TV series, the respondents cannot remember healthcare issues or cures presented by this show. They can only remember different situation that the characters have to deal with.

Figure 3: Do you remember a particular healthcare issue or health cure from the Grey's Anatomy television series?

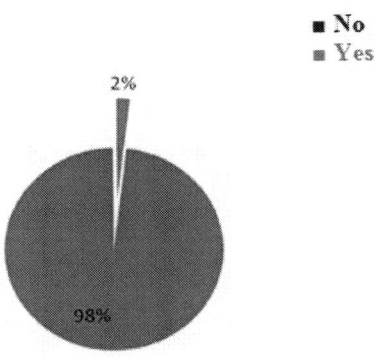

When it comes to the level of trust in the medical advices from Grey's Anatomy, the respondents declare that they do not trust the medical advices from this television series because they believe that the health information available to the public is incomplete, superficial or unreal.

Figure 4: Level of trust in the medical advices seen in Grey's Anatomy television series

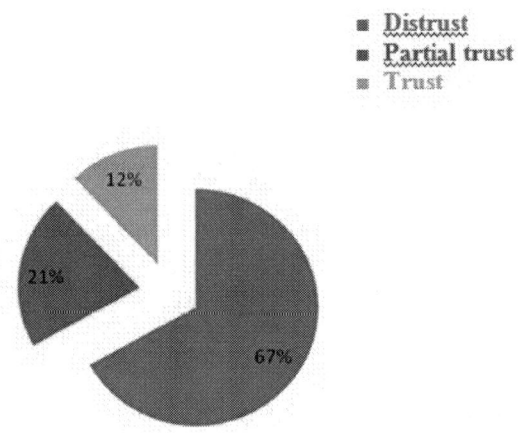

Furthermore, the results show that the respondents think that after watching *Grey's Anatomy* television series they became aware of the fact that eating the right food, physical fitness, strength and happiness are the meanings of a good health (Figure 5).

Figure 5: Romanian People Understandings of Health in Grey's Anatomy

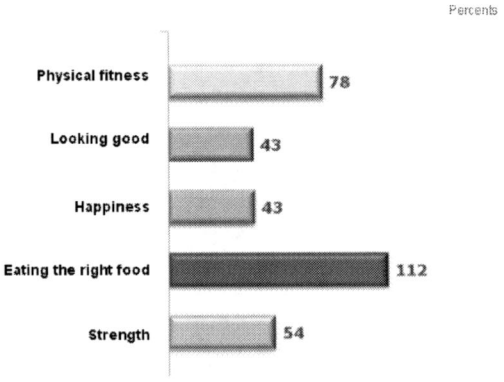

Another important aspect of the survey was to find out what means to be healthy. The respondents believe that to be healthy means having a good diet (95%) or being active and practice sports (87%) as they have seen in *Grey's Anatomy* television series. Also, feeling strong or being fit are arguments for one person's good health.

Figure 6: What does it mean to be healthy for the Romanian people?

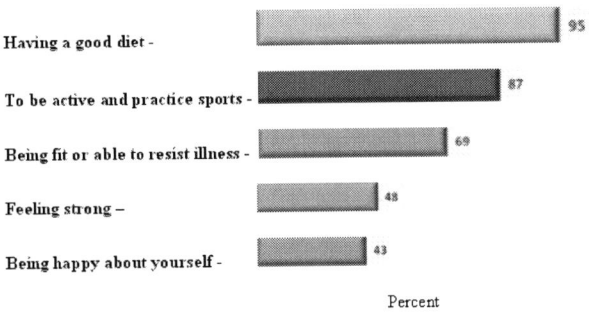

The results show that besides medical television shows, the medical television series also play an important part in shaping people's beliefs and understandings about health. The respondents see television as a positive influence because it raises awareness of some important health issues such as diet and exercise or eating healthy food. This opinion comes in contrast with some scholars that state that the media and especially new media technologies have encouraged an increase in sedentary activities and unhealthy eating (Smith, Green, 2005).

Conclusions

The media is extremely powerful in promoting health beliefs and in creating role models for the contemporary people. It is clear that the media can play a significant role in shaping people understandings of health, as well as in shaping people's health beliefs or food practices, especially through television programs dedicated to health or through advertising. The dominance of television over all other media is rationalized by the popularity and prevalence of the medium. The television should accomplish the role of educating the public. As Lang (1998) also suggested, marketing and branding can change health beliefs or food culture over a relatively short period and most of the people are particularly influenced by these strategies. This article realized an inventory of the main Romanian medical magazines, television shows and television series and also focused on the Romanian people's understandings of health in the medical television series. The article underlined the media effects upon people's health beliefs and behaviours. After a brief overlook of these issues we must agree with Brashers and Babrow when they state that "communication in health and illness constitutes the most vital of human experiences. No other human phenomenon is more elemental than health and illness, none connects us more viscerally with our aspirations, or confronts us more palpably with our limitations (1996: 243).

References

Blaxter, M., Paterson, E. (1982). *Mothers and Daughters: A Three-generational Study of Health Attitudes and Behaviour*, London: Heinemann.

Brashers, D. E., Babrow, A. S. (1996). 'Theorizing health communication', *Communication Studies*, 47, 243–251.

Calnan, M. (1987). *Health and Illness: The Lay Perspective*, London: Tavistock Publications.

Curtis, S. (2004). *Health and Inequality: Geographical Perspectives*, London: Sage.

Curtis, S., Taket, A. (1996). *Health and Societies: Changing Perspectives*, London: Arnold.

Eldridge, J., Murcott, A. (2000). 'Adolescents' dietary habits and attitudes: unpacking the 'problem of (parental) influence', *Health*, 4 (1), 25–49.

Jacobs, J. (2003). *Body Trauma TV,* London: British Film Institute.

Jones, L. (1994). *The Social Context of Health and Health Work*, Basingstoke: Palgrave.

Jones, L. (2000). What is health?. In Katz, J., Peberdy, A., Douglas, J. (eds.), *Promoting Health: Knowledge and Practice*, Basingstoke: Palgrave.

Lang, T. (1998). The new globalization, food and health: is public health receiving its due emphasis? *Journal of Epidemiology and Community Health*, 52 (9), 538–39.

Lloyd, C., Shakespeare, P. (2000). 'The Rise and Dominance of Biomedicine', in Team, K. C. (ed.), *K203 Block 1: Visions and Values in Health Work,* Milton Keynes: The Open University.

Rideout, V. (2008). *Television as a Health Educator: A Case Study of Grey's Anatomy, A Kraiser Family Foundation Report*, California: Henry J. Kaiser Family Foundation.

Signorielli, N., Morgan, M. (eds.). (1990). *Cultivation analysis: New Directions in media effects research*, Newbury Park, CA: Sage.

Smith, A., Green, K. (2005). 'The Place of Sport and Physical Activity in Young People's Lives and its Implications for Health: Some Sociological Comments', *Journal of Youth Studies*, 8 (2), 241–53.

Thomas, R.K. (2005). *Health Communication*, New York: Springer.

Williams, R. (1983). 'Concepts of Health: An Analysis of Lay Logic', *Sociology*, 17 (2), 185–205.

Fiction Television in Brazil: New Perspectives

Lilian Fontes Moreira

In order to offer an overview of the current situation of Brazilian television fiction within the international scenario, the present paper presents a study on the changes that have occurred in the production of television fiction. This has occurred due to the increased pay TV market in Brazil and its interference in the rates of audience, in the programming of broadcasters and in the television fiction products.

In September 2011, new parameters of the 12.485 Brazilian law—called the Law of pay TV—were sanctioned by President DilmaRousseff, forcing cable channels to introduce Brazilian programs, in its programming.

In the case of Brazilianfictional narratives, the soap opera, which has become the public's most accepted genre in various social strata, has undergone a transformation process due to competition presented by the fictional products of cable TV channels, where series prevail, especially the U.S production. Therefore, I will draw a parallel between soap operas and series to assist in the analysis of the differences and approaches of the two genres. As object of study, I present Divã, a series produced by Globo TV in 2011, in which I use basic methodology parameters that can be applied in other fictional television productions.

Introduction

In contemporary times, the television has been presented as an effective vehicle to convey cultural expressions of a country.Among the television programs, one can say that the fictional narratives, through their stories, their dialogues, scenarios and characters, offera portray of the authentic mode of expression of certain population. Every work of fiction—literary narrative, film, theater, television narrative—appropriates elements of reality in the construction of their fictional universes, acting as a mediator between the subject and the existential world. As Umberto Eco says, "the fictional assertions are true within the framework of a possible world of a particular history" (Eco, 1994, p. 94).

In the case of the Brazilian open TV, it is observed that the fictional production, specifically the serial narratives (soap operas, series, miniseries) occupies a large space in the schedule of the broadcasters. However, this situation has been changing due to the expansion of cable TV.

The cable TV started in Brazil, as in the U.S in 1958. Nevertheless, due to communication and economics policies that were forged by the Brazilian executive and legislative forces,its system was implemented only in 1989. In 1991, great media groups began in this field, but it was theGloboOrganization that made the largest volume of investments, creating GLOBO SAT.Today Globo Sat is the largest pay TV in Latin America and the market leader in Brazil, with 37 channels of which 26 channels are in SD 10 + HD channels, and 1 international channel.

The pay TV market in Brazil has grown considerably. In 2000, it recorded 3.4 million subscribers. However, because of the economic stability that Brazil has been experiencing since 2002, classes C and D now have access to pay TV, which changed significantly this setting. In 2007, about five million Brazilians had access to cable TV. In 2011, that number grew to 11 million. Dueto the new pay TV law enacted in 2011, it is expected that by 2015 this number will triple, reaching 35 million.

In September 2011, newparameters of the 12.485 Brazilian law—called the Law of pay TV—were approved,increasing the government investments in the area and forcing cable channels to insert in their broadcasting a definite number ofBrazilian programs. The law would come to boost the market, to stimulate sponsorship, helping independent groups to create products with higher quality, which would portray the rich cultural and geographicdiversity in the country.

Increased access to pay TV, which enhanced the choice of the viewer, would cause changes in thestructures of the companies of broadcast TV. The research whose object of study was the time range between 18 hours and midnight, considered the most disputed broadcast TV in terms of audience, presented by NWP (National Panel Television) show that in 2001 there were 59% of TVs connected. However, in 2010 this number dropped to 56%, registering a decline of 3%, where each point equals 191,000 homes. Interestingly, the same indices PNT show that in the decade there was an increase in the number of connected TVs: 40% in 2001 to 42% in 2010. This reinforces the interference of the audience of cable TV.

This fact particularly interests us since we observed that there was a change in Brazilian soap operas, which now makes attempts to experiment new formats and languages to capture the lost audience. The reasons are varied and embraced by the competition between the open TV channels (due to an enhancement of its programming in recent years), and the new habits cultivated by members of the audience, such as internet access in various mobile devices, and access to payTV.

In the case of television, the audience research is ameter factor point between production and audience reception. The responses of the audience to media messages entail locating the viewer within broader social and cultural contexts. The concept of 'interpretive communities' originated in literary studies, which considers the role of receivers in mass communication should be explained referring to their social and cultural repertoires, in the case of television reception proves to be useful to realize that members of different social classes are classified into different 'systems of meaning', as stated by the theory presented in the book Frank Park David Morley, Television, Audiences y cultural studios (Morley. 1996). The notion of interpretive communities would complement that of socioeconomiccategories using the word interpretative just to explain that the audience, in addition to demographic entities, refer to shared cultural formations and, therefore, share common meanings and ideologies that structure the reception. From this point of view, the content of television production would be subjugated to the interpretation of the audience, being intentionally molded by producers as a strategy to reach the audience.

The receptors, in turn, are designed as producers of meaning that reinterpret and rework the messages of the media, according to characteristics such as age, gender, ethnicity, social group, character and values, thus granting that the behavioral studies would focus more on the individual receptor. The extensive layer of program options transmitted will cause the viewer the need to make choices. We can detect that the selection of the programming is done from the references, desires and needs that punctuate the experience of the individual much more than the needs of the television companies.The interaction of the subject with the referent television, the pleasurable relationship established with the product indicator will be displayed to select television programming.

This parameter points to the issueof "marketing strategies" suggested by Martín-Barbero. The term "product" refers to TV "merchandise", belonging to sphere of values within the sphere of values, use and exchange values. In modern industrial society, the merchandise was described by the classical categories of economy and historical materialism as a product made in the factory. In the transition to a post-industrial and post-modern society, under the interference of new information technologies, communication becomes the central element in the establishment of new relations of production. The temporal sequence production / market / consumer ceases, creating a network of constant feedback between the subject producer-consumer. The manufacture of the object is directly subjugated to the values, habits, tastes, and to the lifestyle of the consumer and its success is subject to the ability to capture the consumer signals. What is produced not only is material goods, but social relations that manipulate increasingly symbols and images.

Thus, the media no longer articulates with a pre-defined ideology, but its strength lies in the ability of persuasion and seduction, incorporating any demands that were not in his speech, working as an instance to organize everyday life and the social imaginary. In the "new capitalism" the audience research for assembling profiles of viewers no longer point to the ratings of social classes but to the mechanisms of individuation, expressions of wishes and interests generated by the technology available in the areas of Information Technology and Telecommunication, integrated with new marketing techniques within the concept adopted since the 1980s called "relationship marketing", which refers to the embodiment of every customer. Relationship marketing, personalized service, market individualism, customization are terms that follow the contemporary trend.

The social networks of the internet, online tools through which users share opinions, ideas, experiences, tastes, habits, friends forming individual profiles of common interest groups have been targeted marketing and advertising.

The structure created by the pay TV would specificallyanswer a customized public and its singularities, offering a range of channels with varied options. There are channels for those who like to watch movies only, for those who prefer other sports, scientific documentaries, cartoons, 24-hour journalism, and so on.

The entry of cable TV in Brazil caused a change in the model of thetelevision business. "It is a service that entered the Brazilian milieu seeking to meet a market segment unattended by broadcast television and also acting to generate new consumption habits." (GoulartRibeiro, Sacramento, Roxo. 2010, p. 227).
As expounded in the 1990s, LuizGleiser, executive area cable TV:

> There has been a very rapid and violent globalization and the distribution of television programming, whose result will be what might be called the end of the national ghettos. Thus, as has happened with the Brazilian national cinema and music, going out of the ghetto in which we live in terms of television. The explosion is inevitable there is no way to prevent it. There is no way to look at the monster and say "you will not get in Brazil." (p. 231).

The progressive migration of an audience of high socioeconomic extract for payTV led to a drop in TV audience.

Considering the significant market growth of pay TV in Brazil, we are witnessing at the moment a transformation in the provision of television products. In the case of fictional narratives, the Brazilian soap operadominates and has become the genre more accepted by the public in various social strata. However, this format has been suffering competition from series presented by pay TV channels, predominantly the U.S. productions.

In the United States, from the 80s, there was a boom in the production of series directed to the public-TV. Television networks, such as Universal Channel, AXN, HBO, Fox, Warner and Sony offer a huge range of options ranging from realistic drama to sitcoms, criminal action, supernatural approach serving a diverse audience, and following the different age groups. There are series that achieved an audience of over 10 million viewers, as was the case of Friends (1996), Sex and the City (1998), The Sopranos (1999 HBO production), Lost (2004), House (2004), Heroes (2006), The Walking Dead (2012)Breaking Bad (2013).

Believing in this niche market, the production of series in the U.S. has become more sophisticated, winning new ranges of audience to the point of calling the attention of scholars in the field of communication.

Considered as a popular fun television, the American series acquired status of work of art. They have deep characters, challenge procedures, and address social issues. The majority of the intellectual public approves these series. However, they are nothing more than a strategy to reach a new market.

In turn, the audience is now seen as "intellectual public ".

"Hollywood is no longer the source of creative vigor of American entertainment. Intelligent life is now on TV," as mentioned in the article presented in Veja magazine, December 15, 2010, signed by Marcelo Martheand Isabela Boscov.

No wonder that filmmakers of works of wide recognition came to recognize the importance of the television market, freeing it from the stigma of "mass culture," and considering it as a means to reach a wider audience than the film disseminating their work, as is the case of the series Boardwalk Empire (HBO) by Martin Scorcese, and Terra Nova (Fox) and Falling Skies (FXUK), both by Steven Spielberg.

Bernardo Bertolucci's, the Italian director, in a statement published in Veja magazine, Editora Abril, on 1/06/2013, said that: "American movies that I like now are not Hollywood, but the television series as Mad Men, Breaking Bad and The Americans."

In the case of productions made in Brazil, it turns out that since 2005 there has been greater interest in investing in fiction television narratives in the format series/serials. As an example one can refer to case of HBO (Home Box Office), an American channel cable TV, which hired Brazilian products, such as the serials Mandrake, Alice, and Children's Carnival. Since then, the cable channels GNT, Multishow Brazil Channel, and Fox began to explore this segment. In 2009, the Brazilian Ministry of Culture (MINC) sponsoredeight projects included in the first stage of the selection FICTV / More Culture—Announcement of Selection of Projects of Development and Production of Serial TV drama to be shown in the channel TV Brazil. As for Globo TV, the largest open TV station in Brazil, one saw that from the year 2009 on, there was more interest in producing series as an attempt to find new languages that are in accordance with the expectations of the XXI century society.

In 2009, 41 television fiction programs wereproduced,being 31 by Brazilian TV Globo. Of the 31 productions, 15 were series, which shows that a new panorama is in activity, demonstrating the willingness to try new formats and new contents to test the public acceptance.

In 2009, a marked increase of formats was also witnessed. Short stories begin to be told, approaching the Brazilian standard model to those thatpredominate in European countries and in the United States, the sitcom format.(Vassalo Lopes, Obitel 2010. p. 143).

Differences and similarities between soap operas and series format

With a specific structure, the contents of soap operas are built with plotof easy acceptance by the public, presenting dramas that permeate the daily lives of the viewers, in an exercise that is intended to prompt identification, rather than the questioning by the introduction of new values. On average, the plot of the soap opera is formed by the central conflicts and side disputes, with various groups of characters and places to be unwound over an average of 160 chapters presented daily. The plot follows a linear narrative structure, in which each chapter is a variation of at least two stops for the entry of commercial or calls from other programs of the network itself.

The end of each chapter presents a thriller that will "tie" the viewer, arousing his curiosity to be present the next day on the same channel, at the same time. Lasting about eight months, only in the last chapter the solutions for all disputes submitted during that timeare presented. It is common, when the end of the drama is near, the outcome of the conflict is resolved according to audience measurement.

Being a product that has the responsibility to meet the needs of a broad and diverse audience, the content tends to gather standardized collective dramas. As Maria Rita Kehl states, "is the image (from television, advertising and journalism) which is the mass moment of reception, because, to achieve the crowds in their diversity and complexity, it is necessaryto put the differences aside."(Kehl, 2005, p.236)

Unlike soap operas, whose narrative construction is nourished by various thematic elements within the melodramatic line, the series follows a different path by proposing specific topics to a particular target audience. The series have short duration, ranging from 8 to 12 episodes for each season presented weekly. The line of narrative construction is based on a single thematic element in order to discuss contemporary issues. The audience of the TV series is tuned to the appeals of contemporary will prefer provocative and unique contents.

Therefore, we may emphasize the following distinctions regarding the analysis of the contents:

Table 1 - Differences between Soap Operas and TV Series

SOAP OPERAS	SERIES
Wide audience, diverse, en masse	Public segmented
Standardizedcontent	Differentiated content
Collective dramas	Individual dramas
Issues of common sense	Themed questions
Identity homogenization	Identity customization

Along with the proliferation of the series format, there is a change in the narrative of the soap operas. What once was based on a central plot and storylines that would go all the chapters in the productions offered by Globo TV since 2008, though we observe he creation of mini-plots within the main plot, with a beginning, middle and end, lasting one week.
In the view of the journalist Arthur Xexéo:

> Brazilian soap operas increasingly approach the format of the American TV series. There is no longer a central plot that tries to hold the viewer from the first to the last chapter. Nowadays there is a group of characters and situations experienced sometimes by one, sometimes by another character. The author does not focus more on the protagonist. Each subplot is in the air for about a week. If the chapters of a week were edited in a product of an hour or an hour and a half, the result would not be very different from an episode of "Brothers & sisters" or "Deadwood." (Xexéo, 2011).

During the years 2009/2010/2011, Globo TV released more than 20 seriesdealing with various themes and productions lasting around 30/40 minutes. All of these programs are presented at approximately 10:40 pm in the evening. The choice of the time is based on two factors:

1 - It does not interfere with the schedule of soap operas, which are presented at primetime, which length generally increases—start at 9 pm and ending after 10 pm, in order to steal the audience of the movies in Telecinenetwork of cable TV that begins precisely at 10 pm.

2 - The late opening allows the discussion on controversial issues such as violence, sex, drugs, and murder. Based on the data measured by the responsible agency, the audience profile of the series released in this schedule time is formed by highest-level women in the economic classes A, B and C, and aged 35–50 +.

An analysis of the series Diva

To assist us in this approach, we chose as the object of study the Divã series, with screenplay adapted by Marcelo Saback and directed by José Alvarenga, and aired by Globo TV from April 2011 to May 2011. This series was addressed tothe middle-aged female audience of literate culture. There were eight episodes of approximately 30 minutes presented once a week, at 10:50 pm in thetime grid in television, with an average of 19 rating points and 40% interest in the time (share).

The series follows the serialization format in which each issue is a complete, standalone story, with a beginning, middle and end, and in which the main characters are the same in all episodes, along with the same intended narrative.

Based on the successful book by Martha Medeiros with the same title, which was unfolded in a play and in a movie, the screenwriter took care in portraying the anxieties and conflicts of a divorced woman with two children, in a language that merges drama and comedy.The cast includes, besidestheactress Lilia Cabral as Mercedes, Totia Meirelles, Duda Nagle, Jhonny Massaro, Marcelo Airoldi, Paulo Gustavo and Julia Almeida.

The character Mercedes, with the end of her marriage and growth of her children, will draw a trajectory that the will live the pleasures and conflicts of a middle-aged contemporary woman. As partners and confidants, Mercedes has the hairdresser Renee (Paulo Gustavo), gay with a sharp tongue, and Tania (Totia Meireles), an independent and sophisticated woman, owner of an art gallery, who had been married many times. Tania will help Mercedes to believe inher abilities as an artist, profession she will tightly embrace after her divorce.

The name Divã refers to the practice of psychoanalysis that the protagonist uses to get to understand her conflicts. Many scenes occur in the analyst's office, but the only character in the screen is Mercedes.

The first and only season, there were eight episodes presenting issues concerning the life of an urban middle class woman, more specifically from the South Zone of Rio de Janeiro, zone that is considered the one that leads the changes in behavior, as itis stated by Gilberto Velho and other anthropologists.

The dynamics of the script is efficient since it merges moments of reflection with dramatic issues that are handled in a good mood. Recorded as if it were a movie, every scene was previously designed with frames and camera movements that are unusual in Brazilian television.

Analysis of the series concerning the discursive strategies

Using the televisual discourse analyzes of authors such as Calabrese (1976), Jost (2001, 2004), Fontanille (2005), Charaudeau (2006), and Veron (1996, 2004), we will distinguish them as the following:

1 - The temporality: the episodes are marked by a rapid pace as befits the format, which requires that, in approximately 30 minutes, the plot is presented in the first five minutes. Divided into flashes that at times expose the action, with the protagonist recounting them, mixed with moments in the office of the psychoanalyst—who the audience does not see or hear—where the main character discusses her reflections.

2 - The use of the spaces: the internal spaces are limited to the Mercedes apartment, with kitchen, living room, bedroom, bathroom and painting studio; the hairdresser's and Tania's gallery, all of themassembled in the studios of Globo Productions. Outdoor scenes expose landscapes of the city of Rio de Janeiro, but the first episode is set in New York, with scenes in the Central Park, an easy ingredient to attract the urban public.

3 - The clothes and characterization: For the character Mercedes it was adopted modern costumes and sober colors, typical of Brazilian urban middle-aged woman whose concern is to look sensual and discreet, hiding the imperfections of age.TotiaMeireles character's costume is more modern in order to characterize it as a vogue and independent woman with exaggerated necklines and sophisticated jewelry; the costume of the character Renee, the hairdresser,is presented in misuse colorful prints, as if it belonged to an imaginary "gay world".

4 - The verbal expression: the speech of all the characters falls under a clear Portuguese discourse, typical of the cariocas, people born in Rio de Janeiro, mixed with numerous contemporary slangs.

5 - As for the topics covered:

a. EPISODE 1 - the fragility of the divorced woman who needs to face new transformations, what makes herrely on psychoanalysis;

b. EPISODE 2 - doing social work in an asylum toescape loneliness;

c. EPISODE 3 - son dating an older woman,and the protagonist's quick affair with a younger man;

d. EPISODE 4 - the main character's insecurity with her appearance, what makes her go to a plastic surgeon, having as the central plot the invitation to the party celebrating the date of her and other friend' graduation;

e. EPISODE 5 - An affair with a virtual boyfriend;

f. EPISODE 6 - A delicate situation with her best friend, Tania, when she discovers that both of them are involved with the same man;

g. EPISODE 7 - the death of a friend of the same age;

h. EPISODE 8 - to bestow a scholarship to study art in Paris. Regarded by the audience, critics and network executives as one of the most highly rated programs of Globo TV in 2011, the series Divã, is an example of qualityaudiovisual production, gathering good texts, clean interpretations, beautiful photography, and a language that suit different segments of the audience.

Final considerations

The objective of this article is to demonstrate the changes that have been occurring in the Brazilian broadcast television networks due to the growth and influence of cable TV. Focusing on the fictional narrative television entertainment product that occupies the largest market of the television industry (Reis, 2004)—my aim is to analyze the differences between the soap operas, genre better accepted by the Brazilian public in various social strata, and the series format that has been proliferating in the worldwide television market.

The hegemonic American audiovisual industry understands the importance of television fictional products as a means to export their culture and customs, thereby achieving exerts domination over the world's imaginary. The success of American series in various cultures—occupying discussion in virtual social networks—has required studies to try to identify the points that win the viewer in all latitudes of the planet.

In Brazil, the new law of cable TV, the increased purchasing power of the population and the access to new technological resources is pointing to a new parameter in the Brazilian television market.

Thinking about the new formats that have been produced for television, we took as a study subject,the Divã series presented by Globo TV in 2011, in which the concern was to establish basic parameters that would help to reap analysis variables observed in this fictional television production. Adopt a research model to the series format production is increasingly necessary as a contribution to the improvement of this type of product, that presents expressive issues about contemporary society.

The many series that have been produced in recent years in Brazil—Divã might work as an example—would fill a new space, presenting a product that requires from the viewer to reflect and observe the society he lives in. Reinforcing cultural Brazilian traits, these series would help to create a small gap in the American television hegemony operating in the world, denouncing other sensitivities, expressing the socio-cultural heterogeneity and, above all, proving their ability to participate as a producer of new styles in a market until now split between the North cone and the South cone. The first is identified as the producing countries, and the latter is seen as merely consumers (Martin - Barbero, org. Lopes , 2004).

References

Corner, J. (2003). Finding data, reading patterns, telling stories: issues um the historiography of television. Media Culture&Society.Universityof Leeds, UK.

Eco, U. (1994) Seis passeios pelos bosques da ficção. São Paulo: Companhia das letras.

Foucault, M. (1979).Microfísica do poder. Rio de Janeiro: Edições Graal.

Frost, François.(2012). Do que as séries americanas são sintoma?. Porto Alegre: Sulina.

Goulart Ribeiro, A. P., Sacramento, I. Marco Roxo. (2010). História da Televisão no Brasil. São Paulo: Contexto.

Jenkins, H. (2009). A cultura da convergência. São Paulo: Aleph.

Hall, S. (1998). A identidade cultural na pós-modernidade. Rio de Janeiro: DP&A.

Jensen, K.B.(1991). 'When is meaning? Communication theory, pragmatism and mass media reception', pp. 3–32 in Anderson, J.A. (ed.), Communication Year-book.

Lazzarato, M. (2006). As revoluções do capitalismo. [Tradução de LeonoraCorsini]. Rio de Janeiro: Civilização Brasileira.

Lopes, M. I. V.(2004). Telenovela: internalização e interculturalidade. São Paulo: Edições Loyola.

Lopes,M. I V. de. Orozco Gómez, G. (2010). Anuário OBITEL 2010: Convergências e transmidiação da ficção televisiva, São Paulo: Ed. Globo,.

Martin-Barbero, J. (2003). Dos meios às mediações. Comunicação, cultura e hegemonia. Rio de Janeiro: Editora UFRJ.

Martín-Barbero, J. (2004). Ofício de Cartógrafo: travessias latino-americanas da comunicação na cultura.São Paulo: Loyola.

Pinsolle, D.,Rindel, A. (junho 2011). Séries de TV para um público intelectualizado. Le MondeDiplomatique Brasil.

Thompson, J. B. (1998) Mídia e modernidade. Uma teoria social da mídia. Petrópolis: Vozes,.

Xexéo, A. (2011). Coluna do Segundo Caderno do jornal O GLOBO, Rio de Janeiro em19/10.

TV Series *Bolji život* (1987–1991): View from the Future[1]

Natasa Simeunovic Bajic

Bolji život (A better life) is the last famous Yugoslav TV Series made in production of Television Belgrade. It was broadcasted in the period from years 1987 to 1991.[2] This period was marked with tumultuous socio-political changes among which most notable were disintegration of Yugoslavia and wars in the region. One of reasons which make it interesting is studying the fact it was created during the mentioned period. Within this period, cultural, political, academic and economic links among Yugoslav republics rapidly collapsed. This TV series includes total of 82 episodes.[3] It was later performed on the program of Radio Television of Serbia (RTS).[4] From 2003 when electronic measurement of television viewing by Peoplemeters[5] started, it was performed in five occasions: 2005, 2006/2007, 2009 in prime time, 2010/2011 in morning and 2012/2013 again in prime time.[6] "Bolji život" is one of the most popular reruns on RTS. Hence, I want to see if and what kind of intersections can be established between watching this TV series and socio-demographic characteristics, and cultural values of the audiences in this time, over 20 years after original broadcasting.

---

[1] This paper is the result of project suported by the Ministry of Education, Science and Technological Development of the Republic of Serbia (grant number 47027).
[2] Within premiere broadcasting, this TV series created large incomes to the television because it was interrupted by long lasting advertising sequences.
[3] This is a short version. Material of extended version is not preserved.
[4] RTS is the successor of TV Beograd and a national public broadcaster in Serbia. There were several televisions in former Yugoslavia: TV Beograd, TV Zagreb, TV Ljubljana, TV Sarajevo, TV Skoplje, TV Titograd, TV Novi Sad (autonomous province of Vojvodina), TV Priština (autonomous province of Kosovo and Metohija)
[5] TV series was later broadcasted during '90s but data about number of broadcasts and ratings are not available.
[6] Great ratings from 2003 to 2012 are achieved by TV series *Bolji život* (12%). The average rating (AMR) in absolute values was about 800.000 viewers per minute, while the total audience (RCH) was 1.379.869. Data are related to Serbia citizens without Kosovo and Metohija, ages of 4 and more years, or to a population of 7.030.479 citizens. The sample includes 2.500 persons from 800 households which have peoplemeters installed. Source: Podaci o rejtingu, Nielsen Audience Measurement and Centar za istraživanje javnog mnjenja, programa i auditorijuma RTS

Literature review: popular TV series in communist countries

After the fall of communism, all European post-communist countries increased their interest for historical, political and sociological context of the communist regime. After that, the research focus was transferred in the area of popular culture, collective memory, nostalgia and everyday life (Volčić, 2009; Luthar & Pušnik, 2010; Ghodsee, 2011; Just, 2012; Todorova & Gille, 2012). However, within the research domain of popular culture, there is a small number of works analyzing TV series. Therefore, they can remain unrecognized as special TV genres and discourses very important for establishing of theoretical and empirical connection between popular culture and collective memory and between special features of television speech and audience forming in communist and post-communist social frame. There is a interesting study of Paulina Bren *The Greengrocer and His TV: The Culture of Communism After the 1968 Prague Spring* among these works. This study uses popular TV programs to review the period of normalization (1969–1987) after the Prague Spring and invasion of the SSSR. For instance, Bren analyses popularity, reception and context in which TV series *The Thirty Adventures of Major Zeman* was made and broadcasted. Elements of "anti-intelectualism", "anti-urbanism" and "anti-Westernism" can be recognized in all episodes:

> "The normalizers (embodied in the heroic figure of Major Zeman) positioned themselves as the antithesis of the 68ers who had brought nothing but disorder and mayhem to Czhehoslovakia and had ridden the waves of mass hysteria to their own advantage" (Bren, 2010: 83).

The connection between discourse of normalization and the TV series *Hospital on the Outskirts* is analyzed by Petr Bednařík in his work *The Production of Czechoslovakia's Most Popular Television Serial 'The Hospital On The Outskirts' and Its Post-1989 Repeats*. Although TV series was useful to communist propaganda and agitation and offered image which is not aligned with reality during the period of normalization, it is interesting to review why it was later performed and why follow up series were made during 2003 and 2008. He concluded following:

"Ratings show that young people born after 1989 are not very interested in these serials. So, the viewers are more likely to be people who share the memories of a television programme they watched in the 1970s and 1980s, just as they share the memories of other cultural objects, books, films, not to mention household artefacts" (Bednařík, 2012: 32).

Jacub Machek used the example of series *Žena za pultom* broadcasted in late '70s (Machek, 2010) to show that TV series was the most important genre of popular culture in the period of normalization.

In order to embrace the wider frame of production, broadcast and great popularity of TV series in Central European communist countries (Hungary, Czech Republic, Poland, Romania) using comparative analysis, Jan Čulík collected texts of several authors and published them as *National mythologies in Central European TV series: how J.R. won the Cold War*. Similar effort was made by editors of the book named *Popular Television in Eastern Europe During and Since Socialism*, although it includes less number of works dedicated to popular TV series. One of them analyses the Polish TV series *Alternatywy 4* which was made in period 1981–82, but it was broadcasted in 1986–87 due to censure. Scenes in this TV series present life of people in one of largest Warsaw city areas in a comic way. Using the Bakhtin's term of carnivalization, Ostrowska analyzed elements through which satiric relationship toward socialistic reality and communistic propaganda can be visible. She concluded that this TV series is a very successful compound of impact of cabaret, satirical theater, culture of student street protests and criticism of the Polish television genre – block of flats (Ostrowska, 2012).

However, unlike other communist countries, Yugoslavia had a specific position because of three reasons at least: it was (con)federation of six different republics; after Tito's breakup with Stalin, Yugoslav soft socialism was developed under major influence of West (especially USA); Non-Aligned Movement was established (1961) as a response to block division of the world. Therefore, the popular culture had in a way different evolution unlike of countries behind the Iron Curtain. Very early, after the so called Tito's "No" to Stalin in 1948, the liberalization of cultural politics started. It contributed to a great development of popular culture. Analyzing music, movies, comics, literature, Zoran Janjetović metaphorically explained the path of the popular culture in Yugoslavia, which moved from the 'International' to the

Commercial (Janjetović, 2011). However, studies in Serbian and English language about TV series as specific discursive practice and rich television genre remained almost untouched research resource.

Bolji život: short description

Photo 1, *Svetlana Bojković, Lidija Vukićević, Dragan Bjelogrlić, Boris Komnenić and Marko Nikolić in TV series Bolji život*
Photo by Danilo Cvetanović,
RTS Television Belgrade, Programme archive, http://tvarhiv.rts.rs/wwdok/Kasete.htm

Bolji život is the TV series which presents the life of members of one Belgrade family Popadić, using well chosen and aligned narrative elements: father Dragiša (soo called Giga Moravac) originating from inside of Serbia, graduated in Law, works in a state-owned company which fails in business and lives in an apartment that belongs to his wife; mother Emilija (professor of Latin language) who plays the piano, noble woman, originates from old and once rich Belgrade family; the older son Aleksandar (Saša) who graduated Law, calm and clumsy, waits to get married and has problems in finding a job; daughter Violeta (Viki) who is an actress, instable, searching the right love; the younger son Slobodan (Boba) who graduated secondary school and has problems with studying and behaviour. The family is in a bad financial situation. Unpaid bills and fines constantly arrive. The whole line of compelling characters that are easy to remember is made through relationships of family members with other people from their closer and further environment. Real lives of members of different generations and social statuses of Yugoslav (primary Serbian) society from late '80s are reflected in their fictive lives. Hence, many scenes show significant changes in society, politics and culture.[7] For example: Boba is in the military service in the JNA (Yugoslav National Army) where conflict between several young men started. They belong to almost all Yugoslav republics and the conflict appeared during the forming of music orchestra and selection of the song (whose song is the best); the superintendent of the company named "Balkan promet" took the social-realistic painting of the wall. This painting presented workers, hammer and sickle. Instead of that, he placed the picture of neutral dead nature so the buyer with private capital would buy this enterprise in a short time; the superintendent addresses employees with "ladies and gentlemen" instead of "comrades"; in the school, the richest student is the son of the craftsman who makes tombstones; all jobs in different institutions are possible to be done if there are personal contacts etc. This series also presents jail, hospital, university, court, store, night club, casino etc. The combination of humour, irony, metaphor, different language resources, family stories, successful acting of most of actors and realistic manner created one of the most popular TV series. However, those are not the only elements which make positive reactions of the audience. There are time of original broadcasting, numerous reruns and long-year transition in Serbia which creates an image for a Serbian citizen that nothing is going to

---

[7] It was a time during which the 8th Session of the Central Committee of the League of Communists of Serbia (September 1987) was conducted. During this session, the Milosević's nationalist currents took the victory. The session was broadcasted in a whole for the first time. Furher, dismissals of editors and journalists and political pressures on news reporting started. Milošević started rapidly to win the way to political power. Cultural, academic and political contacts between Serbia an Slovenia, Serbia and Croatia started to collapse since 1988; at the end of 1989, all economic and trade links between Slovenia and Serbia were broken; the federal budget has dried up since several republics stopped to send their tax contributions to the federal budget in 1990; petty violence increased in a whole country (Ramet, 2009). However, since many academic studies and different foreign media accused Milošević as mainly responsible for the breakup of Yugoslavia and wars on its territory, it does not and cannot be entirely correct interpretation. Gibbs noted several causes of Yugoslav crisis and wars, including the role of international financial institutions. After the period with significant rate of growth of national income, extensive investment in infrastructure and intense increase in labor productivity, a period of economic crisis due to the increase in oil prices on the foreign market and widespread recession started. "Such interpretations follow ignoring of economic crisis which made wars possible and guilts of Western financial institutions (especially IMF) because of their contribution to collapse of economic situation in country. Structural adaptation of economy, which was imposed to Yugoslavia, was not inevitable. It was an option by Western officials in order to provide payback, but they didn't think about social and political consequences of such politics." Gibbs, D. 2001: 210).

change. Therefore, it is necessary to try to determine how the audience reacts to characters and presented situations in this TV series, more than two decades after its premiere broadcasting.

Photo 2, *Rozalija Levai and Josif Tatić in TV series Bolji život*
Photo by Đorđe Čubrilo
RTS Television Belgrade, Programme archive. http://tvarhiv.rts.rs/wwdok/Kasete.htm

Theoretical basis: Active audience

First theoretical analyses about media influence on audience started from maximum direct hypodermic influence[8] (Lubken, 2008) over "two step flow" model of communication (Sparks, 2011) to minimum media influence (Milivojević, 2001). However, the amount of the media influence on individuals and society in a whole cannot be precisely measured even using the best empirical results. It was necessary to observe the audience in a more flexible way in frames of media and cultural studies. It was made by Stuart Hall. In his work *Encoding/Decoding* (1992), the activity of audience is observed instead of its passivity. He considers that there are three possible ways in which audience receives television contents: dominant-hegemonic position (decoding of the code in frames of reference code), negotiated position (composition of adaptive and oppositional elements) and oppositional code

---

[8] It is known as the Magic Bullet Theory or Hypodermic Needle Theory and it is related to an attitude that there is a causal-consequence relationship between content presented by media and audience behaviour.

(decoding of a message in a total opposite way). According to Hall's acknowledgement that the audience can decode different media messages in a different ways, I assume that is important to investigate how much the TV series *Bolji život* is actual nowadays and what the audience exactly "reads" form the content of this fictional world. It is also important because the one investigation noted that the most responses to a question about television reruns were made according to the TV series *Bolji život* (Simeunović Bajić, Vesnić-Alujević, Majdarević, 2012). Data from that research also showed that audience watch TV shows made and broadcasted in former Yugoslavia (movies and series mostly) which broadcast or were broadcasted on most of TV stations with national coverage. However, they do it in casual manner, when have some free time or accidently turn to a channel with such kind of program running.

Methodological frame

The work applied quantitative survey of audience older than 15 years and qualitative interpretative method of unstructured open interviewing. The research used answers of younger generations, but also answers of older generations were observed because of potentially different interpretations of the same television content. The questionnaire included closed type questions and it was conducted during April and May of year 2013 on example of 204 respondents. The questionnaire was passed using the internet to email addresses and there are about 40% of respondents who answered to these questions. The author intended to form a sample of more than 800 respondents but in a lack of financial resources for engagement of interviewers, the advantages of the Internet were used. However, it was very hard to convince respondents to take a few minutes of their time and answer this short questionnaire. According to these initial steps, the investigation can be used as a stimulus to other researchers to conduct further investigation for this subject. Data were processed in software package for statistic process of data, known as SPSS. Beside socio-demographic characteristics of respondents, the questionnaire included 6 questions: Have you watched some of reruns of a TV series *Bolji život* in last 20 years?; Have you followed the last rerun of the TV series *Bolji život* which was broadcasted at the channel RTS1 after Dnevnik[9]?; If you have, can you please explain why?; Do you think that action, characters and described situations in this show are relevant today in Serbia?; Do you think that situations and relationships in society which are presented in this TV show will remain current in Serbia during next years?; Do you think that situations and relationships in society which are presented in this TV show will remain current in Serbia during next two or three decades? For a question: If so, can you please explain why?—five answers were proposed: Because it is the last great Yugoslav TV show; Because it depicts life in realistic manner; Because it is full of humour; Because it was very often replayed; Because of all above. All questions and offered answers were formed according to preliminary unstructured interviews which the author conducted with representatives of different generations during previous years. They implied to the fact that viewers identify themselves with fictional world of this series considering that everything in it is presented in realistic manner with a fine dose of humour. Relying to that, after the conducted survey, the author made interviews with one representative of the each generation.

Bolji život—nowadays

According to conducted survey and unstructured interviews with representatives of different generations, it is possible to describe the view from the future to the series which was made and broadcasted during the collapse of Yugoslav society and country.

The percent of female respondents is nearly twice larger and it was 65.7%. There were 34.3% of male respondents. Among the respondents from different generations, there are most of those who are between 20 and 29 years of age (39.7%), than 29.4% of those 30–39 years, 18.6% of those 15–19 years and 8.8% of those who are over 50 years old. The percent of those who are 40 to 49 years old was 4.4%. There were most of people who lived in urban areas—83.3%, suburban areas—14.2%, and rural areas—2.5%. During last two decades, some of reruns of the series *Bolji život* were watched by 73.5% of respondents. However, the last rerun which was broadcasted in prime-time in 2013 was regularly watched by 13.2%, occasionally by 29.9% of respondents while 56.9% did not watch this at all.

---

[9] Central informative programme.

Among respondents who watched some of reruns of the series (category *didn't watch* is excluded) percents were in following order: *because it was broadcasted very often*; *because it presents the life in a realistic way*; *because it includes all defined reasons*; *because it is full of humour* and finally—*because it is the last famous Yugoslav TV series*.

Table 1. Explanation: If you have, can you please explain why?

		Frequency	Percent	Valid Percent	Cumulative Percent
Valid	Because it is the last great Yugoslav TV show	7	3.4	3.4	3.4
	Because it depicts life in realistic manner	36	17.6	17.6	21.1
	Because it is full of humour	22	10.8	10.8	31.9
	Because it was very often replayed	55	27.0	27.0	58.8
	Because of all above	31	15.2	15.2	74.0
	I didn't watch it	53	26.0	26.0	100.0
	Total	204	100.0	100.0	

The percent of those who think totally or partially that situation, characters and situations in this series are topical in Serbia nowadays: 38.2% and 38.7% respectively. Only 8.3% of respondents consider it is not topical any more. It is interesting that nearly half of respondents—48% (the category—*didn't watch*[10] is not excluded) consider that situations and relationships in society, presented in this series will be topical in Serbia during next years.

---

[10] Answers to questions related to presented situations and social relationships, were obtained by those who answered as—*didn't watch* - for previous questions. It can be explained by the fact that this series is known to entire television audience by several elements so it became a special media discourse.

Figure 1. Situations and relationships in society, presented in this TV series, will be topical in Serbia during next years.

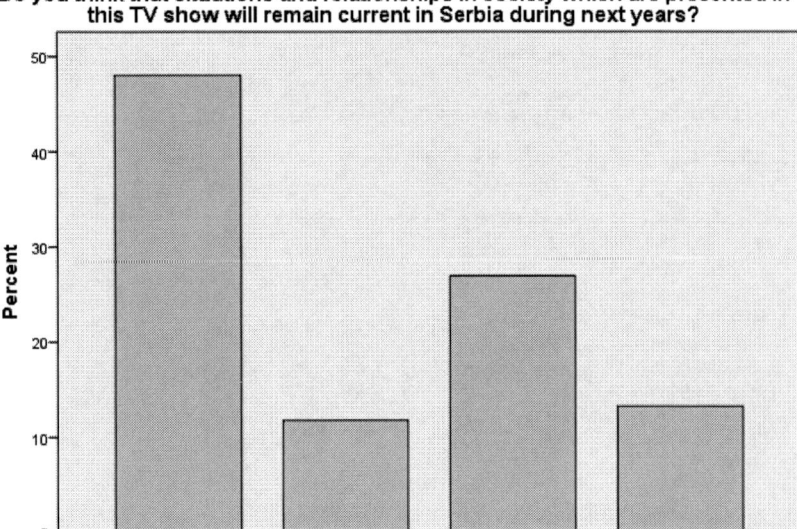

The percent of those who think that situations and relationships in society in Serbia will remain the same during next few decades is also notable (27%). Respondents who are not sure—45.1%; no answer—14.7%.

According to the interview with representatives of different generations, following answers were obtained:

> I love to watch *Bolji život* series because it is our TV series. It is interesting and shows the constant search for a better life. The real life is exactly presents in it. I like the love story between Emilija, professor of Latin language and professor of Mathematics, called Terminator. All farewells in this series are so sad, while Giga Moravac is almost always funny and would like if this TV series could be broadcasted further more." (F, 56, rural area, primary school, unemployed)

> "It is a good TV series. Everything is presented like in a real life. Each detail is well planned. Scenes from the jail and the army are notable for me. Love relationships are more complicated nowadays." (M, 21, rural area, secondary school, employed)

"I watched it when I was a child. It was interesting because nothing more interesting was on television in that time. The series is really realistic. It presents different generations in a right way. It is full of humour. Nowadays, nothing changed in Serbia according to facts presented in TV series. Everything goes using contacts. I forgot most of details but I don't like to watch the rerun. It was broadcasted to many times." (F, 37, rural area, primary school, employed)

"This TV series is tragic-comic for me since everything is the same nowadays. Essentially, nothing has changed. The situation is the same in public enterprises. Act is very good. I like everything in this TV series. The uncle Kosta is the only one who is annoying for me. The most interesting episode is where Giga takes women from the enterprise to the shopping in Thessaloniki. No matter how much it is broadcasted, I would watch it always." (F, 25, urban area, faculty degree, unemployed)

"I loved to watch this TV series. It is tragic and comic at the same time. Actually it is realistic. Directors of public enterprises are most realistic presented. The value system started to collapse in that time. Everything started to fall apart. To date, nothing has been improved." (M, 67, rural area, secondary school, retired)

"I like the TV series very much. I watched it several times. The most interesting part is when Viki married a doctor. I wouldn't change anything in this TV series. I like how everything looked in that time, especially a job in a public enterprise. I think that the way of life in the series is much similar to a life nowadays. Young people are slightly different than in previous time. The humour is present only when Giga makes jokes, and it is most interesting for me. I would watch the next broadcast definitely." (F, 15, suburban area, student)

"For many years, I didn't have time to watch this TV series, but I watched the last rerun. It reflects our time in a realistic way. Little things have changed since that time. I identified myself with Giga, an honest man who cannot find his way through the sea of business frauds. Also, I identified myself with Saša who cannot find a job as a lawyer and with Koka, who has a baby with him with no place to live. The story about heritage is also interesting because we all would like to have a rich aunt who would leave some money after her death." (F, 43, urban area, faculty degree, unemployed)

Described quantitative and qualitative data show that TV series *Bolji život* is very popular. Even those who claim that they did not watch, they know a bit about it. Thanks to many reruns in prime-time, well organized narrative elements, description of all segments of social reality and good acting, this TV series obtained an important media discourse which can be analyzed from several perspectives. First of them relies to an identification of audience with reality of the content of the series. That reality includes detecting of a large society crisis which started in '80s. It is not finished since the transition lasts longer than Serbia citizens expected it. The second perspective, which is connected to a first one implies to an idealistic expectation of a 'better life' which usually never comes, since it is (sometimes black, sometimes bright) something it happens to us right now. Such construction of impossibility to create a 'better life' is incorporated in a wider context of social-historical faith of Serbian people and country. According to that, the identification can be made on a level of myth and mythical image creating. This image about Serbia is always late and it cannot solve basic issues. The third perspective includes the lost of Yugoslav identity since the wider Yugoslav society is transformed into a narrower Serbian society in consciousness of audience. Parts of former Yugoslavia—Slovenia and Croatia are already members of the EU, while Serbia has to pass a long way to achieve that. That way is marked with symbolic transformation of Yugoslav into Serbian. This TV series showed differences and intolerance among Yugoslav republics on the one hand. On the other hand, it tried to override them in some presented links with highlighted Yugoslav value. Actually, the defined symbolic value of presented world needed to be aligned with official ideology. However, the audience does not decode these media messages in a same way. The feature—*the last great Yugoslav TV series* does not mean much to someone. More important thing is the social reality which slowly or poorly changes and influences on a quality of life of an ordinary man.

Conclusion

Production of TV Belgrade, once the largest part of the Yugoslav television production, was very rich. Although the program had to be aligned with ideology of socialistic country, working people, brotherhood and unity, it was quite various and professional standards were taken into account. It was a public television so it was assumed that it is useful to a society as a whole.
RTS as a successor of TV Belgrade is an official public media service of Serbia citizens. Although Serbia has many domestic commercial and foreign television stations, RTS achieves highest ratings for years thanks to its First channel (RTS1) whose contents are adapted to taste and needs of the

audience. New television formats are introduced, sport events are constantly monitored, informative program and domestic TV series are diverse. Since other domestic televisions broadcast cheap Latin American, Indian and Turkish series, viewers will likely to choose local product. Therefore, TV series *Bolji život* has high ratings although it was broadcasted many times. This research shows that large number of reruns has a significant impact on high ratings. If each episode is not viewed, many times people watched several scenes or episodes. This is enough to keep *Bolji život* as a symbol of past and present time in which reality does not satisfy ordinary people.

This TV series creates a very important part of the entire popular culture by representing the everyday life and social reality in historical period and in the area marked with dramatic changes. As a TV discourse, *Bolji život* is connected with values of popular culture which belongs to all social groups. Audience can experience Barth's "jouissance of the text" by discovering of dominant and hidden meanings connected with historical, political and social context. Also, the TV series is an excellent example of evocative power of television and emotionally—affective connecting between audience and fictional event.

Since domestic scientific literature does not include systematic works in this area of study, this chapter can be used as an incentive to researches to analyze the role of TV series and their audience in production of popular culture in former Yugoslavia and Serbia.

References

Bednařík, B. (2012). The Production of Czechoslovakia's Most Popular Television Serial 'The Hospital On The Outskirts' and Its Post-1989 Repeats. *VIEW Journal of European Television History and Culture*, volume 01 issue 03/2013, Retrieved from http://www.viewjournal.eu/index.php/view/article/view/jethc029/54

Bren, P. (2010). *The Greengrocer and His TV: The Culture of Communism After the 1968 Prague Spring*. Cornell University Press. Retrieved from http://books.google.rs/books?id=o2LT7c_Kw80C&source=gbs_navlinks_s

Čulik, J. (Ed.). (2013). *National mythologies in Central European TV series: how J.R. won the Cold War*. Brighton ; Chicago: Sussex Academic Press

Gibbs, D. (2001). Izvori jugoslovenskog ratnog sukoba, *Sociološki pregled*. vol. 35, No. 3–4, pp. 177–211

Ghodsee, K. (2011). *Lost in Transition: Ethnographies of Everyday Life After Communism*. Duke University Press. Retrieved from http://books.google.rs/books?id=Zz8mlzuOjjIC&printsec=frontcover&source=gbs_ge_summary_r&cad=0#v=onepage&q&f=false

Hall, S. (1992). Encoding/Decoding. In: Hall, S. et all. (Eds.) *Culture, media, language: working papers in cultural studies, 1972–79*, (pp. 107–117) Routledge. Retrieved from http://books.google.rs/books?id=jpzEACvzDFoC&printsec=frontcover&hl=sr&source=gbs_ge_summary_r&cad=0#v=onepage&q&f=false

Janjetović, Z. (2011). *Od Internacionale do komercijale*. Beograd: INIS

Just, D. (2012). Art and everydayness: Popular culture and daily life in the communist Czechoslovakia, *European Journal of Cultural Studies*, vol. 15, no. 6, pp. 703–720, DOI: 10.1177/1367549412450637, Retrieved from http://ecs.sagepub.com/content/15/6/703

Lubken, D. (2008). Remembering the Straw Man: the Travels and the Adventures of Hypodermic. In: Park, D., Jefferson, P. (Eds.) *The History of Media and Communication Research: Contested Memories*. (pp. 19–69) Peter Lang. Retrieved from http://books.google.rs/books?id=Vo7goofWc28C&pg=PA251&dq=media+impact+hypodermic&source=gbs_toc_r&cad=3

Luthar, B., Pušnik, M., (2010*) Remembering Utopia: The Culture of Everyday Life in Socialist Yugoslavia*. New Academia Publishing. Retrieved from http://books.google.rs/books?id=S0x0vUKAhbIC&dq=yugonostalgia+communist+countries&source=gbs_navlinks_s

Machek, J. (2010). The counter lady as a female prototype: prime time popular culture in 1970s and 1980s in Czechoslovakia. *Medijska istraživanja/Media research*, vol. 16, no 1, pp. 31–52. Retrieved from http://mediaresearch.cro.net/clanak.aspx?l=en&id=378

Milivojević, S. (2001). Javnost i ideološki efekti medija. *Reč*, 64/10, pp. 151–213, Retrieved from http://www.fabrikaknjiga.co.rs/rec/64/151.pdf

Ostrowska, D. (2012). The Carnival of the Absurd: Stanislaw Bareja's Alternatywy 4 and Polish Television in 1980s. In: Havens, T., Imre, A., Lustyik, K. (Eds) *Popular Television in Eastern Europe During and Since Socialism*. Routledge, Retrieved from http://books.google.rs/books?id=giO-NS4Uu08C&source=gbs_navlinks_s

Podaci o rejtingu. Nielsen Audience Measurement and Centar za istraživanje javnog mnjenja, programa i auditorijuma RTS

Ramet, S. (2009). Jugoslovenska kriza i Zapad, Retrieved from http://pescanik.net/2009/10/jugoslovenska-kriza-i-zapad/

Simeunović Bajić, N., Vesnić-Alujević, L., Majdarević, A., (2012). Televizijsko repriziranje kao moguća strategija kulturne politike i odgovor publike. (pp. 455–467) In: *Kultura i društveni razvoj*, Conference Proceedings "Kulturna politika, umetničko stvaralaštvo i medijska praksa u funkciji održivog društvenog razvoja", Belgrade: Megatrend university.

Sparks, G. (2011). *Media Effects Research: A Basic Overview*, 4th ed. Cengage Learning. Retrieved from http://books.google.rs/books?id=ScB1ps0iDD0C&dq=media+impact+The+TwoStep+Flow&source=gbs_navlinks_s

Todorova, M., Gille, Z. (2012). *Post-Communist Nostalgia*. Berghahn Books. Retrieved from http://books.google.rs/books?id=j33ZkSLqSQAC&source=gbs_navlinks_s

Volčić, Z., (2009). *Neither East nor West: the past and present life of Yugoslav identity*, CAS Working Paper Series No. 2/2009, Retrieved from http://www.cas.bg/uploads/files/Zala%20Volcic.pdf

The *X-Factor* of Singing Competitions TV Series

Maria Dicieanu

Introduction

The X Factor, The Voice, Idols, Got Talent[1]... if none of these names sounds familiar, you most likely have had your TV turned off for the last years. With a rather simple structure aiming to find and grow a superstar under the viewers' watchful eyes, these singing competitions have proved to be the golden goose of the new millennium in TV series, having been adapted and embraced in over 40 countries worldwide[2]. According to a International Television Expert Group study, during 2006–2008, both Got Talent and Idols were in the top 10 of the most successful formats around the world, on the second and ninth positions[3].

Despite the success in terms of audience engagement, the shows have more often than not, failed to accomplish their designed purpose of creating and launching superstars. Even more, internationally acclaimed musicians such as Sting[4] and Plan B[5], have severely criticized the formats, considering them to have taken a toll on the music industry through the promotion of cover artists, rather than singers with an "unique signature or fingerprints"[6]. This however, has not stopped TV producers to continue investing in such

---

[1] *Got Talent* is not exclusively a singing competition being open to all kinds of talents, however I have decided to included in this paper as it is part of the Simon Cowell empire
[2] According to Wikipedia: *The X Factor* has been adapted in 41 countries, *Idols* in 48 countries, *The Voice* in 49 countries and *Got Talent* in 54 countries
[3] 'Global TV trading and most successful TV formats worldwide' December 2009, Last consulted 30th June 2013 <http://www.international-television.org/tv_market_data/international-tv-format-ranking-and-trading_2006-2008.html>
[4] Collett-White, Mike. "Sting calls X-Factor 'appalling'". Reuters blog. November 11th, 2009. Last consulted 30th June 2013 <http://blogs.reuters.com/fanfare/2009/11/11/sting-calls-x-factor-appalling/>
[5] Fletcher, Alex. "Plan B criticizes 'X Factor' celebrity and image focus ". Digital Spy, July 19th 2012. Last consulted 30th June 2013 <http://www.digitalspy.co.uk/tv/s103/the-x-factor/news/a394159/plan-b-criticises-x-factor-celebrity-and-image-focus.html >
[6] Collett-White, Mike. "Sting calls X-Factor 'appalling'". Reuters blog. November 11th, 2009. Last consulted 30th June 2013 <http://blogs.reuters.com/fanfare/2009/11/11/sting-calls-x-factor-appalling/>

shows, raising the stakes more than ever with larger awards and even commissioning multiple seasons a year.

This paper wishes to have a deeper look at how singing competitions work, comment on the duality between the shows and the reality, together with discussing whether we are currently witnessing the slow death of these formats due to lack of relevance in the real world, or if we should expect the TV to prevail despite "killing the radio stars"[7].

The Beginnings

Television is a medium which is constantly reinventing itself. It might seem that Idols, X Factor, The Voice are fresh formats that have captured the world, but in truth many key aspects embraced in these post 90s singing competitions, can be traced to older TV contests and talent shows. For instance, the audience's voting for its favorite acts and choosing which ones to put through in the next stage of the competition, was also featured in the ITV's Opportunity Knocks talent show, aired between 1956–1978. It was for the first time in a British talent show, when the power of decision shifted from a panel of judges to the public at home and their telephone votes. The system proved so effective that it has been embraced by all the Idols – type[8] shows, despite of the judges being the deciding factor in the early stages of these competitions. Even more, telephone votes (together with the text message extension) remained the only accepted voting method until 2011 when online voting was introduced.

Opportunity Knocks was also the first show to highlight the drawbacks of the home voting system. In 1974, the show was won by a singing Jack Russell Terrier dog, to the detriment of the emerging comedy actress and singer Su Pollard[9], which would later find real fame through a series of sitcoms. Despite the fair warning, similar outcomes would inevitably be registered in contemporary singing competitions as well: Oscar-winner actress and singer Jennifer Hudson placed seventh in her American Idol season,

---

[7] The Buggles. "Video Killed The Radio Star" song from The Age of Plastic album released by the Island Records label, September 7th 1979

[8] The notion "Idols – type" refers to the X Factor, The Voice and Got Talent shows as well

[9] BBC Home. "Great Nottinghamians: Su Pollard". BBC.co.uk. Last updated March 2003. Last consulted 30th June 2013 <http://www.bbc.co.uk/nottingham/features/2002/11/great_nottinghamians_su_pollard.shtml>

Susan Boyle didn't win Britain's Got Talent but went on to become the most successful star produced by the franchise, One Direction—currently a worldwide phenomenon and platinum selling artists—lost the X Factor UK title to an artist dropped from his recording contract after only two years[10].

The voting system was however not the only element imported by Idols franchise in their formats. The New Faces talent show airing between 1986 and 1988 featured a panel of very outspoken judges, the most famous being Tony Hatch, dubbed as 'The Hatchet Man' due to his severe criticism delivered to contestants[11]. This very direct manner of offering critique has been embraced by both Nigel Lythgoe, called "Nasty Nigel" during his judging time on Popstars[12], and by Simon Cowell, known for his sharp-tongue when judging American Idol, Britain's Got Talent, The X Factor UK and The X Factor USA contestants. Featuring comments like "You look like an elephant"[13], "God doesn't want you to win this competition"[14], "It's the way you look that's putting us off"[15], "The audition, if I'm being honest with you, was horrible"[16] became regular practice on the shows, while the audience genuinely seemed to embrace the ruthless-ness. Simon's comments became so popular, that the best and most comical ones were even published as a collection put together by his older brother Tony Cowell[17]. And it was not just Nigel and Simon embracing the Hatch method: Britney Spears also proved quite blunt in rejecting contestants during the X Factor USA auditions mak-

---

[10] The Sun. "X Factor Curse Hits Matt Cardle". The Sun. Last updated 24th May 2012. Last consulted 30th June 2013. <http://www.thesun.co.uk/sol/homepage/showbiz/4331540/X-Factor-curse-hits-Matt-Cardle.html>

[11] Vallantine, Stuart. "UK Television Talent Shows Through the Ages: The Not So Perfect Ten". East of the M60. July 9th 2010. Last consulted 30th June 2013. <http://mancunian1001.wordpress.com/2010/07/09/uk-television-talent-shows-through-the-ages-the-not-so-perfect-ten/>

[12] Wikipedia. "Nigel Lythgoe". Last modified June 30h 2013. Last consulted June 30th 2013. <http://en.wikipedia.org/wiki/Nigel_Lythgoe>

[13] Youtube. "Simon Cowell nasty comments 1". Youtube.com. Uploaded on 26th August 2010. Last consulted June 30th 2013 <https://www.youtube.com/watch?v=rJo7jbZZv5k>

[14] Ibid. 12

[15] Youtube. "Simon Cowell nasty comments 2". Youtube.com. Uploaded on 30th August 2010. Last consulted June 30th 2013 <https://www.youtube.com/watch?v=ZrGdyT8ltO4>

[16] Ibid. 14

[17] Cowell, Tony. "I Hate to Be Rude, But...: Simon Cowell's Book of Nasty Comments", Publisher John Blake, February 1st 2006 <http://www.amazon.com/Hate-Be-Rude-But-Comments/dp/1844542254>

ing Cowell admit that "She's surprisingly quite mean" and "I've grown to like her a lot"[18]. Hoping that they might have discovered a female version of Simon Cowell, producers even featured a montage of Spears' various nasty remarks for the premiering episode of X Factor USA's second season, which was heavily promoted in the media[19]. Disappointingly however, Spears couldn't keep up with the nasty-ness once the live shows started.

In 1996 The Big Big Talent Show was launched on ITV, searching for the best variety acts and giving the viewers the possibility to vote for their favorites. The general format was quite similar to what was going to become later the Got Talent franchise, to the point of even having the same main award[20]: the opportunity of spot during the Royal Variety Performance[21]. The show however 'died' after two seasons, only to be revived and slightly revamped ten years later when it proved to be a big hit.

One can start wondering why, if originality was not the element making Idols become a worldwide phenomenon, earlier shows didn't meet with a similar impact and level of success. A possible explanation comes from the emphasis on the "reality factor" which older shows lacked. At the beginning of the 1990s the introduction of Avid systems and non-linear editing gave producers the possibility of effectively working with larger quantities of filmed materials while also cutting down the costs of post production all together[22]. This ultimately opened the door for reality televison and shows like Big Brother, Survivor, The Real World or Changing Rooms. In his article Making Over the Talent Show Guy Redden proposes that it was the combination of life style and reality with the classical talent search which turned

---

[18] Hyman, Dan. "Simon Cowell on Britney Spears: 'She's Surprisingly Quite Mean'". Rolling Stone. September 7th 2012. Last consulted 30th June 2013 <http://www.rollingstone.com/movies/news/simon-cowell-on-britney-spears-shes-surprisingly-quite-mean-20120907>

[19] Robinson, Shaun. "Is Britney Spears The New Simon Cowell On The X Factor". AccessHollywood.com. Last consulted 30th June 2013. <http://watch.accesshollywood.com/video/is-britney-spears-the-new-simon-cowell-on-the-x-factor/1831341649001?utm_source=accesshollywood.com&utm_medium=referral#>

[20] This prize is only valid for the winners of the UK edition.

[21] Vallantine, Stuart. "UK Television Talent Shows Through the Ages: The Not So Perfect Ten". East of the M60. July 9th 2010. Last consulted 30th June 2013. <http://mancunian1001.wordpress.com/2010/07/09/uk-television-talent-shows-through-the-ages-the-not-so-perfect-ten/>

[22] YouTube. "Charlie Brooker's Screenwipe—Reality TV Editing". Youtube.com. Uploaded on 1st March 2007. Last consulted June 30th 2013 <http://www.youtube.com/watch?v=BBwepkVurCI>

these shows into "an international killer application"[23]. The writer also concludes:
The new talent searches can be viewed as part of a longstanding swathe of game-oriented programming in which ordinary people appear as participants in some form of competition and are rewarded (or not) relative to how well they do something. [...] What is most distinctive about the new talent shows is their premise to change people. The reward is not to be a richer version of yourself empowered with a cash prize to use as you will, nor enjoyment of commodities you have somehow earned. Rather, it is the exchange of your old self for a new one. The older talent shows focussed mostly on the moments of performance and their assessment by judges. In the new crop with their higher stakes, real job prizes, the central moral focus behind the ordinary contestant formats is the guarantee of a new life for the single winner".[24] (Redden, 2008)
People found it easier to engage in series that dealt with special phenomena (turning a regular person into a national idol) while also being able to identify with the typologies among the contestants. The new forms of talent shows have made a purpose for instance, of inserting shots of the very commonly looking families of the contestants, either cheering for them or offering support and consolation in case of failure. The audience is thus constantly reminded that it is looking at regular people dreaming big. Later in the shows, the contestants are occasionally seen returning for a visit to their family and friends. These visits allow the audience to see how much the lives of the contestants have changed. Suddenly everybody in their home town knows their names, they authorities award them special distinctions and they can fill stations of people wanting to show their support and listen to them singing. Thus, the reality factor together with the emphasis on the life-changing experience played a significant role into the success registered by these franchises.
However, as the Popstars / Pop Idol formats showed, it it also a matter of having the right type of format at the right time. Popstars was a series first launched by Jonathan Dowling in 1999 in New Zeeland. The show aimed at

---

[23] Redden, Guy. "Making Over the Talent Show" chapter in Exposing Lifestyle Television: The Big Reveal edited by Gareth Palmer. Ashgate Publishing, ltd., 2008, p.130
[24] Redden, Guy. "Making Over the Talent Show" chapter in Exposing Lifestyle Television: The Big Reveal edited by Gareth Palmer. Ashgate Publishing, ltd., 2008, p.135

documenting the creation of a new successful band from scratch, and then following the launching of their first single. Through a series of auditions, a jury would pick the best singers and they would later perform in live shows. One by one, the aspiring talents would get eliminated, until five of them remained and ultimately formed the band.

Quite significantly, the first British season of Popstars was actually billed as a documentary rather than a singing competition[25], and lacked the inclusion of the public's vote. Though the format proved successful, being sold to more than 50 countries, the decision of leaving the audience out proved not so wise, as it gave Simon Fuller the opportunity of launching Pop Idol—a similar but ultimately more successful format, featuring the addition of the public's vote element. In later seasons of Popstars, the audience will be the one with the ultimate choosing power, however this twist will not manage to save the show's being dropped from broadcasters all around the world, after an average of 2 seasons. The only notable exceptions were encountered in Germany, Slovakia and France, where the shows reached 10, 8 and respectively 5 seasons. France is also the only country to still be broadcasting the show, most states having dropped Popstars by 2004.

Another downfall for the show proved to be the over-all context. While vocal groups were still on top of the charts when the show was launched, the early 2000s saw break-ups and hiatuses from the most successful of the branch such as Spice Girls, Backstreet Boys, N'Sync, 5ive and All Saints. A show entirely dedicated to forming and promoting top-charting bands became an unrealistic format with an irrelevant-for-the-music-industry goal, despite the rather successful results from putting together the groups Girls Aloud in the UK and No Angels in Germany.

Pop Idol meant to bring more versatility, by promoting individual artists. Created by Simon Fuller and featuring Simon Cowell as one of the judges, it was launched in 2001 and broadcasted on ITV. By 2002 it was picked up by Fox in the USA while 2003 saw 14 new adapted versions worldwide. The show became a smashing televison series with an average of 4 broadcasted seasons per country, yet it was dropped in UK (the originating state) after only 3 seasons. Part of this was caused by Cowell's wish to launch his

---

[25] Wikipedia. "Popstars". Last modified May 28th 2013. Last consulted June 30th 2013. <http://en.wikipedia.org/wiki/Popstars_(UK)>

own similar format[26] The X Factor which would not only allow him to be in control of the discovered artists but also open the stardom opportunity to groups and people over 25 as well as young boys and girls. Moreover, Pop Idol had the draw-back of being tied to a specific music genre in a time when diversity, uniqueness and recognizably were gaining ground in the music industry. Great Britain was the only country in which "pop" was present in the show's name, the other versions either choosing the American example of emphasizing the national dimension (Australian Idol, Greek Idol, Indian Idol etc.) or simply sticking to an Idol / Idols name.

Ultimately the Pop Idol / Popstars situation got to show that the success of a TV series depends not only on being able to create the perfect format, but also releasing it in the right context, making sure the audience is prepared to embrace it, taking care that the form is adaptable enough to withstand certain trends' shifts while also assuring a perfect collaboration between the key team members.

The American Idol and its Legacy

"American Idol" would not be only the "game changer" that Mr. Grushow and Fox had been searching for. It would be a business-changer for all of network television. (Bill Carter, 2006)[27]

The show that redefined the television's standards and expectations in terms of programming, that inspired many other formats such as So You Think You Can Dance, America's Best Dance Crew and arguably even The X Factor and The Voice and that contributed to Fox's industry record of eight consecutive season victory among adults between 18–49[28], was on the verge of not being picked up by any main American television network. Despite the success registered in Britain by its predecessor Pop Idol, a

---

[26] In 2004 Simon Fuller filed a law-suit against Simon Cowell claiming that *The X Factor* copies the *Pop Idol* format. The legal action was settled with Fuller's becoming a joint partner of *X Factor* and with Cowell's agreeing to remain as a judge on *American Idol* for five more years.

[27] Carter, Bill. "How A Hit Almost Failed its Own Audition". The New York Times.30th April 2006. Last consulted 30th June 2013. <http://www.nytimes.com/2006/04/30/business/yourmoney/30idol.html?pagewanted=1&_r=0>

[28] The Futon Critic. "FOX Sets New Broadcast Industry Record With Eighth Consecutive Season Victory Among Adults 18-49". TheFutonCritic.com. 24th May 2012. Last consulted 30th June 2013.<http://www.thefutoncritic.com/ratings/2012/05/24/fox-sets-new-broadcast-industry-record-with-eighth-consecutive-season-victory-among-adults-18-49-614111/20120524fox01/>

singing competitions did not seem at all appealing to broadcasters especially considering the fact that Popstars had failed to become a phenomenon in the previous years. Accounting the events that had the show in limbo status before being finally picked up by Fox, Bill Carter acknowledges that "music had already failed in the United States in reality format on two networks"[29], hence the format proposed by Cowell and Fuller was met with skepticism. It took the salutary intervention of Elisabeth Murdoch, daughter of Rupert Murdoch founder and chief executive of the company owning Fox, that had previously been exposed to the Pop Idol phenomenon, to have American Idol broadcasted in the summer of 2002. The show proved an instant hit with 10 million viewers on its premiere and by 2004 it would become one of the biggest shows on the American networks.

Even with Fox's agreeing to give the show a chance, Idol could have still potentially failed if the producers would have made it a more standard American show. The format was initially commissioned for an 8 episodes summer show, which would have radically changed the British format. Luckily due to Mr. Murdoch's interest in the show, the same amount of episodes of Pop Idol were kept[30]. Instead of going the safe way and hiring American figures from music industry as judges, producers chose to "import" Simon Cowell as well, despite his initial fears of not knowing what is relevant in U.S and being too brutally honest for its audience.

> At first he [Simon Cowell n.b.] had doubts about whether he knew enough about American music to judge American singers. [...] He expected that some genius at the American network was bound to try to water down the show, and especially his honestly acerbic comments. He would have no interest in a sweetened version of "Pop Idol." (Bill Carter, 2006, p.4)[31]

Carter notes that producers also expressed doubts regarding the show's having two hosts which would make things seem too "cluttered",[32] and four judges which in situations of a tie, would grant all decision power to Simon Cowell. Although the number of hosts didn't prevent the first season to become a hit, from season two onwards only Ryan Seacrest would be presenting the show. With respect to the number of judges, despite the initial

---

[29] Ibid. 26
[30] Ibid. 26
[31] Ibid. 26
[32] Ibid. 26

plans, only three judges could be arranged for the first season, and they remained in that formula until the eighth installment.

Bill Carter also notes Simon Cowell's resistance against embracing the Hollywood model of working with everything scripted, keeping up with being his natural self and improvising lines on the spot. The judge proved to be a true asset of the show his ruthless-ness becoming a trade-mark for such competitions.

But while Cowell was striving for genuine, the show was anything but such, a lot being put together and manipulated for the cameras. The auditions with the judges which were presented as the first stage of the competition and dubbed as the first step made by contestants to follow their dreams, were actually the end point of an already long process in which contestants had to sing for various scouts and producers. In his article "Secret Rituals of American Idol Auditions Exposed" Richard Rushfield, a dedicated journalist to the American Idol phenomenon, revealed several myths regarding the auditions including the fact that producers occasionally told contestants which songs to sing, deliberately advanced to the later auditioning stages untalented acts which the audience can later make fun of, and mislead the public with regards to the number of people that sing in front of the judges. Shots of thousands of people are shown lining up at a specific location, while only a couple of hundreds actually get to perform in front of the judges.[33]

An interesting phenomenon occurs with respect to this manipulation. While the audience is actually aware that they are being misled, it doesn't seem to influence at all its relationship with the show. This is even more evident in The X Factor format, where at a certain moment in the selection procedure, the contestants are being taken to the "judges' houses". It was revealed on numerous occasions[34] that the houses which supposedly belong to Simon Cowell, Britney Spears, Sharon Osbourne and the other judges, are actually specially rented by producers for this stage of the competition, as the stars don't actually want to have their privacy invaded by contestants and filming crews. In an interview for BBC, a spokeswoman for the show

---

[33] Rushfield, Richard. "Secret Rituals of American Idol Auditions Exposed". TheDailyBeast.com.January 19th 2010. Last consulted 30th June 2013. <http://www.thedailybeast.com/articles/2010/01/19/secret-rituals-of-american-idol-auditions-exposed.html>

[34] BBC News. "Walsh's X Factor house 'not his'". BBC.co.uk. November 29th 2005. Last consulted 30th June 2013. <http://news.bbc.co.uk/2/hi/entertainment/7040283.stm>

claimed the audience was never mislead as The X Factor had never stated that the houses belonged to the judges, nor did they call them "judges' homes".[35] Whether the subtle language difference was actually caught up by the audience or not, cannot be estimated, but the revelation didn't affect in any way the ratings. Despite this clarification made public in 2007, The X Factor UK's viewer's numbers continued to steadily increase until 2010.

The public apparent ignorance to being manipulated can be extrapolated also to the declared purpose of the shows. While American Idol has constantly claimed to be in search of the next big name in music industry, it more often than not failed at finding them. The most successful and well know Idol alumni remained Kelly Clarkson, the original winner of season one. Other winners such as Carrie Underwood (season 4), Jordin Sparks (season 6), Phillip Phillips (season 11) and Scotty McCreery (season 10) enjoyed various levels of worldwide success, but the fact remains that hundreds of contestants, winners included have long been forgotten and fallen in anonymity.

Also, while standard phrases such as "record numbers of people auditioning", "record number of recorded votes" and "record number of downloads" are customarily used each year, trying to imply that the current season has always the best talent while the winner will quite likely become even more successful than the previous ones, record sales had failed to sustain the theory.

Despite the flaws however, American Idol did serve as main source of inspiration for other singing competitions, such as The X Factor a British production created in 2004 by Thames, FremantleMedia and Syco Entertainment and The Voice, a Dutch format by John De Mol produced from 2010 by an Endemol and Talpa collaboration. Both formats could in fact be seen as reactions to American Idol.

Clash of the Formats

While it was clear for everybody that the audience craved for singing competitions and discovering new talent during the years 2000s, none of the producers were actually able to deliver the format that would make all others irrelevant. This resulted in the shows' running simultaneously, splitting

---

[35] Ibid 32.

ratings and over-crowding the market, which both audiences and producers considered problematic.

In some countries the competition seemed to be welcomed and embraced. Such was the case of Romania, where both The X Factor and The Voice where launched in the same year and in the same period of time by rival television stations willing to dispute their supremacy. In the UK as well, The Voice was scheduled by BBC in such a way as to overlap with ITV's much older and famous show Britain's Got Talent, in an attempt to crush the competition with a new and fresh format. In the US, The Voice also proved eager to compete, scheduling two seasons per year so that it would clash both with the freshly launched version of Simon Cowell's The X Factor, and with the more experienced and renowned American Idol. Behind the scenes and despite this apparent show-off however, things were far from being perfect, and the once easy to read and please audiences, became a wild card.

In the Netherlands for instance, The Voice managed to apparently reach the ideal stage by eliminating all the other competitive formats. It swiped away Popstars which it was scheduled against, and it also eliminated The X Factor broadcasted later in the year. Not even a fresh revamped version of Cowell's format, featuring as a judge Ali B, one of the Voice's mentors, could compete with de Mol's production. The Dutch were clearly embracing the show created in their own country, preferring it to the international formats, but more importantly, they were stating that the market was no longer accepting multiple singing competition formats. Even though in the past X Factor and Popstars had been happily co-existing, the years 2010[36] and 2013[37] showed two singing competitions per year, were one too many for the Dutch environment.

A similar statement seemed to be made by the British public, this time The X Factor being the favored one. In spite of the show's initial positive response, BBC's large budgets allocated for the production and of the big names attached as mentors, The Voice UK simply failed to make a lasting impression. Although in its first season it did scare Britain's Got Talent,

---

[36] 2010 was the year The Voice of Holland was launched. It registered record audiences, considerably higher than Popstars.

[37] In an attempt to re-create some competition for The Voice, following two years in which it had been the only singing competition on the Dutch landscape, a new version of The X Factor was launched. The show considerably flopped and has failed to be renewed.

making it register low ratings, it could not touch The X Factor, allowing the Cowell franchise to regroup, recover and, become winners of the 2013 clash. The fact that The Voice UK failed to created the hype it was aiming for, its long term future being now put to question, in a context in which X Factor's ratings seem to be independently[38] falling each year and there is no other singing competition show in the mix, reinforces the idea that cracks are beginning to show in what used to be 'gold mines' formats.

In the USA's landscapes, things were more muddy, but nonetheless bleak. The Voice and The X Factor, once again featuring the acid Simon Cowell as a judge, were released in the same year. Everybody expected the former to fail and the latter to succeed, yet the novelty of the blind auditions were preferred to the usual Cowell's spicy remarks. The Voice became a serious contender, even for clashing with the giant American Idol, while The X Factor slowly lost its grip. Not even the format changes seemed to be able to salvage the show, and its third season recently ended without any announcement with regards to its future, without any relevant artists launched and discovered, despite the massive 5 million dollar prize, and with some of the lowest ratings yet[39].

The X Factor's abrupt exit from the mix, is not however significantly improving American Idol's and The Voice's situations. The former has been struggling with keeping audiences engaged during the past year and the last season has registered a set of absolute lows in terms of numbers of viewers. The Voice has been gaining popularity, but not at the rate the other singing competitions are losing it. Also, up until now it has failed to produce a genuine contender for stardom, American Idol still being the only show in the US currently running, which has accomplished this goal.

At the moment, we seem to be witnessing an interesting phenomenon with regards to these shows. On one hand, the public seems to be fed up with the manipulation, stereotypy and predictability of American Idol. Take for instance the 5 seasons in a row of only white-males-playing-guitar winners, most of them coming from Southern states. By the time Candice Glover fi-

---

[38] There is no reason to assume The Voice UK had a doing in this ratings' drop, as it was already happening before the show was launched, and The Voice's presence did't seem to influence the drop rate.

[39] Wikipedia. "The X Factor (TV Series)". Last modified June 29th 2013. Last consulted June 30th 2013. <http://en.wikipedia.org/wiki/The_X_Factor_%28U.S._TV_series%29>

nally managed to break the strike, it seemed producers had been trying so hard to have a female winner, that they didn't even genuinely attempt to put through decent male singers contenders for the title. This artificiality has certainly harmed the show's overall image, as season 12's peak rating of 17.93[40] million viewers was less than half of what it had been back in 2006 and 2007[41]. On the other hand, American Idol remains up to this date, the undeniable star generator. None of the contestants of X Factor and The Voice have managed to even come close to the level of success registered by some of the Idol alumni. This argument seems to considerably weight down in the eyes of the public, as American Idol remained the most watched singing competition of 2013.

However, even if the Voice will eventually surpass American Idol, traditional reality TV will still suffer a back-lash, as the drama, tears, social cases, public humiliation and the other secondary elements that play a significant role in the story-telling of Idol and X Factor, are being down-played in de Mol's production, which does indeed focus on the voice, live performances and the work with the mentors.

The clash of the formats extended also to the content of the shows, and not just in their fights for ratings. Several elements migrated from one competition to the other, each aiming to fill in the gaps the other formats were exploiting to their own advantage. For example, in Romania, The X Factor embraced the rule that each mentor would eliminate one of their own acts each week, until the semi-finals when the public would be the only deciding factor. This procedure is more similar to The Voice's format during the live shows, rather than the classic X Factor elimination procedure. Also, the US version of the X Factor almost eradicated the classic boot-camp all together (including the traditional Judge's House stage) replacing it by a four chair challenge. Incidentally, a 'four chair turn' was a term made popular by The Voice, referring to the artists that managed to make all the four judges turn during the blind auditions. The two selection procedures are in effects quite different, but the terminology clearly underlines that the shows are trying to

---

[40] Wikipedia. "American Idol". Last modified June 30th 2013. Last consulted June 30th 2013. <http://en.wikipedia.org/wiki/American_Idol_%28season_12%29>
[41] Wikipedia. "American Idol". Last modified June 30th 2013. Last consulted June 30th 2013. <http://en.wikipedia.org/wiki/American_Idol#cite_note-ratings-1>

come up with responses to the creative elements featured by their competitors.

Several elements from The Voice were embraced by American Idol as well, such as having two competing artists sing the same song and then having the judges decide which one did it better. The exchange worked however both ways, The Voice embracing the idea of home visits (which had been missing from its initial season thus resulting in a more dry relation between the audience and the contestants), popularized by Idol, and that of duets with famous artists, which first appeared in The X Factor. Having some of the last remaining contestants perform on a tour is yet another element originated by Idol and then further embraced by The Voice and X Factor alike.

While in the media each of the shows' representatives were claiming their format is the best and the only one worth watching, behind the scenes another story unraveled, production teams paying close attention to their competition, striving to gain inspiration that could ultimately make their own formats better.

Conclusions

> "Pop Idol won the prestigious Golden Rose of Montreux in 2002. It was cited by the judges as 'perfect television'." (Biressi, Nunn. 2005)

There is no denying that in spite of the flaws, singing competitions have accomplished a series of things no other formats have managed to do. The simple concept of finding an artist or talent among ordinary people, has proven so effective, that several versions of format could be simultaneously broadcasted and watched by the public within the same time frame. Most of the countries that are currently showing their own versions of The Voice, Idols, X Factor or Got Talent, actually broadcast at least one other show from the list as well, and very often, even two. The fact that audiences can withstand so many variations, without being bothered by the inevitable repeatability, gets to show the versatility of the format and, indeed, its out of the ordinary characteristics.

America's choice of broadcasting five of these programs per year (taking into account The Voice has two seasons) shows there is still an interest in the market for singing competitions and that ultimately each form has its qualities. In the same way, it is quite evident the audience is not yet ready to give up growing talents under their own watchful eyes. And it's not just singers that people wish to discover and develop in this way, but also dancers, performing groups, chef cooks, top models, clothing designers and even dog groomers. Whether it's the direct implication in the making of a star, the illusion that they are even in a small proportion, responsible for the artist's success, or simply a need for people to observe other subjects fulfilling their dreams, there's a definite edge that keeps the public tuning in and consuming these types of shows.

This involvement however, also has a down side as people can't be continuously deceived about what they think they are accomplishing. The decreasing tendencies in the viewing numbers suggest that if stars fail to arise from these competitions, people will eventually stop watching as they can't continue to both emotionally and materially invest and support ultimate failures. The growing process, though captivating, is not strong enough to keep the shows going indefinitely, especially considering the relatively large number of such formats currently being broadcasted.

We have seen that throughout time, the singing competitions have adopted different elements one from the other. The fact that the shows are continuously clashing and competing against each other, does keep them somewhat fresh and sensitive to the public's wishes and expectations, thus resulting in better programs.

Ultimately however, what will ensure a longer TV life for these shows is their ability to create relevant artists. If they are slowly but steadily reaching the end of their "15 minutes of fame" is entirely dependent on who they will launch in the following years. So we'll just have to keep on watching and see who the winners are and what they do...

References

Biressi, A., Nunn, H. (2005). "Reality TV: Realism and Revelation". A Wallflower Press Book published as an e-book by Columbia University Press.
BBC Home. "Great Nottinghamians: Su Pollard". BBC.co.uk. Last updated March 2003. Last consulted 30th June 2013 <http://www.bbc.co.uk/nottingham/features/2002/11/great_nottinghamians_su_pollard.shtml>
BBC News. "X Factor copyright case settled". BBC.co.uk. October 11th 2007. Last consulted 30th June 2013. <http://news.bbc.co.uk/2/hi/entertainment/4482216.stm>
BBC News. "Walsh's X Factor house 'not his'". BBC.co.uk. November 29th 2005. Last consulted 30th June 2013. <http://news.bbc.co.uk/2/hi/entertainment/7040283.stm>
Carter, B. (2006). "How A Hit Almost Failed its Own Audition". The New York Times. Published 30th April 2006. Last consulted 30th June 2013. <http://www.nytimes.com/2006/04/30/business/yourmoney/30idol.html?pagewanted=1&_r=0>
Collett-White, M. (2013). "Sting calls X-Factor 'appalling'". Reuters blog. November 11th, 2009. Last consulted 30th June 2013 <http://blogs.reuters.com/fanfare/2009/11/11/sting-calls-x-factor-appalling/>
Cowell, T. "I Hate to Be Rude, But...: Simon Cowell's Book of Nasty Comments", Publisher John Blake, February 1st 2006 <http://www.amazon.com/Hate-Be-Rude-But-Comments/dp/1844542254>
Fletcher, A. "Plan B criticizes 'X Factor' celebrity and image focus ". Digital Spy, July 19th 2012. Last consulted 30th June 2013 <http://www.digitalspy.co.uk/tv/s103/the-x-factor/news/a394159/plan-b-criticises-x-factor-celebrity-and-image-focus.html >
Hyman, D. "Simon Cowell on Britney Spears: 'She's Surprisingly Quite Mean'". Rolling Stone. September 7th 2012. Last consulted 30th June 2013 <http://www.rollingstone.com/movies/news/simon-cowell-on-britney-spears-shes-surprisingly-quite-mean-20120907>
International Television Expert Group. 'Global TV trading and most successful TV formats worldwide' itve.org. December 2009, Last consulted 30th June 2013 <http://www.international-television.org/tv_market_data/international-tv-format-ranking-and-trading_2006-2008.html>
Redden, G. (2008). "Making Over the Talent Show" chapter in Exposing Lifestyle Television: The Big Reveal edited by Gareth Palmer. Ashgate Publishing, ltd.
Robinson, S. "Is Britney Spears The New Simon Cowell On The X Factor". AccessHollywood.com. Last consulted 30th June 2013. http://watch.accesshollywood.com/video/is-britney-spears-the-new-simon-cowell-on-the-x-factor/1831341649001?utm_source=accesshollywood.com&utm_medium =referral#>
Rushfield, R. "Secret Rituals of American Idol Auditions Exposed". TheDailyBeast.com. January 19th 2010. Last consulted 30th June 2013. <http://www.thedailybeast.com/articles/2010/01/19/secret-rituals-of-american-idol-auditions-exposed.html>
The Buggles. "Video Killed The Radio Star" song from The Age of Plastic album released by the Island Records label, September 7th 1979

The Futon Critic. "FOX Sets New Broadcast Industry Record With Eighth Consecutive Season Victory Among Adults 18–49". TheFutonCritic.com. 24th May 2012. Last consulted 30th June 2013. <http://www.thefutoncritic.com/ratings/2012/05/24/fox-sets-new-broadcast-industry-record-with-eighth-consecutive-season-victory-among-adults-18-49-614111/20120524fox01/>

The Sun. "X Factor Curse Hits Matt Cardle". The Sun. Last updated 24th May 2012. Last consulted 30th June 2013. <http://www.thesun.co.uk/sol/homepage/showbiz/4331540/X-Factor-curse-hits-Matt-Cardle.html>

Vallantine, S. "UK Television Talent Shows Through the Ages: The Not So Perfect Ten". East of the M60. July 9th 2010. Last consulted 30th June 2013. <http://mancunian1001.wordpress.com/2010/07/09/uk-television-talent-shows-through-the-ages-the-not-so-perfect-ten/>

Wikipedia. "American Idol". Last modified June 30th 2013. Last consulted June 30th 2013. <http://en.wikipedia.org/wiki/American_Idol#cite_note-ratings-1>

Wikipedia. "Got Talent". Last modified June 27th 2013. Last consulted June 30th 2013. <http://en.wikipedia.org/wiki/Got_Talent>

Wikipedia. "Idols (TV Series)". Last modified June 24th 2013. Last consulted June 30th 2013. <http://en.wikipedia.org/wiki/Idol_series>

Wikipedia. "Nigel Lythgoe". Last modified June 30th 2013. Last consulted June 30th 2013. <http://en.wikipedia.org/wiki/Nigel_Lythgoe>

Wikipedia. "Pop Idol". Last modified June 2nd 2013. Last consulted June 30th 2013. <http://en.wikipedia.org/wiki/Pop_idol>

Wikipedia. "Popstars". Last modified June 22nd 2013. Last consulted June 30th 2013. <http://en.wikipedia.org/wiki/Popstars>

Wikipedia. "Popstars (UK)". Last modified May 28th 2013. Last consulted June 30th 2013. <http://en.wikipedia.org/wiki/Popstars_(UK)>

Wikipedia. "Su Pollard". Last modified June 18th 2013. Last consulted June 30th 2013. <http://en.wikipedia.org/wiki/Su_Pollard>

Wikipedia. "The Voice (TV Series)". Last modified June 30th 2013. Last consulted June 30th 2013. <http://en.wikipedia.org/wiki/The_Voice_%28TV_series>

Wikipedia. "The X Factor (TV Series)". Last modified June 29th 2013. Last consulted June 30th 2013. <http://en.wikipedia.org/wiki/The_X_Factor_%28TV_series>

YouTube. "Charlie Brooker's Screenwipe—Reality TV Editing". Youtube.com. Uploaded on 1st March 2007. Last consulted June 30th 2013 <http://www.youtube.com/watch?v=BBwepkVurCI>

YouTube. "Simon Cowell nasty comments 1". Youtube.com. Uploaded on 26th August 2010. Last consulted June 30th 2013 <https://www.youtube.com/watch?v=rJo7jbZZv5k>

YouTube. "Simon Cowell nasty comments 2". Youtube.com. Uploaded on 30th August 2010. Last consulted June 30th 2013 https://www.youtube.com/watch?v=ZrGdyT8ItO4

TV Drama as a Narrative form: Scenes from a Gendered and a Sacralized Cultural Sphere in Turkish Society

Nuran E. Işık

Introduction

Turkish society has characteristics which oscillate between traditional, modern and postmodern ways of seeing the world. Turkish popular cultural texts offer us an opportunity to study the complex relationship between the societal and political change, and the rhetorical characteristics of different cultural genre. The formation of everyday life in contemporary Turkish society can be clearly observed through an analysis of the relevant genres, which include television dramas, adaptations of fiction, different types of reality shows, health programs, and so called 'magazine' programs. These textual formations represent indicators of the different ideological and cultural transformations underlying cultural and sociological changes in Turkey: There are a number of other processes which additionally serve for the construction of the symbolic marketplace. These are the privatization of television channels, the impact of the globalization processes on different segments of society, the integration of banking and advertising industries into the global markets, the boom in domestic consumption, a visible increase in formation of identity claims through the media and the pluralistic nature of the popular cultural sphere in terms of being a venue for different cultural voices.

As is well known, the literature on television studies offer research based on cultural studies as well as critical theory. However, instead of simply borrowing from one of these approaches, this paper takes an innovative approach, aiming to analyze the ways in which different narratives and rhetorical markers impose themselves on audiences by employing discursive strategies which have a claim deriving from 'real life'. As Casey point out, television has successfully uncovered its constructedness, discursive and mediated nature; furthermore it keeps presenting itself as a neutral, unmediated and objective medium by hiding all processes in the production of meaning. (2002: 48). When it comes to revealing such constructedness, the narratives positioned within different genres provide important clues about the prioritization or subordination of certain meaning makers, such as beliefs deriving from religious texts, hegemonic values presented within the framework of normalcy, and rhetorical tactics for silencing atypical or unwanted voices. As Valaskivi (2000) notes, genre formulates and limits expression in relation to the visual dimension of the programme, the amount of dialogue used, the appearance of the setting, and the degree of 'realism'. Most of the TV drama form, to which unique genre characteristics have been attributed (e.g. Mafia TV serials) ironically label themselves as a series of narratives borrowing from 'real life situations'. By doing this, they seem to have constituted a sense of 'authenticity', expressed through various different forms of aesthetics (masculine/feminine, pre-modern, nostalgic, moral). As Nelson (1997) vividly emphasizes, one of the reasons for the continuing dominant influence of realism on television is that it corresponds to human beings' strong inclination to make sense of the world, through the use of narratives. The following evaluations aim at revealing the ways in which different narratives (which take the form of highly masculinized and pious aesthetics) offer themselves as major claims in Turkish culture, constructed as a sphere which needs to be portrayed within the framework of authenticity.

The following have emerged as the most important sociological features of Turkish society: tensions between secularism/laicism and Islamization; identity markers of Kurdish versus Kemalist ideologies; the masculine versus feminine worlds; and class divisions. The evolution of TV dramas in Turkish society has reflected these sociological divisions and tensions in such a way that the mediatization of daily life can be clearly observed in different segments of society. TV dramas have reproduced narratives stemming from ideologies and discourses, some of which have been articulated through popular culture. In such a context, role and function of TV as a "super-narrator" has been gaining importance: The mediatization of everyday life is becoming increasingly reflected on the vocabulary of people so as to create a series of neologisms which can be exemplified by daily linguistic rituals. Some of the heroes of TV drama have been glorified to the extent that children are named after them. Housewives' daily conversations often center on the most famous characters in TV dramas. Furthermore, a certain material culture reflecting TV drama settings has been produced and marketed for large audiences and children or teenagers often role play the main characters. The settings where these serials were recorded have become tourist attractions for those who identify sorrows and successes with the characters through photographs and souvenirs. TV dramas not only functioned to reproduce or accommodate local characteristics into a mediated world, they also became a cultural signifier at transnational level: Several Turkish TV dramas are exported, creating a new venue for the political economy of the media; some have become extremely well known in countries such as Morocco and Tunisia, so that everyday life of these societies have also been affected by this 'exported' cultural marker. In other words, Turkish TV dramas have become an important cultural signifier and mediator at national and transnational level. In this paper, such a complex and multidimensional process will be evaluated with an emphasis on a gendered cultural sphere, and the rise of popular religion. The first theme will be exemplified by a type of hegemonic masculinity reproduced and glorified in many TV dramas and narratives. The second theme is the illustration of "religionization in Turkish media" as depicted by popular religious tools.

Gendering Popular Cultural Narratives: The Identity of "Delikanlılık" (Crazy Blood) as a Form of Hegemonic Masculinity

With the rise of commercial channels in the 1980's, television has become the most significant medium of entertainment in Turkish society. As a result of this dominance, it has become increasingly difficult to prevent the dispersal of cultural identities in the public realm; it has been widely argued that developments in global media culture have eroded state hegemony in the cultural realm, making the fragmentation and dispersal of cultural identities inevitable (Öncü 2006).

The examples of media texts and genre in Turkey manifest the hybrid character of cultural and sociological characteristics, which have been affected by the way in which media industries have evolved in time. The privatization of TV channels after the 1980's is considered the most important period in terms of the integration of the Turkish cultural production world into the neoliberal logic of media institutions. The increasing integration of political institutions and the media created a new equilibrium, which allowed the major cultural and political actors to negotiate over the meaning-making processes in the popular cultural sphere. The support of political actors on the issue of facilitating investments in the media demanded compensation, in the form of the creation of a world of spectacle a la Debord (1967), that is, the creation of 'stars' as the major figures or persona in the media texts (Ergur 1993). The function of the media began not only to embrace not only a wider spectrum in every aspect, from the observer/consumer to the spectacle itself, but also led to the participant/actor becoming more actively involved in creating media texts. Eventually, the media became a major agent in society, and in this new role, it was able to reveal the mundane, sacred, modern, traditional, hybrid features of various different cultural routines. The Turkish media became more flexible, increasingly able to reflect different cultural styles and values. The cultural and political ties developed with international institutions and organizations signified a new trend in mediation, in terms of rapid circulation of all kinds of symbols in social life. As the struggles over political and cultural issues emerged in different mediation processes, media texts increasingly articulated tensions caused by identity crises, social problems and social pressures to become part of the globalization process. Of all media, television has been one of the most important in the formation of a cultural public sphere.

While the 1970–1980's witnessed the domination of foreign productions such as the series 'Dallas', the production of national TV dramas peaked at the end of the the 1990's, highlighting the role of media technology, the adaptation of local genres and the reflection of struggles between many different identity markers, including as secular, traditional, masculine, feminine, Turkish, Kurdish, sunni and heterodox (Alevi). Because of the highly competitive market in their productions, TV channels employed an innovative approach to language use, which aimed to stimulate both the senses and the emotions.

Such a multidimensional process is also an outcome of a need to articulate a narrator for "multiple realities" (Schutz 1964). These realities cannot be fully explained either through orientalist framings nor occidentalist tendencies, which are simplistic angles produced by the TV narratives themselves. Instead, the way in which these constructed dualisms are legitimized and reproduced by daily rituals and discourses should be considered as a major problematic within the framework of media studies. TV drama has the power to reveal the unexplored potential of reality. Its perspectives which often pass unnoticed, and can bring repressed experiences out it into the open, and thus enlightens that which is invisible and anticipates the unexpected and the unforseen. As Ridgman writes, texts constructed via TV narratives can illustrate masculinized experience of historical drama as an indicator of 'patriarchal politics' (Ridgman 2000). TV drama offers narratives which provide a stage for social reality, and organizes and displays the dramaturgy through which society is able to represent itself to itself. The concept of "indigenization" (Buananno 2008) helps us to understand how society is representing itself to itself via TV drama in Turkish society: The concept of "indigenization" refers to "the process through which forms and expressions of external cultures, elaborated by other societies, are appropriated, re-elaborated, and restored by diverse local societies in configurations that are consistent with their own home-grown systems of meaning" (Buananno 2008: 88). The examples of TV drama cited below also depict a process whereby non-local materials are transformed to provide new configurations of local tastes and sentiments.

After the 2000's, television serials reflecting the difficulties of daily problems became a very popular genre. The portrayal of ethnic identities in drama serials created the opportunity to discuss the existence of groups with different identities, alternative ways of living and other invisible, previously ignored features of social life. One of the most significant features of the serials is their ability to create a sense of continuity in narration by breaking down the structure of fiction into predictable stages, such as beginnings and endings; this is a process which emphasizes the affective role of the narrative in terms of emphasizing curiosity. Such narrative characteristics facilitate the audience identification with the main characters. Eulogies from admirers in the newspapers on the death of leading characters reveal a sphere where the lines between reality and fiction have been blurred (Ahıska and Yenal, 2006). The claims about authenticity and realism emphasized above have been exemplified by such incidents as well as different examples of mediatization of everyday life (the intensity of discussions about TV drama in social media, popularity about the increasing status of actors and actresses playing in TV dramas, and other popular cultural discourses).

Although the themes of these dramas vary, a great majority employ characteristics adopted from the classical Turkish movies of the past, such as melodrama. Love and lust, action and heroism, vengeance and glorification, materialism and altruism are among popular themes, all of which reflect a negotiation among pre-modern, modern and postmodern ways of living. The genre has become so popular that it has created a culture industry marketing products identified with the sentimentalized reflections about the ambivalences of Turkish modernity.

The role of TV drama as a super narrator has increased the visibility with the growth of cultural tensions and social cleavages: The more such visibility increased, the greater the role of TV dramas in mediating identities and voices in the cultural public sphere, especially as understood from a gendered perspective. The classical Turkish film genre reproduced categorizations generally recognized as codes of modernity such as East versus West, masculine versus feminine, and poor versus rich. TV dramas produced after the privatization of TV channels also reproduced similar dualisms by re-appropriating local cultural codes such as masculinity as part of a nationalistic discourse.

In order to exemplify the arguments made in this paper, texts from a very popular 1990's TV drama have been selected: Crazy Heart (*Deli Yürek*)[1].

Deli Yürek is a story about a very brave young man, a worker, Yusuf, who seeks justice and morality in his life. He lived a normal life until selected by his commander to become a special agent in a fight against the enemy. Yusuf is brave, charismatic, handsome, genuine, honest, and passionate about justice; his life is guided by the imperative to 'do the right thing'[2]. Yusuf becomes a hero, fighting against villains, the members of the mafia world. He is engulfed in the negative world of these evil people on the one hand, but on the other, is able to continue his existence in the 'normal or 'moral' world of friends, relatives and others who live according to moral standards. The binary opposition between the positive and the negative worlds is the main theme of the story, which is based on the events and in-

---

[1] Crazy Heart (*Deli Yürek*): The production, directed by Osman Sınav, started in 1998. It was on the air for four years. The feature film which was produced after the TV serial has ended was entitled: The Crazy Heart: The Hell of Bumerang.

[2] His name comes from the well known story of Josef. Yusuf is believed to have been the eleventh son of Jacob (Ya'qūb), and his favorite. Of all of Jacob's children, Joseph was the one given the gift of prophecy. Joseph is admired as a great preacher of the Islamic faith, who had an extremely strong commitment to God and one who tried to get people to follow the path of righteousness. In the TV serial, too, Yusuf has been struggling to follow the same path.

cidences designed to illustrate that the immoral and criminal world can only lead to further evil and misdeeds. The epideictic character of the narrative dictates how the text praises, affirms or condemns the major values of the heroes and/or villains.

Yusuf's relationship with his best friend, the bird man (*Kuşçu*), his moral mentor, is the key to understanding the aesthetic sensation, which is created by the utilization of the power of engaging discursive tools such as parables. The birdman, so named because of this habit of feeding birds on the roof of an apartment block, is Yusuf's moral guide in resolving the numerous dilemmas he experiences in the cruel world of the evil characters. Yusuf is a powerful man who will only accept as the birdman, portrayed as having spiritual powers as his interlocutor. This spiritual righteousness is occasionally implied through the narrative power of his stories, which act as a force of mediation between the evil and the spiritual worlds. The birdman can mystically make predictions about the future, and his dreams have significance for Yusuf's life. He makes implications about the importance of virtuousness in life. However, he never openly and directly imposes his caveats, preferring to storify these as parables in the serial. The birdman gives advice through the stories of his own experience, or refers to various proverbs, verses, hymns, mystic figures, poems of spiritual nature, and interpretations of dervishes, which all signify folkloric wisdom and telos.

The mafia leaders generally portrayed use an array of sophisticated strategies, some of which are violent; the hero therefore has to learn how to survive in this battle; he not only shows a moral standing, but also acts through a series of rules and norms which are described by the term 'crazy blood' (*delikanlılık*) in Turkish culture. A person described as having crazy blood (*delikanlı*) is honorable, never using unfair means against his enemy; he is honest, virile, courageous, sincere, and protective of women without accepting them as equals. The term refers to a constructed identity which is savage, serving to produce an expression of manhood which rests on a history of subjectivities shaped by different mentalities and cultural configurations. Just as the father protects the family, the state has a duty protect the society. The state coded as a father figure, and the motherland, a woman needing protection. The ways in which masculine identity and nationalism are interrelated in this drama also creates an aura whereby a mentor is represented as having the moral powers needed to theorize and justify the deeds and duties of the hero.

Since the production of *Deli Yurek*, most Turkish TV dramas prioritized the hyper masculine identities which constitute "delikanlılık" (crazy blood) over other identities. This serial signified the beginning of a new era where a gendered mediated cultural sphere was reproduced via an ironic combination of codes, such as masculinity and nationalism, as part of a savage world, a world where rational-legal rule in Weberian sense is not possible. Instead, the survival of the fittest became the main code, elevated to a level where notions such as civilization and reason are seriously threatened. *Deli Yurek* has become a symbol of masculinism and bravado, re-appropriating 'authentic' cultural features of Turkish society, thus, bringing a new voice to enhance the understanding of the gendered reality depicted in such TV dramas[3]. Thus, the way in which such an example of a TV drama is glorified and presented as the ultimate aesthetic genre contributes to the process of indigenization, so as to reposition the local and the global as an intersection.

Hypermasculinity can also be read as a backlash against those gender roles which were created by Turkish modernity, and thus modeled on Westernization. The men of Western appearance were always portrayed as anti-macho, or, virile enough. The TV dramas produced for private channels, portrayed the lives of 'regular guys', or, the men on the street, and covered themes such as divorcees, large families, men and women living in neighborhood, the love affairs of the wealthy, the moral dilemmas experienced by different types of people, the domestication of everyday life, traditional life styles with a touch of modernity, idealists trying to achieve a collective goal, and family quarrels. These themes required a gendered language which was able to expose what is unspoken. In other words, TV dramas brought about configurations on the private lives of individuals representing different life styles, which created a cultural baggage for daily conversations. The type of masculinity which had previously been coded as 'Eastern' or 'savage' was re-introduced as an ideal type. The types of ideal

---

[3] These interpretations have been elaborated based on comments made by the producer of Deli Yurek, Osman Sınav during a personal conversation in 1999. He stated that only TV dramas which would portray the 'real' and 'authentic' characteristics of Turkish society would survive (at that time, there were more than eighty TV serials on air).

women also changed correspondingly: Although the 1990's witnessed a series of TV dramas in which modern women were portrayed as positive elements for the society, this could not persist in the long run, and most TV drama later normalized women's roles within the patriarchal structure of society. The type of woman who supports herself financially and independently is a rare case in TV dramas produced after 2000's. The current ideal type of would be a beautiful, educated, reproductive woman with the expectation of marriage to a rich but morally dubious husband. The 'indigenization' process emphasized above has been complemented by tendencies such as re-invention of traditions.

Although there seems to be a need for a full understanding of the geneology of TV dramas in Turkey, it can be clearly stated that the late modern Turkish society in general has been witnessing a process called the re-sacralization of cultural sphere, a comprehensive term incorporating all types of sacred symbols used in the public sphere. Although much has been written in recent years on conservatism and the rise of Islam in Turkish society, it is possible to argue that glocal transfusions and interpenetrations have also played an important role in transforming Turkish society in terms of making Islam and Islamization more visible. TV dramas produced for private 'Islamic channels' have normalized religionization in terms of the interpenetration of (non-heterodox) religious affairs into the daily lives of individuals. Thus, the contested area of cultural sphere was made more visible via these productions, which emphasized various aspects of the new approach to sacralization

The Rise of Popular Religion in Turkish TV Drama

Popular piety is constructed through a process, facilitated by the media, of mediation, that is, the mutuality between new forms of communication and the institutionalized form of communication. As Meyer and Moors (2006) emphasize, religion cannot be analyzed outside the forms of mediation that define it. Religion and media need to be understood as co-constitutive, therefore it makes little sense to claim that the former exists prior to the latter (Meyer 2006). The media offerings tend to be formularized, predictable, and sentimental, with positions on good and evil clearly defined, very similar to folk narratives (Hinds, Motz, and Nelson 2006). The emergence of new cultural publics in Turkish society signified a new era in which both traditional and modern lifestyles could be represented as contributing to the negotiation of what constitutes a moral, good or ideal life. The circulation of such symbols representing traditional, sacred, religious, and spiritual aspects became increasingly visible in different formats, an outcome of the internet and digital technology. The integration of neoliberal and Islamic publics into Turkish society created the need for a new interpretation of the role of mediated religion, with its reflections in other spheres of life, such as politics, business, and culture.

As Asad (2001) argues, in identifying religion, we need to delve into its materialities which constitute its form and being. It is thus important to denote sufficient attention to the practices of both the religious and the secular in order to account for the emerging piety culture. The particular emphasis of this paper on the concept of piety contributes to an understanding of the way faith is revealed through different devotional practices aimed at creating religious virtues (Asad 2001: 142). In addition, research on Islamic piety movements has shown, in regard to for individuals who actively seek to inhabit ethical norms and cultivate Islamic virtues, how submission and 'agency' are mutuality constitutive processes (Deeb 2006; Mahmood 2005). In Turkey, the "politics of patience" (Duran, 2008) has had an impact on the different forms of the piety culture, and has led to the construction of a distinctive vocabulary. Various kinds of different pious performances have started to accompany 'modern' ways of living, and these performances claim to carry their own authenticity and priority over other signifiers, such as the secular and Western. Similar to the struggles and meanings of secularism and laicism, the competition between various pious sensibilities and ethical selves can be seen as indicators of inconsistencies and contradictions in Islamic identity formations, and as such, are worthy of study.

Lipstiz (1990) emphasizes the popularity of television which is due to its familiar and recurring story narratives, and their similarity to tabloid tales and folklore. Turkish TV's repackaging of both the teachings and cultural manifestations of Islam include the production of programs and genres such as live broadcast of religious ceremonies on sacred days (e.g. the birth of Muhammad), prophetic stories, religious prayers, descriptions of Qur'anic verses, conversations about the Qur'an, the preaching on Islamic rules and deeds, religious drama, call-in shows, live conversation programs, inspirational fiction, religious music programs, adaptations of other literary genres, and, most importantly, TV dramas, as a site of highly conservative narratives. In addition, there emerged programs on unconventional approaches to the interpretation of Islam: e.g., rituals involving different interpretations of Qur'anic verses, a variety of New Age themes such as reiki, astrology, feng-sui, some of which are infused with Islam. Considering the whole range of relevant programs can lead to a fuller understanding of the televisual moments of Turkish 'media-scape' formulated by Appandurai (1990).

The majority of secular and non-secular narratives which employ rituals of storytelling on television tend to borrow from discursive markers of religious piety. In addition to those exemplified in this paper, other dramas and also other genres have involved a similar process, whereby groups are invited by an interlocutor to resolve the tensions stemming from the problems covered in the narrative. This creates a spiritual sensitivity through which the audience learn 'lessons', and also receive weekly affirmations functioning as moral prescriptions. With regards to Islam, the narratives on prophetic legends and also dervishes are considered to have instructional as well as moralistic implications. Also very common is the extensive use of folklore and tales as a foundation for supernatural events, characters and anectodes involved in the occurrence of miracles (*karamat*). Accordingly, the articulation of storytelling features in TV dramas creates an atmosphere of openness to the possibility of spiritual influence and awakening.

Conclusion

There can be no culture, except one which is isolated, that does not incorporate 'a different mixture of alien ideas' (Robertson 1995, p. 41). The audiences as well as producers adopt and adapt different global/local forms of narratives as a part of the process called "indigenization", which gives rise to forms and expressions with hybrid and syncretic nature. In this paper, two important complementary narratives, those of masculinity and popular religion, are identified as factors characterizing the aesthetics of various TV dramas in Turkish media. Through exposure to a world of hypermasculinity recontextualized in different genres such as TV drama, it is expected that audiences will form a linkage between their moral selves and just deeds. It has become evident that TV dramas glorifiying certain concept of heroism would justify a world of power, in which Machiavellian tools are considered superior to more egalitarian approaches. Therefore, the TV dramas are not only aesthetic sites of entertainment, but, they are also powerful genres which set the agenda for certain angles or approaches to the politics of everyday life. It is therefore necessary to understand and evaluate the different narratives and genres which produce a language of their own, in order to construct identities. It would be interesting to see how different processes such as 'narrativization of selves' are relevant to understand different rhetorical strategies. In addition, there is a need to integrate literary and rhetorical approaches to television studies so as to decipher the intricate relationship between the unacknowledged role of popular piety on the one hand, and the gendered sphere on the other. The intersection between these spheres would provide us the ways in which different discursive and rhetorical strategies have been reproduced and improvised so as to reveal ambivalences in cultural sphere.

In Turkey, in addition to the visibility of Islam, as well as the religionization of the cultural sphere also affected the media world, in terms the development of media narratives which served the dominant ideological markers, such as conservatism, as a hegemonic framework. The creation of a re-gendered or a hyper-gendered space has opened up a new sphere for media scapes which place a strong emphasis on such dutiful, obedient, conforming, pious, and patriarchal subjects. Based entirely on fiction, TV dramas can offer a wide range of imaginative themes, stemming from a variety of values and world views. These include love, altruism, varying life styles, emotions, collectivism, individualism, all of which stem from different values and worldviews. There appears to have been a certain pattern in Turkish media in terms of linking specific values with certain identities in order to present a unified world, characterized by diversity. The process of sacralization and re-gendering attaches a feature of authoritativeness, which precludes the voices of independent individuals who are the authors of their own lives. For example, the most popular serial in 2013, *Muhteşem Yuzyıl* (The Magnificent Century—referring to the Magnificent Suleiman), has been formulated as a historical soap opera depicting the Ottoman Empire as an underappreciated period in Turkish history. While the past is historicized through the romantization of the relationship of the sultans and their subjects, it also has the effect of dislocating the present moment through aestheticizing political entities which glorify the Empire-like political entities. This empire culture has been perpetuated through the above mentioned narratives of heroism/hypermasculinity, as well as a gendered aesthetic culture. Once again, the mediated function of TV drama goes hand in hand with the 'ontological security' (Giddens 1991) it provides for individuals, who are inspired and encouraged in the face of the difficulties presented by the problems of society. The need to rely on a super-narrator seems to be an indicator for a search for security for the political classes who themselves feel less than entirely secure.

References

Ahıska, M., Yenal, Z. (eds.) (2006). *Türkiye'de Hayat Tarzı Temsilleri,1980–2005 (Representations of Life Styles in Turkey)*, Istanbul: Osmanlı Bankası Arsiv ve Arastırma Merkezi.

Appadurai, A. (1990). 'Discuncture and Difference in the Global Cultural Economy'. In Szeman, Imre and Kaposy, Timothy (eds) *Cultural Theory*, London: Blackwell, 282–296.

Asad, T. (2001). 'Reading a modern classic: W. C. Smith's 'The meaning and end of religion', *History of Religions* 40(3): 205–222. In Rianne Subijanto (2011): 'The visibility of a pious public', *Inter-Asia Cultural Studies* 12:2: 240–253.

Buananno, M. (2008). *The Age of Television: Experiences and Theories*, Chicago: The University of Chicago Press.

Casey, B. (2002). *Television Studies: The Key Concepts*. London: Routledge.

De Bord, G. (1983). *The Society of Spectacle*, London: Rebel Press.

Duran, B. (2008). The Justice and Development Party's 'new politics': Steering toward conservative democracy, a revised islamic agenda or management of new crises? In: Cizre Ü (ed.) *Secular and Islamic Politics in Turkey*. London: Routledge, pp.80–107.

Ergur, A. (2002). 'Gerçeklik tanımlayıcısı olarak görsellik ve Türkiye'de siyasetin gösterileşmesi', (Visuality as marker for reality and the spectacularization of politics in Turkey), *Toplum ve Bilim*, 93: 7–29.

Giddens, A. (1991). *Modernity and Self-Identity: Self and Society in the Late Modern Age*, California: Princeton University Press.

Hinds, H. E., Motz, M. and Nelson, A. (eds) (2006). *Popular Culture Theory and Methodology*, Madison: University of Wisconsin Press.

Öncü, A. (2006). 'Becoming secular muslims: Yaşar Nuri Öztürk as a super-subject on Turkish television', In Meyers, Birgit and Moors, Annelies (eds.) *Religion, Media and the Public Sphere*, Indiana, Indiana University Press, 227–240.

Lipsitz, G. (1990). *Time Passages: Collective Memory and American Popular Culture*. Minnesota: University of Minnesota Press.

Mahmood, S. (2006). *Politics of Piety: The Islamic Revival and the Feminist Subject*. New Jersey: Princeton University Press.

Meyer, B. (2006). 'Religious revelation, secrecy and the limits of visual representation', *Anthropological Theory* 6: 431–444.

Meyer, M. and Moors, A. (2006). *Religion, Media, and the Public Sphere,* Bloomington: Indiana University Press.

Nelson, R. (1997). TV Drama in Transition, New York: St.Martin's Press.

Ridgan, J. (2000). 'Patriarchal Politics: Our Friends in the North and the Crisis of Masculinity, in *Frames and Fictions on Television: The Politics of Identity Within Drama,* Carson, B. Jewellyn-Jones (edit), Intellect Books, UK: 2000.

Robertson, R. (1995). *Glocalization: time-space and homogeneity-heterogeneity,* in FeatherstoneM., Lash C., Robertson R. (eds.): Global modernities, Sage, London.

Schutz, A, (1964). *Collected Papers,* Vol III, Nijhoff, The Hague.

Valaskivi, K. (2000). 'Being a part of the family? Genre, gender and production in a Japanese TV drama' , Media, Culture, and Society, 22: 309–325.

The hero's journey

*María Teresa Nicolás Gavilán, Lourdes López Gutiérrez,
Carmen Silvia Sánchez Arana, Tania Alejandra Benítez Sánchez*

"We all need heroes"[1] may be one of the certainties of human beings that can explain our astonishment when confronted with the epic fiction. The epic gender introduces the hero's myth, enhancing us through the belief and desire of becoming better.

In Joseph Campbell's works (1991) we can understand how myth is a metaphor to the world's truths; it's a collective dream. This has different functions grouped in four categories: 1) Mystic, which refers to the transcendental consciousness. What's after this and now? 2) Cosmologic, which refers to the understanding of our role in the world, beyond the scientific explanation. This results in a reality sense. 3) Sociological functions, which tend to cohesion the social order from behavior rules. 4) Educational function, which lead to our learning in specific situations in life. And because of this loss one brings up the stories and characters which blend with the different cultures.

Through the assimilation of the fiction's myth we can establish character's models and their constant in actions. This is specially seen in the audiovisual means, so popular nowadays. And the hero's myth is the most popular.

The hero, in any of its presentations, from the historical character to the imaginative cartoons, goes through a path, an itinerary (as Campbell calls it) in which the main character has a specific starting point where he "is", afterward there is a unique detonation that makes him "act" in a special way and then he is confronted to a "mission". When he leaves, in this journey, he is going to confront the "unknown"; interacts with enemies, overcomes obstacles, works out his own uncertainties, shows his abilities on specific tests, including death, and as a last repairing act he obtains the "repairing fulfillment" that allows him to have a strengthen return home. (Vogler, 2002)

The "superhero" is a kind of hero which exhibits some nonhuman qualities. The superheroes become prototypes in the popular (belief) imagination and

---

[1] From Lex Luthor to Clark Kent. Season five Smallville.

they become appealing because of their "super human" qualities and also because of the values and ideals they represent. Superman is an example form heroes' anthology. According to Stan Beeler (2011) "Superman is the non-religious myth which has persisted the most in the modern occidental civilization".

When a serie about a hero is worked out, the biggest challenge is to develop the character with human qualities making him vulnerable, so that the public could be hooked to this character. His personality tells us who he is, his desires, intentions and goals. The public's emotional identification to this character involves the attraction he flows to viewers.

In the serie, the construction of characters reflects two main characteristics: Traces his or her behavior and acts according to the value he or she represents and maintains this coherent structure. Character should be made under the following paradigm: "the character as a person". In other words, he or she lives in a specific social environment, exhibits a real personality, defined by physical atributes. All these make him or her rich enough so to overcome any moral crisis or external factors which make the problem. And this richness is reflected in his or her actions. According to Robert McKee (1997:101): "The real personality is discovered from the decisions taken under pressure, and the bigger the pressure, the deeper the revelation and natural essence of the character".

On the other hand, the empathy felt for the characters is a multilevel process which can increase or decrease. The first level is cognitive empathy which consists in understanding character and circumstances. The second level is an emotional empathy, related to an affective implication with the character. The third level, a superior level, a value empathy which implies the importance given to the character. It also means "I like the character, hence he is good". We aren't referring to a moral judgment but evoking the good feelings from the viewers (remember we are in an emotional level). The last level is projective empathy, that is, the ability to deal with fantasy, to identify oneself with the main character as to become that character, to integrate our life to the life of those characters. And this identification with characters is developed while we experience the different empathy levels.

In Smallville serie the characters follow these principles and its emotional success is seen in the 10 years it lasted. The main characteristics are well supported in their personalities and are well acted out. The viewers have been loyal to the serie, specially the first five seasons. This shows the emotional success.

The story starts with Clark Kent teenager years, the future Superman. He starts to discover his physical abilities and his tendencies to protect humanity. His family plays a main role in his personality, ideals, values and integrity of the future hero.

The importance of the family environment in the development of the main character's personality traits, as well as the antagonist character's traits,have been a priority in the serie. It is so important that the key point of the first season is to present the paternal relationship of several character (Jonathan and Clark Kent; Lionel and Lex Luthor). According to Vogler, we can state that the father is the "mentor" in the hero's journey (Vogler, 2002).

This is why we consider very important to analyze the first season according to the family influences and theirs consequences in the hero's personality. The methodology chosen was the qualitative analysis of the 24 episodes of the first season. In terms of categories, (the hero's analysis according to traits exposed, like personality and values) we studied the following aspects: the conflict, the values used and the decisions taken.

Smallville: Superman's genesis

For 10 years, the serie producers, kept the serie in the best TV schedule because of its high ratings. It was programmed for TV channels like CW and Warner Channel. But what elements could make a difference when it is about the most famous "superhero" already known? What can be the hooking element to an audience that knows the story very well?

To answer this we have to go to key elements: the social context, characters, theme, and the set in stage.

In relationship to the social context, Smallville, was presented by W.C. in October 16, 2001. In general context we find out that the American society, at that moment, was living a fearful and insecure stage after September 11 events in the Twin Towers in New York and the American intervention to Afghanistan. This critical moment modifies the type of viewers. They support new answers and solutions to the social problems. This is a historical opportunity to the serie. It offers teenagers and young adults of America the most famous superhero and his genesis is representing the American values[2].

In the pilot program, the main characters are introduced at the same time the meteorite rain is falling and at the same moment that Clark's ship is landing. Viewers are introduced to Lionel Luthor, Lex Luthor (Alexander), Jonathan Kent, Martha Kent and Lara Lang.

In this episode main information is presented to the viewers so they can identify the real qualities belonging to characters and their basic lines of action.

The two main characters (Clark and Lex) influenced by their respective parents are presented and the main type of relationships they are going to have (three types) are stated: family, sentimental and friendly / antagonist relationship.

As we explore the relationship among them we can draw the following chart from the first season.

Picture 1 - First season

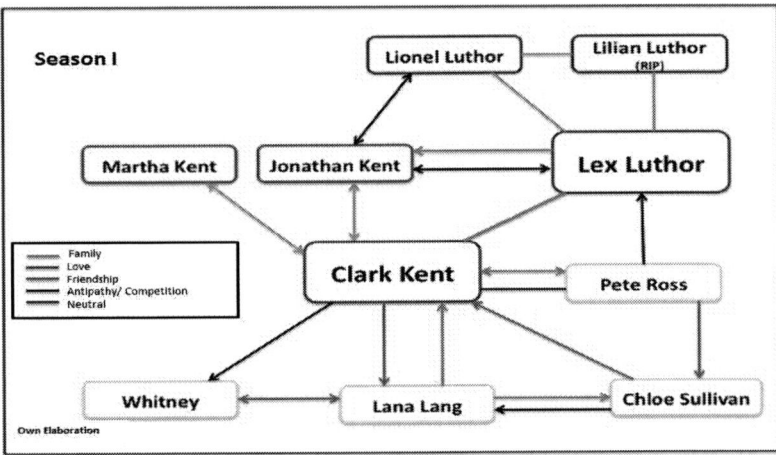

These relationships established in the first season are a referential frame to the rest of the seasons. It helps us to understand the character's actions.

---

[2] We should emphize the important historical context from which this fiction comes from. Superman, first presentation was during the Great Depresion years in the U.S.A. There are several similarities between the first presentation and this one: the intention to state a model being, the desire to tell a myth, the proposal of hope to the audience. Through out the whole story of the "iron man" the serie shows that everything could be possible in America and that it's still a Land of Opportunity.

Besides the main characteristics, we are presented from the first episodes, to an exclusive prototype: "meteor-freaks". These are people who have developed "super powers" because they were also altered by the meteorite rain. These "meteor-freaks" presents other teenagers like Clark who have developed special skills but, differently from Clark, they don't have the family support and encouragement they would need. The narrative goal of these characters is to present a challenge to the main values Clark shows and they test their stability and loyalty. These "meteor-freaks" secondary characters belong to the Volger's prototype called "chameleon".

In terms of theme, Smallville sets out to the audience the fact that this superhero's knowledge is not innate but won through his education and personal development. Through out this growing process he became an "iron man". This learning path was achieved due to his primary social circles: family and friends.

The family environment, differently from other science fiction serie, is very important in the hero's development. He trusts his parents. We can see this from the first chapter, when we are set in present time, Clark is having breakfast and asks his parents permission to play in the football team. The parents don't allow him because of his superpowers, that wouldn't be fair to the other players or team. The antihero, Lex, is also influenced by his father Lionel, who challenges him constantly.

And finally we'll analyze some aspects of what we see on stage which contributes to define the main characters. There are four key elements on stage: the set design, costumes, lighting and action.

These are two main environment to Clark Kent: the farm and the school. Lex's action moves more often between the Luthor's mansion in Smallville and Luthor Corp. From this moment we can see Lex's economic and social superiority in comparison to Clark. Their life's roles are completely different. Kent's farm is a family space which Clark shares with his parents and all of them agree on rules and behaviors[3]. On the contrary, Lex lives alone in a

---

[3] The Kent family meets in the kitchen. It represents the ideal place to chat about what they are going through. The living room looks as cozy as the kitchen but it's the place where they are informed what's happening listening to the broadcasts. The warm colors used for these 2 places (yellow and red) are also helping the setting. Only the basement tends to be gray. Even Clark's bedroom follow these primary colors (mainly blue)

luxurious castle made of cold stone and wood contrasting with Smallville. Wider settings are Smallville high school[4] and Luthor Corp[5].

The character's color palette emphasizes each one's personality. Clark wears primary colors (red, yellow, blue), superhero's colors, known by the public[6]. Lex wears grays, violets, blacks in conservative clothes, not old fashion though. As seasons go by we see his personality gets darker, the same as his environment.

About image design, Clark is in a warm environment and Lex is in cold ones. Lex scenes emphasize shadows on his face, we seldom see a direct light. Even during the day, Lex scenes are developed in a semi dark atmosphere that may come through the castle windows or any other place, but light is never coming directly. At night, candlelights seem to reflect the atmosphere. In any case shadows are always there. While in Clark's scenes, he has a direct and full light, using the sun's light in the day scenes. Yellow tones are often presented and when kryptonite is detected, green tone scenes are showed.

These elements are clearly established since the first chapter. They are starting the iconic traits of this serie. Through the symbolic interaction meaning is given to the actions and situations, and this leads us to identify schemes and types that will make a unique serie[7].

Heroes and antiheroes are created. Analyzing parental marks in Clark and Lex.

We'll describe the parent's influence in the two main characters[8]. Along the serie first season we see Jonathan's teachings on how to control Clark's

---

[4] High school characteristics are completely American using yellow and red as basic colors. It has groups with strong and different identities. Clark will join the groups that are closer to his goals and thoughts. In the first season we see Clark trying to join the football team because he thinks it is a good way to get closer to Lara Lang. School is the starting point of most of the experiences Clark is involved.

[5] Luthor Corp stages are gray and industrialized. This is the setting in which Lex should take decisions, become responsible of his acts and start a new business model from the one Lionel has worked. This is the setting in which Lex is taught without mercy. His anti-values are developed here.

[6] Although there are differences in clothes, these colors are mainly used. Only in those scenes where he exhibits an antagonistic attitude this changes to the usage of red and with leather accessories.

[7] The schemes typification belong to the theory of the social construction of reality which states that those who share a cultural environment share also some schemes.

[8] Martha, Clark's mother, is an important part of the father-son relationship. In Lex's

powers, to use them to help others, to make this helping intention a goal in his life, learning to control selfishness, all these a classic attitude in an archetype hero. Jonathan gives Clark a home's security and a protection. On the contrary, Lionel teaches anti-values, maquiavelic values: achieving and holding power no matter what, vanishing the opponent, using lies and manipulation. Differently to Jonathan, Lionel doesn't present a protective fame for Lex but sends his son to Smallville as punishment.

Although all chapters present the points described, there are three main chapters which we analyze: eight, twelve and seventeen.

In chapter eight we see a comparison between Kent's family and Luthor's family. At the beginning Jonathan and Martha go to Metropolis to celebrate their wedding anniversary while Clark has a small party. Earl, a friend, comes to the party and tells about the epileptic attacks that he is having due to the Kryptonite he's been exposed to at Luthor Corp. The day after Clark's party all the class mates have a guided visit to that factory. Earl kidnaps the students trying to get justice from the Luthor family. Then, by an accident, the plant pressure starts to increase risking all students' life. Clark handles the situation and Earl frees the students. Lionel wants his son to fix out all his problems reassuring his son that Earl is not telling the truth. Things get complicated and Clark saves Lex's life again. Lex finds out Earl is right and his father's lies. Once they work this problem out, Martha and Jonathan give Clark a big hug. Lex sees this and feels envy, we can see this through his face expression. Lionel and Lex have to coldly hug each other in front of the press.

We see how supportive are Jonathan and Martha to Clark; they show love for him and make him know how proud are they because of his brave and generous attitude to help others. On the contrary, Lionel puts pressure on his son, lies to him and behaves with no values for others. Lex is presented as a smart and hard boy who, at the beginning, practices justice and respect. But through out the development of the serie these positive characteristics disappear from him and his father's teachings show out.

At the middle of the season, in episode twelve, the program director experiments with Clark personality and we can see him without his "super powers". We are presented to a different teenager without these "super powers"

---

case, the mother has passed away, and the father is the only one in charge of his son's teachings.

and with non supportive parents. This happen during an electric storm in which Erick, an unpopular and distracted boy, who has a strict father gets Clark's powers. Enchanted by these new powers, he uses them to show off his ego and hurt others. This suggests how a common teenager would selfishly enjoy this situation powers. We see Clark gets hurt by this teenager, bleeding and with ribs fractured. The Kent family always supports the son in any problem he has to face and this reinforce his conviction of being loved by what he really is and not because he has special powers. At the end of the chapter he regains his "super powers" and all this teaches him another life's lesson.

In the seventeen episode, Clark's father positive influence is shown at the same time that we also see the opposite situation in Lex. The antagonism between Lex and Lionel becomes stronger. Dominic Senatori is sent by Lionel to check Lex unusual expenses and they find out Lex used them to investigate Clark. Lex does all this trying to understand what happened the day of the accident, when Clark saved his life. We can see how Lionel, in his obsession to prepare Lex to become the master of the world, makes Lex to develop a shield against his noble feelings.

We also notice a big difference on how each family see the future for the son. Lionel thinks Lex's future is given by one important fact: Lex is Lionel's son and that entitles him to all the power and richness[9]. While Jonathan thinks Clark owns his destiny but as a result of his actions. This is expressed orally in episode six when Clark knows a psychic, Cassandra and Jonathan tells Clark he is his own destiny[10].

This conflict between the character and his believes improves the drama. We also have to analyze the similarities between Clark and Lex: they both have been "different" to the rest of the children; they have special "powers" that allow them to help (or not) others. All these make them have a hard time to integrate with friends. Clark and Lex, both are full responsible to make this planet become a better place to live. Nevertheless, they will fol-

---

[9] Lionel Luthor wanted to make a strong son. He wanted his son to understand his destiny of greatness. This can be seen from chapter one, when Lionel says: " The Luthors are not afraid of anything. We don't have that luxury, we are leaders".

[10] Cassandra is a psychic Clark asked her to see his future and she can't see anything. Lex didn't believe in Cassandra's power but he wants to know what she could see in this future. When Cassandra touches him she dies. The viewers are allow to see Cassandra's vision: a sunflower field where rain is blood.

low very different paths in which they will stumble in their decisions and will try to hide their flaws. In this development they will make themselves an unforgettable legend.

Conclusion

This serie is a social event transformed to literature as science fiction and presented on TV since 2001. It tells, in a unique way, the life and actions of an "alien superhero".

This drama presents a scientist whose planet is going to be destroyed by meteorites rain. The paternal love makes this scientist build a small ship to save his son's life. If all of them had to die, at least his baby son should survive. The father sends this ship to space with good hopes, love and his best wishes of that his son could arrive to some other place where he can be well and act well. This baby lands on Earth and achieves this first objective: to survive. A couple without children, the Kent family, finds out this baby. They consider him a blessing and they welcome him. The empty space of the son they never had is now occupied by a loved one. From that moment on we are dealing with a fullfill and fortunate home.

During the first season we find contrasts between the Luthor and the Kent families. In this Alfred Gough and Miles Millers's world, the family atmosphere to which our heroes and antiheroes belong plays an important role. It is not only a catalyzing agent of the action but also a creator of personalities and values.

Smallville myth means the hero genesis favored by those characters who supported the myth when the hero was just developing and transforming to a full heroic character: the family.

For each character the social development and specially family, determined how they used their power and as a result it traced its use in favor of cohesion, pacific interaction, and experiences in their community. It is summarized as good or bad according to their actions.

Its teaching, though, is not in a black and white view, because it doesn't build a behavioral manual. This is clearer through out the facts of the story. The dialogues lead the character to action but also give him freedom to decide and act out.

These are the fundamental elements influencing the character and transmitted to the audience. The characteristics agreed and shared in the relationship between the main character and the audience are held here. Superhuman powers and qualities are resources which allow the development of such fantastic situations, uncommon situations: flying, unusual strength, vision across matter. All these are the characteristics defining the superhero and helping him to be accepted. He is seen as an example because of this power and his teaching lessons. All this will make an inner charge that will allow emotion in the viewer.

Heroes show social values that help us to make distinction between the right and wrong, the good and the evil. However, there will always be uncertainty experimented by the characters and viewer, which makes them get together, emotionally, and go through the journey at the same time. This explains the myth: the teaching experience.

This serie emphazises our best traits so we can be aware that in our life struggles, we are a balance between matter and spirit. All the inner strength, has a base of love story, sacrifice, values, which support the beneficial results our hero is obtaining now and gives a hope to humanity for a better future.

References

Aristóteles. (1989). *Poética.* Editorial Gredos, Madrid, 1989.

Beeler, S. (2011). "From Comic Book yo Bildungsroman: Smallville, Narrative and the Education of a Young Hero", en *Geraghty, Lincoln, Smallville: chronicles.* Scarecrow Press, Maryland.

Campbell, J. (1901). *El poder del mito. (En diálogo con Bill Moyers).* Emecé editores. Barcelona.

Casetti, F., Di Chio, F. (2007). *Cómo analizar un film.* Paidós Ibérica. Barcelona.

Lipovetsky, G., Serroy, J. (2009). *La pantalla global.* Anagrama. Barcelona.

McKee, R. (1997). *Story: substance, style and the principles of screenwitting.* Harper Collins, New York

Tubau, D. (2011). *El guión del siglo XXI. El futuro de la narrativa en el mundo digital.* Ed. Alba. Barcelona.

VV.AA. (1988). *Historia de la literatura I. El mundo antiguo.* Editorial Akal. Madrid.

Vanoye, F. (1996). *Guiones modelo y modelos de guión. Argumentos clásicos y modernos en el cine.* Paidós, Barcelona.

Vogler, C. (2002). *El viaje del escritor.* Ediciones Robinbook. Barcelona.

Volpi, J. (2011). *Leer la mente. El cerebro y el arte de la ficción.* Ed. Santillana. México

About the contributors

Dr. Bajić, Nataša Simeunović holds Ph.D. She is Research Fellow and Assistant Professor at the Faculty of Culture and Media (Megatrend University, Belgrade, Serbia). She teaches courses in Models of cultural policy and Communication history. She published one book, several book chapters, numerous scientific papers in domestic and foreign journals and involved in several conferences in Serbia and abroad. Scope of her research is wide (media, popular culture, discourse, public opinion, cultural politics, ethnic minorities, marginalized groups, literature). She often combines quantitative and qualitative methods in her work. Currently, she is engaged in two projects supported by Ministry of Education, Science and Technological Development of the Republic of Serbia.

Dr. Branea, Silvia is Associate Professor at the Department of Cultural Anthropology and Communication in the Faculty of Journalism and Communication Sciences at the University of Bucharest, and Associate Researcher at the Laboratory "Sociology of Communication and Public Space", at the Institute of Sociology of The Romanian Academy. Apart from her teaching and research activities, she has also collaborated with Radio Romania Cultural, the public radio broadcasting company. Her main areas of research are communication and globalizatio; the reception of TV series among youth; organizational sociology; and the analysis of online inter-ethnic forums. Her publications comprise author volumes (two single author books and two co-authored works), as well as studies published in both Romanian and international journals, including *Romanian Journal of Journalism and Communication*, *Journal of Community Positive Practices*, and *Journal of Media Research*.

Dr. Dicieanu, Maria is currently an independent researcher focused on new forms of media, particularly transmedia narratives and interactive story-telling. She combines writing with being a film-maker, in the attempt of better mixing theory and practice. In 2008 Maria completed a BA in Multimedia Sound and Film Editing at National University of the Arts of Theatre and Cinema "I.L. Caragiale", Bucharest , Romania, and later, in 2009, a MA in Film Studies at University of Amsterdam, the Netherlands. She is in the process of having published a chapter entitled: "Adaptations: Primitive Transmedia Narratives?" in the "Words, Worlds and Narratives: Transmedia and Immersion" volume initiated by Inter-Disciplinary Press. She has also presented papers in November 2013 in Amsterdam, the Netherlands, during the European Fandoms conference, and in February, 2014 in Caen, France during a Characters Migrate symposium. Maria is currently based in the Netherlands where she is working as a free-lance multimedia artists, having projects ranging from film editing, curating artistic content for the online platform Submarine Channel and helping promote the best student films via the Breaking Ground organization.

Dr. Fuchs, Michael (www.fuchsmichael.net) holds a Ph.D. in American Studies from the University of Graz, Austria, where he teaches media studies and American literature. Michael has co-edited *Landscapes of Postmodernity: Concepts and Paradigms of Critical Theory* (2010), *Placing America: American Culture and its Spaces* (2013), and *ConFiguring America: Iconic Figures, Visuality, and the American Identity* (2013). Currently, he is working on a book on traces in horror movies, a project on cities in audio-visual, and a project on the imaginary construct that is 'America' in video games.

Dr. Galvez, Raquel Crisóstomo teaches in Communication Sciences Faculty at the Internacional University of Catalonia, in the studies of Advertising, Audiovisual Communication and Journalism. She has been professor of a serial narrative course for three years at the Faculty of Humanities at the University Pompeu Fabra. She also has a Degree in Business Communication Techniques of IDEC (Pompeu Fabra University). Her PhD in Humanities at the Pompeu Fabra University (2011), was titled *Art Spiegelman's Maus. A dissociation of roles through the semiotic genealogy of cats and mice in the literature, the graphic novel and the visual culture*. Crisostomo's research area covers the comics, the serial narrative in general, but especially television fiction from the perspective of cultural studies. She has published several academic articles on television seriality as "The Mystery Box: matryoshka and hypermediatic narrative at J.J. Abrams" or "The enemy is at the gates. The new domestic enemy status in contemporary American seriality. *Dexter* and *Homeland*". In 2014, she collaborated in the Massive Open Online Course "The third age of television", a project coordinated by Jordi Carrión and Alberto Scolari at the University Pompeu Fabra. Nowadays she is coordinating the book *Mad Men in the glass*, along with Enric Ros, an approximation to the Mathew Weiner's tv show.

Dr. Gavilán, Maria Teresa Nicolás Director of the Communication DegreePanamerican University, Campus DF. Mexico.PhD in Communication by the Navarra University, Spain. Master in Social and Political Science by the Navarra University, Spain and Law degree by the Panamerican University, in Mexico. She has stay as researcher at the Hebrew University of Jerusalem, Israel. Currently she is a member of the National System of Researchers of the National Council of Science and Technology, in Mexico. She belongs to several international institutions associated with the area of Communication: Latin American Association of Communication Researchers. At present she is the Chair of the Working Group Ethics of Society and Ethics of Media, of the International Association of Media Communication Research. She also belongs to the International Peace Research Association, in the peace journalism area. She has published extensively in the field of Intercultural Communication, Communication ethics and Peace journalism. Her commitment to the Mexican society expressly takes shape like National Committee member and the Ethics Formation Committee of the Association in pro for the best.

Dr. Gutierrez, María de Lourdes López is educator; BA in Communication with a specialization in Film Studies, from the *Universidad Iberoamericana* in Mexico. Master in Education Sciences from the *Universidad del Valle de México*.At the *Universidad Panamericana*, in Mexico, she is Coordinator of the Master's degree of narrative and digital production, and she is in charge of the Narrative Analysis module and analysis project of television series of the Department of Graduate Studies in Communication. She has been teacher in the cinema areas, art history, screenwriting, ethic and regulations of communication at the undergraduate and postgraduate level at the *Universidad del Valle de México*, the *ITESM Campus* Mexico City, the *Universidad de la Comunicación* and the *Universidad Panamericana*.She is writer and conductor of the media analysis program *Dos Dedos de Frente*, in the Civilian radio of the *IMER*.Author and/or coordinator of the books *"La comunicación que necesitamos, el país que queremos"* (CONIECC-UIA, 2010) and *"Qué enseñamos las escuelas de Comunicación"* (CONEICC_UCSJ, 2912) as well as of a number of articles on art and communication.She was Member of the Valley of Mexico region of the National Council for Education and Research of Communication Sciences (CONEICC) in 2009–2012.She performed as a Member of Advisory Board of the Canal of Congress and the National Jury Prize for Journalism, 2013.

Dr. Işık, Nuran Erol is Professor at the Department of Sociology, Izmir University of Economics. Her research interests include research methods in media, popular religion, the sociology of media and popular/political culture. Her recent publication has been about popular religion reflected in Turkish drama: "Parables of Indicators of Popular Wisdom: The making of piety culture in Turkish television dramas", (2013) European Journal of Cultural Studies,16,5, 565–581.

Dr. Kroener, Oliver completed his Master's degree in the Department of Theatre and Film Studies at the University of British Columbia in November 2013. He recently co-edited *Cinephile 9.1: Reevaluating Television*. Oliver also holds a M.A. (Magister Artium) in American Studies and Sociology from the Goethe University in Frankfurt am Main, Germany.

Dr. Marinescu, Valentina is a PhD Reader at the Faculty of Sociology and Social Work at Bucharest University. She teaches undergraduate and graduate courses in media and society, and methods of researching mass communication. Her interests lie in media and communication studies, with a specific focus on East Asia. She has also published articles and book chapters on those subject matters. She was a fellow at the Academy of Korean Studies, Republic of Korea.

Dr. Mendelyte, Atene is a Ph.D. candidate in film studies at the Centre for Languages and Literature, Lund University, Sweden. Prior to that, she studied media (film, television, new media) at the University of Amsterdam and was affiliated to the Netherlands Institute for Cultural Analysis. She also studied literature and intermediality at Vilnius University (Lithuania) and English literature at University College Cork (Ireland). She is currently researching American avant-garde films in relation to Deleuzian film-philosophy, mental- and neuroaesthetics. Previously, she worked with Samuel Beckett's television plays as well as his theatrical notebooks, concentrating on either film-philosophical or intermedial aspects of his works. She, too, did some research on William Butler Yeats's Noh plays, attempting to unmask their Romanticist nature. She has published a number of articles on a range of subjects including philosophy, cultural studies, music and theatre. Her interests lie in various forms of media and artistic expression, (primarily continental) philosophy with a specific focus on mind/perception.

Dr. Mesonero, Rodrigo Born in Madrid, Spain, in 1980. PhD in Communication at Universidad Europea de Madrid (UEM) with European mention, he has developed his career in different communication companies and lecturing at University. His academic background includes studies in screenwriting for television and cinema, a Bachelor in Journalism and a Master's Degree in Television Production. He has developed his professional career working initially as a journalist for the national newspaper ABC and later on television, as a screenwriter in national sitcoms *Aída, 7Vidas* and *A ver si llego*. He has also worked in production and direction departments at production companies like Cuarzo or Videomedia. Nowadays he reconciles lecturing screenwriting and television production and direction courses at the Spanish university UEM with freelance collaborations as writer, director, producer and transmedia adviser. His academic research focuses on transmedia storytelling, with special emphasis in audience interaction and audience participation in television, cinema or any other audiovisual content.

Dr. **Mitu, Bianca** is a Lecturer at the University of Bucharest. She has a PhD in Communication Science, and was a Visiting Scholar at CAMRI, University of Westminster, Faculty of Arts, Media and Design, London, in 2011. Her research interests lie in media and communication studies, with a specific focus on political communication and television studies. She has an outstanding international scientific background, and has published in international journals from the UK, Italy, Germany and USA. She is an active member of important international scientific associations, including IAMCR, ECREA, and the UK Social Policy Association, and an active editorial board member of *Journalism and Mass Communication Journal*, *Interpersona*, and *Management Dynamics in the Knowledge Economy*.

Dr. **Moreira, Lilian Fontes** Graduated in Architecture and Urbanism at the Santa Ursula University (1981), Masters in Communication from Federal University of Rio de Janeiro (1997) and Ph.D. in *Communication and Culture* (2009) from Federal University of Rio de Janeiro. Since 2010, develops research FICTION TELEVISION in Federal University of Rio de Janeiro, with support from Foundation Support Research in Rio de Janeiro (FAPERJ / CAPES). Has experience in the area of Arts, with an emphasis on Brazilian literature, cultural studies, in communications with an emphasis in journalism and television, in the area of architecture and urbanism. With training multidisciplinary, has a background in philosophy courses not institutional.Born in Rio de Janeiro and is the author of essays, novels, biographical profiles, and has participated seven collections of short stories.

Dr. **Perelló-Sobrepere, Marc** is a Communications Professor at Abat Oliba CEU University and the International University of Catalonia in Barcelona, and has been a Visiting Researcher at City University London. He has taught Sociology, Theory of Information, Professional Journalism and New Media, among others. His areas of expertise and research are information technologies, political and social activism, deliberative democracy, digital journalism, television narratives, cultural changes, cognitive processes, and sociological theories. He is an international member of the Media Ecology Association. He belongs to different research units and is an active speaker at conferences. Besides his academic work, he currently operates as the Communications Directors of an important consulting firm in Barcelona. Previously, he held different positions in the media industry. He served as the Assistant Editor to the multi-awarded cultural quarterly Literal Magazine, based in the United States, and published both in English and Spanish. He also co-founded the Catalan digital newspaper Revista Mirall, and wrote in many others.

Dr. Pierre, Mathieu is teaching Literature and Cinema in High School and at the University of Lille 3 (France). In 2011, he begins a PHD under the direction of Giusy Pisano at the University of Paris 3 La Sorbonne-Nouvelle where he questions the fantastic in the contemporary television series. He's the author of articles on the narrative tension, the importance of religion and music in those series. He will speak at the international conference on the television narratives at the University of Montreal in May 2014.

Dr. Sánchez, Carmen Sylvia was born in San Juan, Perto Rico qhere she studied her bachelor.Degree in Literature, Universidad de Puerto Rico.She studied a Master degreein ;iddlebury College, Vermont.She studied in University of Paris III foe a year, where she took post-graduate courses.She studied a PHD in Western Pacific University and PHD courses at Universidad Nacional Autónoma de México.She has been university professor for the last 30 years.

Dr. Schlütz, Daniela (PhD 2002) is lecturer at the Department of Journalism and Communication Research at the Hanover University of Music, Drama and Media. Her research focus is entertainment research (especially TV series), advertising communication as well as empirical research methods.

Dr. Schneider, Beate (PhD 1973) is professor at the Department of Journalism and Communication Research at the Hanover University of Music, Drama and Media. Her research foci are national and international media systems, media politics and media production.

Dr. Wayne, Michael L. is a graduate instructor in the Department of Media Studies and a PhD candidate in the Department of Sociology at the University of Virginia. His dissertation, "Television as New Media: Post-Network Reception Practices, Distinction, and the Splintering of the Mass Audience," examines the emergence of niche television audiences in light of the medium's recently elevated cultural status. Using data gathered from qualitative interviews with more than sixty young-adults, he finds that the consequences associated with the increasing legitimacy of post-network television programming vary with social location. Specifically, Wayne finds that more privileged respondents in the sample are more likely to understand post-network television as a form of cultural capital and use high-status shows to bond with similarly positioned peers. In contrast, respondents from less privileged backgrounds are more likely to experience anxiety around watching television and tend to emphasize the importance of reading. Wayne is also the managing editor for UVA's media studies journal *The Communication Review* and an adjunct instructor in the Department of Sociology at Virginia Commonwealth University where he teaches "Mass Media & Society." Wayne's work has been published in Cinephile and he is contributing chapters to two edited collections, *An Academic Love Affair:*

Teaching The Wire *in the College Classroom* (McFarland Publishing) and *Using HBO's* The Wire *to Teach Urban Issues*, (McFarland Publishing) based on his experiences using television in the classroom. Please visit www.mikewayne.org for more information.

Dr. Zofio, Enric Ros is a Spanish Screenwriter, Cultural Journalist and Cinema Professor. He has a BA (Hons) Degree in *Audiovisual Communication* (Ramon Llull University). Also he studied *Advanced Studies in Theory, Analysis and Documentation of Cinema* (Pompeu Fabra University) and *Cinematographic Script* (Scriptwriters' Workshop of Barcelona). At present, he teaches *History of Cinema* and *Television Fiction Writing* in ECIB (International School of Cinema of Barcelona), as well as open courses about *History* and *Analysis of Cinema* in several education centers at Barcelona. In 2011, he wrote the essay *"It's Not TV. The Serial Fiction at the Post-TV Age"* (*Taller de Guionistas* Publishing House), about the narrative trends of the television contemporary fiction. He has written widely about cinema in Spanish specialized publications such as *Contrapicado* or *Cine Archivo*, and also in many DVD classic movies collector's editions. In addition, he has written in non-specialized digital magazines about literature, comics and classical music.Previously, he was the Director and Professor of the *Master of Theory, Analysis and Critical Studies of Cinema* (*Estudiodecine*, Barcelona) and he also coordinated the *R+D Department of Television Fiction* at Scriptwriters' Workshop of Barcelona. Beforehand, he worked as Professor of *History of Cinema, Analysis of Cinema* and *Television's Script* in several academic centers; and also he was Copywriter for several advertising agencies. Currently, he coordinates (with Raquel Crisóstomo) a project book about the TV show "Mad Men". His main research interests are popular culture, television fiction narratives, History of cinema analysis, the language of comics, visual *motifs* and myths legacy in contemporary culture.

***ibidem*-Verlag**
Melchiorstr. 15
D-70439 Stuttgart
info@ibidem-verlag.de

www.ibidem-verlag.de
www.ibidem.eu
www.edition-noema.de
www.autorenbetreuung.de